ALL YOU NEED TO KNOW™ ABOUT COMMERCIAL AWARENESS

2007/8

Christopher Stoakes

LONGTAIL

> **Ask any head of graduate recruitment or HR or training or learning & development what they want from their young hires and they all say the same thing: commercial awareness. They want people who are not just technically competent but who are interested in business, who can relate to clients and – above all – who can contextualise their advice. Clients complain that they get professional advice these days that is precisely right but completely useless. Professionals don't understand the client's business, strategy, industry or personal goals. So they give advice that is complex, qualified and expressed in language that is stilted, without any sense of what the client is going to do with it – how he or she will act upon it. So this book is designed to help young professionals relate to their clients, as organisations and people. It looks at how business works, at strategy, funding, at the big themes affecting all businesses. Then it looks at clients as individuals and how to relate to them. It looks at how to communicate with them and win business from them. At the end, the reader will have grasped the fundamental truth about commercial awareness: it's a mindset, an outlook, an attitude of mind; and once you have got it your clients will love you and your career will take off.**

Christopher Stoakes has been a City lawyer and a financial journalist. He taught on an MBA programme for 10 years and has written research reports for one of the top management consultancies. He is also a management consultant himself, specialising in the field of PSFs (professional service firms). It's this varied background and experience that he brings to bear in this book. He has also been a marketing director and set up and run his own business.

Chris is the author of the companion volume *All You Need To Know About The City* also published by Longtail. He was a scholar at Charterhouse and at Worcester College, Oxford where he read Law.

Anyone with comments or questions about this book should feel free to contact him at: chris@longtail.eu

WARNING

This book is a simple and concise guide to a complex, multifaceted subject that is changing all the time. Given the need to simplify an inherently complex subject, this book is not comprehensive or definitive. Readers must not rely on this book except as a general, schematic overview. Accordingly neither the author, the publisher, their agents, consultants nor employees accept any liability for any loss (direct or indirect; immediate or consequential; contractual or tortious) however caused from use of this book or reliance upon it.

First published by Longtail Publishing Limited 2006
Tel: 020 7938 1975 Fax: 020 7938 3861 Email: info@longtail.eu

Publisher:	James Piesse
Assistant Editor:	Samuel Tombs
Sub-Editor:	Monica Kendall
Typesetting:	Louise Downer
Art Director:	Andrew Debens

Written at The Scripto KT, Jan-May 2006
© C F Stoakes 2006
Author photo © Fraser Deeth & Dion Lucas/Kingston College 1st Diploma Art & Design – many thanks to Patricia Ayre

ISBN 10: 0-9552186-1-6
ISBN 13: 978-0-9552186-1-3

Printed by: CPI Bath Press

For John Stoakes in memory of Frank Stoakes

CONTENTS

INTRODUCTION *IX*

PART 1: UNDERSTANDING CLIENT ORGANISATIONS

1. WHO'S EATING MY LUNCH? *1*

Why companies have strategies – talking to clients about strategy – vision and mission – normative strategy – Porter's Five Forces – SWOT – matching to the external environment – PEST – scenario planning – top-down and emergent strategies – Mintzberg – Drucker – Boston Consulting Group – balanced scorecard – content and process – the CEO's strategic concerns

2. MONEY, MONEY, MONEY *17*

Cashflow v. profit – income v. capital – working capital requirement – equity v. debt – security – sole trader – partnerships – private and public companies – directors – shareholders – entrepreneurs – venture capital – accounting terms – factoring – invoice discounting – balance sheets and P&Ls

3. GROW OR DIE: GOING PUBLIC AND DOING M&A DEALS *33*

Exit route – listing, flotation, going public, IPO – listing requirements – underwriting – institutional investors – secondary issues – sectors – multinationals – B2B (wholesale) – B2C (retail) – franchising – mergers & acquisitions – competition policy, monopolies and cartels – takeover timetable – Takeover Panel and Takeover Code – non-core assets – hive-downs – MBOs – private equity – golden hellos/parachutes – corporate governance – reading the financial pages

4. BONDS, LOANS AND THE FINANCIAL MARKETS *51*

Public companies as issuers – bonds – basis points – credit rating agencies – junk/high-yield – investment banks – commercial banks – syndicated loans – asset finance – acquisition finance – foreign exchange – spot market – forward – direct and indirect investment – trade finance – inflation and interest rates – risk management – hedging – derivatives – insurance – Lloyd's – shipping

5. BIG ISSUES FOR BIG BUSINESS 71

The accelerating pace of change – the knowledge economy – technology forcing platform and content convergence – impact of the web – disintermediation – business process re-engineering – outsourcing, offshoring – quality systems – supply chain management – consumerism – data mining and warehousing – client relationship management – mass customisation – longtail effect – globalisation – knowledge economy – privatisation, commercialisation and market liberalisation – corporate social responsibility – corporate governance – what all this means for smaller businesses – government, economics and statistics – innovate or die

PART 2: UNDERSTANDING CLIENTS AS PEOPLE

6. IT'S A PEOPLE BUSINESS 95

Active listening – EARS – open questions, follow-up questions – be interested not interesting – personality types – organisational politics – asking about a client's role – the client organisation's business, structure and purpose – contextualise the advice – how is the client going to use it – roles and functions – other professionals and what they do – working together – commercial conflicts – referrals

7. DOING THE WORK 123

Your first client is your supervisor – being delegated to – feedback – appraisals – team working – Belbin – project management – time management – managing client expectations – handling complaints – empathy and rebuilding trust – problem-solving – telephone technique

8. GET TO THE POINT 139

Say upfront what it's about – put conclusions first – write the way you speak – simple language and short sentences – getting rid of the structural scaffolding – what readers want – emails – being personal – using visuals – presentations – writing for profile – using stories in brochures – no conclusions, just stop

9. MAKIN' MONEY 153

The levers of profitability for PSFs – working capital – pricing – what clients mean when they ask about cost – scoping – using previous transactions – alternative pricing structures – risk allocation – value for money – commoditisation of services – post-project reviews – portfolio-managing clients and work types – pricing as a strategic tool

10. BUSINESS DEVELOPMENT 177

'Meeting clients' needs profitably' – building your network – multipliers – client relationship management initiatives – pitching process – hot buttons – turning features into benefits – moving the goalposts – follow-up

PART 3: UNDERSTANDING YOU

11. YOUR FUTURE – THE ROAD AHEAD 193

Becoming a 'reflective professional' – development opportunities – improving incrementally – living with shambolic organisations

12. WHAT ELSE TO READ, WHERE ELSE TO LOOK 197

APPENDIX: JARGON BUSTER 201

INDEX 241

INTRODUCTION

If you want to be a successful professional, you need to have commercial awareness. It wasn't always so. When I started out (as a young lawyer) it was enough to know the law and how it affected corporate clients. After all, the law was the difficult bit.

But that isn't good enough any more.

If you want to be an accountant, actuary, architect, advertising executive, banker, barrister, broker, engineer, fund manager, headhunter, HR professional, ITC specialist, legal executive, management consultant, marketing adviser, patent attorney, property surveyor, PR expert, quantity surveyor, recruitment consultant, solicitor, tax adviser – whatever it may be – you need to master your own discipline and, on top of that, you need to be commercially aware.

And the sooner you start doing that, the better. It's crucial to becoming a successful professional. This book helps you achieve it.

WHAT COMMERCIAL AWARENESS IS

Ask anyone who works in professional life what they mean by 'commercial awareness' and they will give you a different answer. I've asked a load of them and the following is a pretty good smorgasbord of what commercial awareness encompasses:

- A basic understanding of business – how companies are organised and the issues that affect them, from globalisation and channels to market to supply chain management, knowledge management, customer value management, data mining, ERP, offshoring and outsourcing

- An overview of finance – the importance of cashflow, the difference between debt and equity, how companies fund themselves, and an overview of the financial markets and the role of banks
- A grasp of what motivates and drives the people in organisations – their functions and roles
- Use of the language of business – how to communicate in the way clients want
- Insight into some of the common management models that people are taught on MBAs, especially in the field of strategy
- Recognition of the need to market yourself and build your own professional network – how to go about building professional relationships and a personal reputation

WHAT'S IN THIS BOOK...

At heart, commercial awareness is about being able to talk to clients, finding out what they want, why they want it, what they will do with it and what they are prepared to pay, and then delivering it in the way they want. To do that you need to understand how organisations work, the issues they face and the role of people within them. So this book does that and then helps you focus on how to deliver the service clients want.

In short, this book is a rag-bag of stuff, most of it gleaned over the 25 years I've spent working in a commercial context as a lawyer, management consultant, marketing director, MBA teacher and financial journalist, working as an employee, employer and entrepreneur.

If you know these things before you attend your first meeting with a corporate client, you will be fully prepared to make a good impression and start to build a professional relationship that will launch a career filled with demanding clients, stimulating work, interesting colleagues and (let's not beat about the bush) loads of dosh – all of which will make you a sexy proposition to a future spouse or partner. You will be valued, people will seek your views, your voice will be heard, your opinion will matter and your life will make a difference. You'll become a top dog.

And if there's more to a successful professional career than that, I'm a monkey.

...AND WHAT'S NOT

A word of warning – there's tons of stuff that's not in this book: economics, for a start; and if you want an in-depth analysis of accounts and accounting standards, look elsewhere; ditto if you want to know what makes companies successful; and there's not a lot on management; and only a bit on financial markets.

This book is a beginning. I know you're young and have got plenty of better things to do and – according to people of my generation – can't read anyway. So I've stuck in the minimum.

THANKS

I'd like to thank the following who, over the years, have contributed to my understanding of commercial awareness (which doesn't necessarily mean they will agree with anything I've said here). They include: Mark Allatt, Anna Baptist, John Bennett, Chris Blackhurst, Steve Blundell, Julian Boardman-Weston, David Bowen, James Bowman, Jane Chapman, Tom Cook, Ann Marie Cooper, Barry Dean, Andrew Dines, Jason Ellis, Christopher Elwen, Richard Ensor, Richard de Friend, David Finch, Suzanne Fine, Simon Firth, Andrew Freeman, Bernard George, Stephen Gillespie, Anthony Hamilton-Briscoe, Brian Harris, John Heaps, Martin Hill, Alan Humphreys, Sarah Hutchinson, Richard King, Mark Lewis, Simon McCall, Ian McLachlan, Henry Marsden, Rick Marsland, David Martin, Stephen Mayson, Katherine Meade, Johnnie Milne, Des O'Connell, Duncan Ogilvy, Christopher Owen, Nigel Page, James Piesse, Gwyn Price, Giles Proctor, Denis Reed, Tony Reiss, Nigel Savage, Scott Slorach, Paul Smith, David Spencer, John Stoakes, Mark Taylor, Christopher Tite, Philip Tranter, Des Woods, Sally Woodward. Thank you all.

PART 1: Understanding Client Organisations

Chapter 1

WHO'S EATING MY LUNCH?

SPEED-READ SUMMARY

- Successful companies pursue effective strategies

- Strategy matches the organisation's capabilities to its external environment

- Strategy comprises a destination (vision) and a map to get there (mission) – which in turn embodies how a company differentiates itself from competitors and establishes priorities; anything not in the plan does not attract resource or investment

- An organisation's culture ('how we do things round here') has a major impact on how it develops and is called its normative strategy

- There are various management techniques for looking at strategy – these are called 'models' and are generally pictoral

- The most well-known strategy models include Porter's Five Forces, SWOT, PEST and scenario planning

- Consider using strategy models to generate discussions with clients about their own organisation's strategy – and try to find out what your organisation's is too

- Process is how you arrive at a strategy; content is what it consists of

- Using flipcharts and pictures helps – business people are often more visual than professionals who are often more literate and numerate

---

Once upon a time there was a frog, sitting in a pan of water, minding its own business. The water was nicely tepid. Over time the water became warm, then warmer, then hot. However, the change in temperature was sufficiently gradual from moment to moment for the frog to acclimatise itself to the increasing heat. Which is how the frog got boiled alive: by the time the frog realised the water was too hot for comfort, it couldn't get out. Its legs were no longer able to propel it up and out of the pan (though I expect they tasted good).

This parable, minted by management guru Charles Handy, is every chief executive's nightmare (the CEO or chief executive officer is the person in charge of a company, also known as the managing director). The point is that the world is constantly changing and companies have to change and adapt or else go out of business. The problem is that by the time many of them realise their world has changed, it's too late. That, Handy says, is the risk that businesses run if they do not have a strategic sense of their environment and how it is changing around them.

This is why every CEO worries constantly about who is about to eat his or her lunch – in short, which competitor is about to take his or her customer base away. Business is about competition – being the biggest, best, cheapest, quickest (a bit like sport, which is why business people often like sport). Businesses cannot afford to stand still. If they do, they will die – they will be overtaken by competitors who will copy their goods or services, produce those goods or services more cheaply and steal their customers away.

The best businesses – the market leaders – are aware of what makes them stand out in the market (what **differentiates** them from their competitors). They call this their **Unique Selling Proposition** (USP). How you achieve your USP is your strategy. If you want to understand your client, make sure you grasp its strategy.

Whole libraries have been written about strategy – what it is and how to do it. Management consultants (you may be en route to becoming one) earn fortunes telling businesses what their strategy should be and how to implement it. But the concept of strategy is really quite simple. It is knowing (1) where you want to go and (2) how you are going to get there. It's about having a destination and a map. (Here's a tip: if you are a job-seeker, be sure to ask prospective employers about their strategy.)

VISION AND MISSION

Knowing where you want to get to is sometimes called the strategic goal or **'vision'** – the best business leaders can paint a picture of what their organisation, markets and clients will look like in, say, five years' time. How you get there – the route map – is sometimes called the **'mission'**. The reason why it's the organisation's mission is because there must be something unique about the organisation which gives it the ability to achieve its mission: its differentiating factor; its USP. Sometimes the mission is described in terms of an organisation's **values** or **culture**. As a partner from McKinsey, the famous management consulting group, once said: 'Culture is the way we do things round here' and strategy is sometimes described in value terms, in which case it is called **normative strategy** ('norms' being the principles that regulate behaviour within the organisation).

For example, take the Body Shop: its strategy was to create a brand built on environmental values – that's what made it different. Likewise, the Cooperative Bank's strategy is based on being ethically-led. A more straightforward strategy was adopted by General Electric, the US company, immediately after the 1939–45 war which was 'to put a refrigerator in every home'. Similarly, Microsoft's was to put a PC on every desk. The American space programme's vision was – and is – to put man into space, to conquer this final unknown frontier. Its mission in the 1960s was 'to put a man on the moon'.

ASK CLIENTS

A good way of engaging with a client is to ask them what their organisation's strategy is. Business people who are any good at what they do love talking about their business and its strategy. This chapter gives you some of the language and models you need to initiate and sustain that discussion, so that you can see how the work you are doing for a client will further their strategy.

It also helps if you are aware of your own organisation's strategy: usually, if you ask, you will be told or be able to find out – organisations used to be secretive about their strategy but are now more open, at least with their own people. You can then see how working for a particular client fits your own organisation's strategy.

Do all organisations have a strategy?

Yes. Not having a strategy is itself a strategy. It's a bit like steering a supertanker: even if you're not steering it's still being blown in some direction – probably sideways on. This means that you can cast off and set sail without any idea of where you want to go. But you'd be better off knowing where you are going (vision), how to get there and the obstacles and pitfalls en route that you will need to navigate round. In which case you will probably realise that it would help to have a map or chart (mission).

Now, if you do know where you are going, it is easier to decide which actions are useful (because they help you get there) and which you can ignore (because they won't). In other words you can establish a set of priorities – things you need to do and in which order. And this applies in business: you can decide where to channel your resources – what to invest in and what not to.

Now, if by contrast you do not have a strategy, you have no idea where to focus your efforts so you will waste a lot more time, energy and money doing things that may or may not be beneficial. One advantage of having an explicit strategy is that, in developing it, you will almost certainly have thought about the risks and pitfalls you may encounter and – crucially – how to overcome them. These contingency plans mean that you will be prepared. And this is what makes the difference: strategising isn't about predicting the future; it's about being prepared for whatever the future holds.

What follows is a brief discussion of a small number of models (a 'model' is management-speak for a way of thinking, a template, which is usually expressed visually) that business people are familiar with. If you want a more detailed discussion, look in any good management or strategy book.

PORTER'S FIVE FORCES

There is a risk that organisations become inward-looking as they try to examine what their USP is. It is just as important to look outwards, at the external environment, and to define your USP in relation to competitors.

So the most important thing about strategy is to look outwards, beyond the organisation's boundaries, to see how the world out there is changing – something the frog failed to do. One of the most famous management models to encourage business people to do this was formulated by Michael Porter in the 1970s.

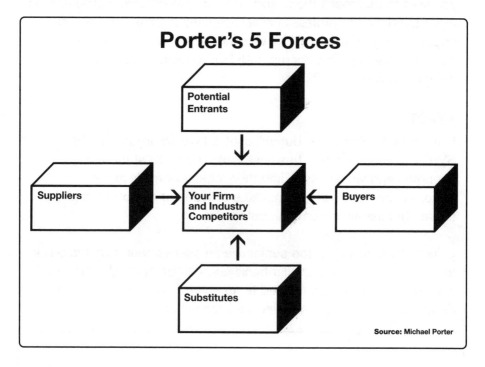

Porter said that any business was subject to five competitive pressures from:

- Industry **competitors** (other organisations in the same sector competing for the same customers)
- Potential **entrants** – organisations in other sectors that might enter this sector
- **Buyers** (customers) – because they are constantly shopping around, seeking increased quality at lower cost
- **Suppliers** – because the business has to buy in goods and services and the price it pays will affect its own profitability
- **Substitutes** – where customers decide to do it themselves or find an alternative which means they don't buy the business's goods or services at all

This model was – and remains – so influential that it is sometimes dismissed as old hat. But it's still good. For a start, it prompts business leaders to focus on **barriers to entry** – how easy or difficult it is for a new entrant to the market to gatecrash and move into your business. It also means that when focusing on customers you start to **segment** them, sorting them into different categories. In order to adapt it to professional service firms (PSFs) – the sort of organisation you are or will be working for – you need to read 'suppliers' as meaning 'recruits'. All PSFs compete for talent – people like you.

SWOT

Even more hackneyed – but still useful, I would argue – is the SWOT analysis. Here, a business looks internally at its own strengths and weaknesses and then looks externally at the opportunities (such as new markets or types of customer) and the threats (for instance from competitors).

Critics say this can be too subjective an assessment. But it is quick to do and repeat on a regular basis and can be applied at any level in a business. It can be applied to an entire PSF or the different departments, practices and service lines within it.

Strengths What's good about the organisation	**Weaknesses** What's bad about the organisation
INTERNAL	
EXTERNAL	
Opportunities What markets / clients can the organisation seek	**Threats** What poses a threat in terms of external competitors or changes to the market place

STRATEGY AS A MATCHING OPERATION

You are probably beginning to see how important an analysis of the external environment is. In an ideal world, you would scan the horizon, identify a commercial opportunity and then set up a business to exploit it. But most businesses have to start with what they are and what they've got by way of people, assets and expertise. Grant is one of many strategy writers who acknowledges that, in practice, strategy is a matching operation, as this diagram shows.

You can see on the right-hand side the reference to the industry environment – which is what Porter's Five Forces is about. The macro-environment is about the Big Things (what economists call the 'secular trends') that affect all our lives.

PEST

PEST is the acronym that covers these Big Things or secular trends. It stands for the Political, Economic, Social and Technological forces that shape our world and necessarily affect commercial activity within it. PEST reminds us to consider the

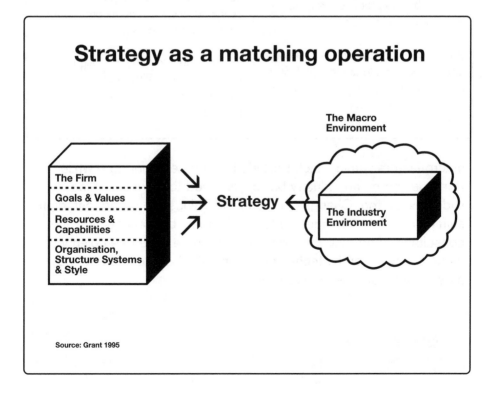

Strategy as a matching operation

The Macro Environment

The Firm
Goals & Values
Resources & Capabilities
Organisation, Structure Systems & Style

Strategy

The Industry Environment

Source: Grant 1995

7

The language of business: process v. content

The most common distinction in business is between 'process' and 'content'. Process is the way in which something is done or discussed. Content is the actual subject-matter. So, strategy consists of the actual plans themselves (content) and the way in which they are developed and implemented (process). This is a useful dichotomy.

Take a meeting. You get together a room full of people who all have great ideas. But before you know it they are all talking over each other, trying to express their views, making their own notes, and after a while the meeting breaks up without any apparent progress. There's been plenty of content but no process – and so, therefore, no progress.

So, instead, you kick off the meeting by getting everyone to agree how long they want the meeting to last and what the outputs should be: in terms of outputs they may agree that it's too early to do anything concrete except have an exchange of views; you may then need a further meeting to take the ideas expressed forward. Eventually you will need some outputs – who will do what and by when. When everyone has agreed, you now have a process. Now you can start discussing people's ideas – the content.

It's always good to use a flipchart so everyone can look up at a single focal point and concentrate on listening and speaking rather than looking down as they make their own notes. The flipchart sheets can be typed up afterwards and the notes circulated. It sometimes helps to have a facilitator, a third party who keeps the discussions on track and on point, who ensures the meeting keeps to time and achieves its desired outputs, and who enables everyone to speak and records what is agreed on the flipchart.

So learn how to write in straight lines and clearly on a flipchart (or smartboard) without feeling self-conscious: it will always come in handy.

macro-factors within which Porter's Five Forces operate – while Porter is fine on an industry basis, you need to consider these wider issues too. Changes in these Big Things are called 'paradigm shifts' or 'secular changes' or 'step changes' by management consultants. And over the past 30 years there have been plenty of these, many driven by technology (think of PCs, the internet and mobile phones) – see Chapter 5.

The CEO's role: being strategic

If you see any bigwig from a company being interviewed, they will rapidly start talking about the market for their goods or services and the competition (other companies providing the same or similar goods or services at an equivalent price). Companies are acutely aware of who their competitors are, what goods or services they provide and at what price.

A company only makes money and stays in business – in other words, survives – if it provides goods or services that people want to buy at a price they are prepared to pay. It offers its goods/services to the market and those people in the market who buy its goods/services become customers. But those customers will only stay loyal if its goods/services remain attractive – i.e. represent value for money (quality commensurate with the price).

I've worked for a number of CEOs and the best have one particular attribute in common: they are always thinking about the business and where it is going.

For example, I once worked for a financial publisher. My CEO would take me to meetings with advertisers (customers). The taxi would stop at a traffic light and a cyclist would go past. 'Are more people cycling to work?' my boss – who had no small talk at all (true of many CEOs) – would ask. I had no idea, so I said nothing. At the next red lights we'd stop outside a builder's merchants and my boss, gazing in through the window at the bathrooms on display, would ask: 'Are more people taking showers rather than baths?' No idea. Nor did I have any idea why he was asking me these weird questions.

Then, over time, I twigged. My boss was constantly thinking of our products (in those pre-web days, books and magazines). If more people were cycling to work, fewer would be commuting by train or bus so fewer would be reading our products (you can read a book on a bus but not on a bicycle). If people were taking showers rather than baths, they wouldn't be reading our products in the bath (in the shower they'd go soggy). So he was constantly thinking about where the business was going and what was changing in people's behaviours that might affect it.

This is the single most compelling reason for being commercially aware: the best business people (the sort of people you want to have as clients) are switched on, interesting, interested people. They are helping to change the world – before it changes them.

CORPORATE PLANNING DEPARTMENTS

Given all of this, you can possibly begin to see that it might be tempting to try to predict these changes and to try to predict how the external environment (including customers, markets and competitors) will change. For a long time, companies tried to do this:

they had corporate planning departments that did huge amounts of research and analysis, devised strategies and then handed them down for the company to implement (at one point it was rumoured that Sony had a 500-year plan). These plans had the attraction of looking scientific. The problem was that they were still a guess or a series of guesses; and were just as likely – or even more likely (predicting the future being what it is) – to be wrong rather than right. Which seemed a pretty risky way of doing things. What's more, these strategies didn't prepare companies for unexpected changes – the paradigm shifts mentioned above.

SCENARIO PLANNING

So over the past 30 years companies have ditched this central 'command and control' approach in favour of 'scenario planning' – this is where you don't try to predict the future but you imagine a series of possible scenarios and plan what you would do if faced with any of them. This set of plans then becomes part of your strategy: when one of these eventualities comes to pass, you reach into your desk drawer for the appropriate plan of action.

There is a well-known Gary Larson cartoon in which a dinosaur is standing on a stage, at a podium, delivering a speech to a congress of fellow dinosaurs (by a strange quirk the crest on the podium bears a striking resemblance to that of RICS – the Royal Institute of Chartered Surveyors, but nothing should be read into this coincidence). Mr Dinosaur is saying something like, 'Gentlemen, the future's bleak. The ice age is upon us, we lack warm blood and we have brains the size of peanuts.' I like this cartoon because it demonstrates simultaneously why scenario planning is essential but why, like all planning, it is not fool-proof.

Scenario planning is 'what if' or contingency planning. You posit a number of scenarios and work through the consequences for your business. The scenarios can be as absurd or as extreme as you like. A certain amount of lateral thinking and doomsday scenario setting is a good thing. After all, an ice age was a doomsday scenario for the dinosaurs above: if they had addressed the possibility millions of years before, they might have been able to evolve into creatures able to withstand it. 'What ifs' can include everything from 'What if the government is thrown out at the next election?' to 'What if they turn the street in which our office is located into a pedestrian precinct?'

Whether these scenarios actually happen is almost irrelevant. The point is that they make an organisation lighter on its feet. It gets into the habit of thinking about where the threats and opportunities lie. This is important because like the water in the pan containing the frog, nothing remains the same, whatever it may appear to be doing. This is not about trying to predict the future (although 'futurologists' who specialise in this kind of thing may claim they can). Businesses that are successful in coping with the future are able to do so not because they can predict it but because they have learnt how to cope with its uncertainties. That is why many large companies have ditched their formal planning departments in favour of something more dynamic, able to deal with previously unforeseen business disruptions such as terrorist bombs in city centres.

EMERGENT STRATEGY

There was another problem with central corporate planning: getting 'buy-in' from the people at the organisation's coal-face. If a strategy was handed down loftily from above, there was no guarantee that the people further down the organisation would do much to implement it and this issue became more pressing as companies dismantled their hierarchies in order to get closer to their markets and customers. The 'flatter' organisations became – often in response to cost-cutting measures which stripped out tiers of middle management – the less bureaucratic they were and the less easy it was to tell people to do things.

It was at this point that a celebrated management writer called Henry Mintzberg came to the rescue. He said that strategy could be 'bottom-up' as well as 'top-down' (top-down being the old style of command-and-control corporate planning). Strategy is particularly bottom-up in PSFs: here, the fee-earners are at the coal-face dealing daily with clients and getting a sense of what is happening in the market from that constant interaction with clients. The fee-earners can then feed this information up the organisation. Mintzberg also said that strategy can be 'emergent' – you can see an organisation's strategy evolve in the way it responds to these external market stimuli. Provided, of course, that this isn't used as an excuse for not having a strategy at all.

Mintzberg did businesses a big favour in emphasising that what matters is having the mindset to keep constantly attuned to your external environment or as the maxim has it: 'Planning is everything, plans are nothing'. What matters is the activity rather than the output: in other words getting into the habit of strategic thinking rather than worrying about the look of any resulting document. If you keep surveying changes in the external environment, responding to those changes and planning how to respond to further changes, it is that strategic activity that matters, not what the individual plans themselves say. Or, to put it another way, it's no good having a beautifully presented 40-page strategy document that sits on a shelf gathering dust.

PETER DRUCKER

No mention of strategy is complete without reference to Peter Drucker, the finest management thinker of the last century. It was Drucker who pointed out that we now live and work in a knowledge economy where what a business knows matters more than what it makes.

He also talked about the 'theory of the business', saying that implicit in any business are assumptions about:

- the environment of the firm, its marketplace, customers, technology and society
- the organisation's specific mission
- the core competencies required to achieve its mission

He said these assumptions must fit reality and not be just some kind of wish-list. He also said that the theory of the business must be known and understood throughout the organisation – easier to do the smaller and younger it is. And he said the theory of the business has to be constantly tested. What is right today may not be right tomorrow.

Drucker said that successful businesses think through what it is they really offer they customers and why it is their customers buy their product or service in preference to anyone else's. This leads us to what businesses actually produce.

BOSTON CONSULTING GROUP MATRIX

Talk of strategy can be vague and 'high level' (another useful business term meaning that it lacks detail). But the BCG matrix – devised by another famous consulting group – focuses on the products themselves. It highlights something called **product lifecycle** – the idea that products are eventually superseded or become obsolete, because competitors bring out better ones.

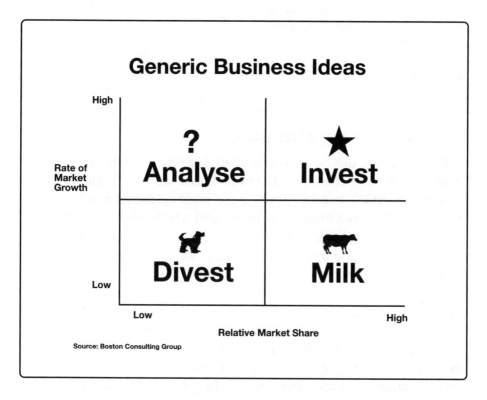

Generic Business Ideas

Rate of Market Growth — High / Low

Relative Market Share — Low / High

? **Analyse**

★ **Invest**

Divest

Milk

Source: Boston Consulting Group

The point here is that the 'cash cows' (mature products) provide the money to allow an organisation to invest in its 'stars' (the new ones). The 'dogs' need to be sold off and the question marks need to be examined and investigated further to see whether they have the potential to become stars. Over time, stars become cash cows and cash cows become dogs. So there is always a need to innovate – the bit of the business known as **R&D** (research and development).

THE BALANCED SCORECARD (KAPLAN & NORTON)

Businesses, as we shall see, focus on money. But you need to worry about more than money to create a successful business. The management academics Kaplan & Norton identified three other areas that an organisation needs to focus on to secure its long-term success:

- **clients** – obvious, really, since without clients there is no business

- **processes** – this is more subtle and means that an organisation has to look at everything it does in terms of how efficiently it does each of those things, from R&D to management

- **learning** – this is more subtle still, and means that an organisation has to be developing and 'learning' all the time rather than standing still; particularly relevant in a knowledge economy where a business's success depends on know-how and keeping that know-how up-to-date

A FISHY TALE OF SARDINES

Talk of products brings us to two other aspects of strategy. The first is that the goal of strategy is to create sustainable competitive advantage (SCA). In other words there must be something a business offers that makes it different and which others cannot easily replicate: otherwise it won't be around for the long term. Which means – and this is the second point – that it must make something that people actually want to buy.

You've heard about the frog. Now let me tell you about the fish – sardines to be exact. This is an old story about two merchants who buy and sell a consignment of sardines to each other. Each time one sells the consignment to the other, he's able to book a profit and the other does the same when selling it back (the price escalates each time, but that's not the point of the story).

Then one day, the second merchant says to the first: 'Where are the sardines you're due to sell me?'

'Oh, I've sold them to a customer,' says the first.

'You've what? What's he going to do with them?'

'He's going to eat them.'

'Eat them? But they're not for eating. They're for buying and selling!'

The point of this story is that in the business world there is a lot of 'buying and selling' – the passing of goods up and down a chain for notional profit. But businesses only prosper in the long term if they produce something customers actually want to 'eat'.

So don't be afraid to ask good basic strategic questions when you're talking to clients about their products, such as:

Is this a product people will want to 'eat'?

Why should they want to 'eat' this product rather than any other?

How can it be improved – and is the improvement worth the cost involved?

How are people going to be made aware of the product and how will it reach them?

As a professional you don't need to have answers to these questions. But clients will appreciate your interest and concern in asking them, because what ultimately drives business people is making money.

But even something as basic as money is, as we shall see, a little more complicated than it might at first appear.

Chapter 2

MONEY, MONEY, MONEY

SPEED-READ SUMMARY

- Cashflow is more important than profit

- Income or turnover is generated from sales, whereas capital is money used to fund the business

- Capital is either debt (loans or bonds) or equity (shares)

- Loans are often secured, using a charge over the borrower's assets

- Businesses like debt because it is tax-deductible whereas dividends are paid out of taxed profit so debt is cheaper

- The business vehicles are sole trader, partnership, limited liability partnership, private company and public company

- Companies are owned by shareholders who appoint directors to run the business

- Entrepreneurs are people who start businesses – success doesn't depend on the originality of their business idea

- Small businesses go to business angels and venture capitalists who provide funds for growth in return for an equity interest (shareholding)

- The two main accounting analyses of a business are its balance sheet and its profit & loss account

- A balance sheet gives you a snapshot of a company at a particular moment – what capital is used in the business, what it's used for and where it's come from

- A profit & loss account tells you how much profit (loss) a company has made over a period, usually a year

- There are various accounting terms for different aspects of money in a business

- Factoring and invoice discounting are ways of boosting cashflow

Strategy is the 'big picture' stuff. Now we need to look at the nuts and bolts of business: money.

Money plays two roles in business. First, it helps a business to keep score, to know how well it is doing, by the amount of **profit** it makes. Second, money is needed to keep the business going: without strong **cashflow** the business will go bust. In this sense, money to a business is like petrol to a car: run out of the stuff and the car won't go. If you keep these two roles of money apart in your mind, you won't go wrong.

CASHFLOW V. PROFIT

Profit is calculated by looking at a business's **income** (the amount of money it receives over a period, usually a year) and deducting its **expenses**. The difference is profit. Of course, if expenses exceed income, the business makes a loss. Income is also called **sales** or **turnover** or **gross revenue** (this term revenue has nothing to do with tax although the UK government body that collects tax is called Her Majesty's Revenue & Customs) and it simply means the total income generated by sales. You take the turnover or gross revenue, deduct the expenses and what you are left with is **net revenue**, which is the same term as profit. Expenses are also called **outgoings**.

Don't worry about these different words: in business there are many different words for the same things. The term 'net' means after expenses have been deducted. It can apply in lots of different situations. If I am owed 10 marbles by one friend but owe another six, my net position is four.

When a business generates a profit, either that money can be left in the business to fund its expansion, or it can be paid out to the owners.

Cashflow is how much money there is going through the business. Let's say you own a shop. You have to pay suppliers for the stock you put on the shelves, you have to pay the rent and rates of the premises and you have to pay staff. These are all outgoings. But at the same time you have income from customers as they buy things.

You want to make sure you have positive cashflow – in other words, you have money in the till at all times, so that whenever you have bills to pay there is enough cash in the till to do so.

Whether you make a profit – in other words, whether you are selling your goods at a price that covers your costs of doing business – is a calculation you can make only after you've been in business for a period (profit is usually calculated annually). But what matters on a day-to-day basis is having enough cash in the till. You might, on paper, be a very profitable business. But if you don't have the cash to pay the outgoings, the business will have a cashflow crisis and – unless you can get money from somewhere – have to close.

Ways of helping cashflow

Cashflow is so critical to business that banks have devised various ways of helping it (for a fee, of course). Two common methods involve (1) getting paid early and (2) paying in instalments.

Methods of getting paid early include **factoring** and **invoice discounting**. Factoring is where a bank buys a company's **receivables** (i.e. the money it is owed by customers) for immediate cash: so, let's say, I sell lots of widgets but I don't want to have to wait for my customers to pay up or chase those that don't. What I want is the cash now, to enhance my cashflow. So I sell those debts to my bank for, say, 90% of their value. I get 90 pence in the pound immediately for no hassle and the bank gets the other 10% for chasing up the debts and, also, as interest on the 90% between the time it pays that money to me and when it gets paid by my customers. A lot of businesses use factoring – it's a specialist area of banking in its own right. Invoice discounting is a variation of factoring.

Ways of paying by instalments include **hire-purchase** and **conditional sale**. These are both examples of **asset finance** (see Chapter 3). It's a bit like paying off a loan – I pay regular instalments and when the cost of the asset (and the interest on that amount) has been paid off, I get title to the asset – in other words, I become the legal owner. But, the good thing for me is that I've been able to use the asset in my business right from the start even though I couldn't afford to buy it in one lump sum.

This distinction between profit and cashflow can be hard to grasp. It certainly took me time. Don't worry about that. It's like riding a bicycle. One day you will suddenly 'get it' and you'll be fine.

It's the reason for the following two strange-but-true statements:

- A business can be very profitable but still go bust
- A business doesn't have to make a profit in order to keep going

Weird, huh? Let's take a closer look.

Let's say that your shop has an annual turnover of £100,000 but each year you make a loss of £1,000. If you could borrow £10,000 (which on a turnover of 10 times that amount you probably could), you could carry on for 10 years without making a profit.

By contrast, let's say you sell high-value items, such as sailing boats. Each boat costs £20,000 and you sell five a year, each one generating a profit of £4,000. So over the year you make a profit of £20,000. It's a good business. But it's a lumpy business because you never know when you're going to sell the five boats. If you don't sell any over winter, for instance, you may run out of cash to keep the business going.

So you can have a profitable business on paper, but find that you run out of cash before you've been able to generate the expected profit. So what matters to business is cashflow first, and profit second. It's why business talks about 'cash is king' (a 'cash crunch' is a lack of cashflow). If you run out of money and you are a company, you become **insolvent** and are **wound up**. If you are an individual you become **bankrupt**.

A cashflow problem is caused by the 'gap' between a business receiving money from buyers and having to pay money out to suppliers, employees and other creditors. This gap is called the business's **working capital requirement** and is usually funded by a bank loan or (if there are any) retained profits from previous successful years. (By the way, 'requirement' doesn't mean it's a rule or anything – it just means what a particular company requires and it differs from business to business.)

INCOME V. CAPITAL

Another distinction to get your head round is between income and capital. **Income** is what a business or individual earns on a day-today basis from trading or working (as mentioned above it's also called revenue or turnover). **Capital** is the money a business needs in order to be in business, in order to fund its premises, equipment and so on, which are called its **fixed assets**.

By the way, don't be confused by that earlier term 'working capital requirement'. Although it contains the word 'capital' it is really an income issue and is only called 'capital' (I imagine) because you need a slug of capital to fill the cashflow gap.

Business formats

You can work on your own as a **sole trader**. Plumbers, market stall-holders, authors, decorators — these tend to be **self-employed** individuals who work on their own for themselves.

If two or more sole traders or self-employed people get together they may form a **partnership**. Each partner is liable for the debts of the partnership as a whole — this is called **joint and several liability**. The partnership does not have a separate identity from that of the individuals within it. However, some large accountancy and law firms have become **limited liability partnerships (LLPs)** and they function more like companies: the individual partners are not liable for the LLP's debts.

A **firm** is, technically speaking, a partnership. But people usually use it to mean a business. And businesses tend to be companies. A **company** can be either **private** or **public**. A private company only needs one shareholder. You can buy an off-the-shelf company for about £100 from company formation agents. So you can become a company director (sounds important) just by spending £100 and filling in a form. Amazing, huh? By contrast, a public company is listed on a stock exchange and has to go through all sorts of hoops to get listed and stay listed (we will explore this later).

All companies (private and public) have **limited liability** (it's why they are called 'limited') which means that if the company goes bust, neither its **directors** (who run it) nor its **shareholders** (who own it) are liable for its debts. So companies are good vehicles for business because of their limited liability status. However, if the directors have been guilty of **misfeasance** (wrong doing) they may be liable.

SOURCES OF CAPITAL: EQUITY V. DEBT

There are two sources of capital: **equity** and **debt**. Equity is money that people invest in a business in return for (1) a share in that business which they hope will grow in value and (2) a share of its profits which they receive as **dividends** (but only when a company has profits to distribute). So they hope to receive dividends paid out of the profits. They also hope that the better the business does, the greater the value of their shares in it. They **realise their**

Entrepreneurs: the people who start businesses

Entrepreneurs are businessmen who build businesses from scratch. Alan Sugar and Richard Branson are famous entrepreneurs. The term suggests an appetite for risk-taking and the ability to be innovative. **James Dyson**, for example, invented the bagless vacuum cleaner and turned it into a business. But you don't have to be original to be successful.

Bill Gates, the world's richest man (net worth: approx $50 billion), didn't invent the operating system that powers Windows. It was called DOS ('dirty operating system' – 'dirty' meaning it wasn't perfect) and was invented by some geeks in a Californian garage. He simply took the idea (and I don't mean steal) and turned it into a business – this was at a time when the dominant player in the computer industry, IBM, thought that the world would be dominated by a small number of machines (under a dozen) that did everything and would be served by men in laboratories wearing white coats. Gates thought the opposite: that everyone would have one and they'd be commodities. **Michael Dell** took this idea of commoditisation further by showing that you can sell computers without people seeing what they are buying till

they've got it – and not making one until someone has ordered it.

The **McDonald** brothers were ranchers who ran a diner on the side selling beef burgers made from their cattle. Ray Kroc was a salesman who sold soda siphons to restaurants and bars. He sold several to their diner. Surprised at how many they needed he sat in their car-park all day watching customers come and go, then went back to the brothers to suggest a joint venture, setting up diners all over the country to sell their hamburgers. The brothers weren't interested but franchised the idea to him. So the ultimate franchisor was originally a franchisee (for more on franchising, see the next chapter).

John Madejski, who owns Reading Football Club and has done more to transform that town than anyone else, made his fortune from a magazine called *Auto Trader* in which people advertised cars for sale. It wasn't his idea. As a student he went to America and saw that car-sales magazines had pictures of the cars in them so people could actually see what a car looked like before deciding whether to make inquiries. In Britain we didn't do that (this was when Britain was still a grey, run-down economy and pictures weren't serious). So when he returned he started his magazine with pictures. And made a fortune.

investment (turn the value of their shares into money) by selling the shares.

Debt is money that is lent to a business, usually by a bank. In return the bank gets **interest** and gets repaid the amount it originally lent (the **principal**).

Businesses that incorporate start off as private companies. They are owned by a small number of shareholders. Their shares are not traded on a stock exchange and, generally, the people who own them work in them. Most small and medium-sized businesses (called **SMEs** – Small and Medium-sized Enterprises) are private companies. A company (private or public) is separate from its directors and shareholders. It is said to have **legal personality**.

EQUITY FUNDING

Initially an entrepreneur will raise equity finance from friends and family. But as the business grows and expands he or she may need further sources of equity funding to support that expansion. These sources are called **venture capitalists** and they provide **venture capital** ('venture' being an old-fashioned term for something risky – an adventure). Wealthy people – individuals – who do this are called **business angels** (like theatrical angels who fund West End productions). But most venture capital providers are either independent **boutiques** ('boutique' in this context meaning a financial 'shop') or are part of a **bank** (but even when they are part of a bank they are still providing equity capital, not debt). Some are public companies in their own right, such as 3i, Electra and Candover. Some **institutional investors** – pension funds, insurance companies and fund managers – also provide venture capital.

All venture capitalists invest to make a **return**. Their expertise lies in identifying small businesses to invest in, nurturing those businesses and then, once those businesses are bigger and stronger, selling their shares for a big profit, then using that profit to invest in more small businesses, and so on. It's risky: many small companies go bust within the first five years. So when venture capitalists put money into a business they like to have a large shareholding so that when they come to sell, their profit more than

Security

Banks will always seek security – i.e. assets that they can sell if the borrower **defaults** (fails to pay interest or repay principal). Security can take the form of a **charge** over the borrower's assets. A charge may be **fixed** (over particular assets) or **floating** (which allows the borrower to deal with those assets). If the borrower doesn't repay the loan on time or pay the interest when due, the bank can **enforce** its security and sell the charged property in order to recover the money it is owed.

If the company is part of group, there may be a **guarantor** that guarantees payment of the interest and repayment of the principal. The guarantor is usually a parent company (i.e. which owns the borrowing company) hence the guarantee being known as a **parent company guarantee.**

An assurance that falls short of a full guarantee is called a **comfort letter** to reassure the bank that, as the company's principal or sole shareholder, the parent company will keep the company in funds and not allow it to become insolvent. It may or may not be legally enforceable depending on its precise wording. Some guarantees are known as **standby guarantees** – they can be called upon automatically if there is a financial shortfall.

compensates them for those other investments which have gone bust. Some entrepreneurs don't like giving up this degree of ownership and control – but often they are doomed to remain small through lack of investment and vulnerable to competitors who are better funded and resourced. This comes back to issues of competition and strategy.

DEBT FUNDING

If you borrow money, you take out a **loan** and this is a **debt** you have to **repay**. Most people get loans from banks. In return for lending you money the bank receives **interest** from you. It may want **security** for the loan (if you're buying a flat or house this security is called a mortgage). Paying interest on the loan is called **servicing the debt**.

BUSINESS ATTITUDES TO BORROWING

Businesses treat borrowing differently from you and me.

I expect some of you may have a fair amount of debt from your student days. And most people either have or want a mortgage. But generally individuals don't like being in debt. As a student you will have known that by getting a degree you were increasing your earnings potential: so taking on that debt was a sort of investment in your future. Same with a flat or house. People want to buy their own place with a long-term loan because they know they will always need a place to live. So that kind of debt is considered OK. Currently, credit card companies are trying to persuade us to borrow and spend. But each of us knows in his or her heart-of-hearts that it's dangerous stuff – interest rates can be high – so we try to avoid it. In an ideal world, you live within your means and set a little aside for a rainy day or your pension (which may or may not be worth doing – as we shall see).

Making sense of numbers

Accountants use a variety of terms in connection with businesses. Here are some of them:

- **ROI (return on investment)** – the amount of income that is expected to be generated by investing a given amount of capital in a business or project
- **Net present value** – the value of a future return discounted (i.e. reduced by the interest implicit between now and then) to give a current value
- **Amortisation** – the reduction in debt by repaying it in instalments
- **Depreciation** – the reduction in the value of an asset in the business to reflect the wear and tear it suffers and to allow for the cost of its replacement
- **KPI (key performance indicators)** – the principal financial measures which tell a business whether it is on target
- **Budget** – a plan setting out how much can be spent in the business over a given period
- **Business plan** – often underpins a strategy, setting out future income and expenditure as well as items such as level of staffing, size of premises, etc.
- **Forecast** – prediction of future sales/turnover
- **Report** – financial review of a period just ended
- **Quarterly** – every three months
- **First quarter** – first three months of the financial year (often written as Q1, with the others as Q2, Q3, Q4)
- **Financial year** – the 12-month period at the end of which the business draws up its annual report; can be the same as the calendar year (January–December) or the tax year (April–March) but doesn't have to be
- **Balance sheet** – periodic snapshot of the capital (equity and debt) employed in the business and the assets that capital is funding
- **Profit & Loss** – statement of income and expenditure over a period showing whether or not a profit or loss is generated

But businesses are different. They like debt. In fact they are encouraged to use debt, because the cost of servicing a loan (i.e. paying the interest on it) is **tax-deductible**. I know anything to do with tax sounds boring but this is important: businesses are taxed on their profit. But the interest they pay on debt is deducted from taxable profit, which reduces the tax bill (which is good, because paying a lump of tax will reduce your cashflow). So businesses like to borrow.

Contrast this with the dividends they pay to their shareholders. Whereas a business must pay interest on its loans or face being sued by the lender, dividends are paid only if there is sufficient profit – **dividend cover** – for a company to do so. And dividends are paid out of **taxed profit** – they are not tax-deductible. So debt can be a cheaper way of raising funds than equity. This is why businesses routinely have more debt than individuals. And they are constantly **refinancing** it – finding cheaper borrowing offers and options.

One reason why companies like to borrow as much as they can is that the more money you have available to you, the quicker you can grow and achieve your strategy. A business starved of investment cannot expand as quickly as one that has access to money – and so it risks being overtaken by richer competitors.

ACCOUNTS

You may well be a young accountant: if so, don't bother with the rest of this chapter. For the rest of you, I will try to make this as short as possible.

There are two accounting documents which relate to companies that you need to know about. One is the balance sheet. The other is the P&L (profit and loss) account. They do different things.

The **balance sheet** tells you how much capital is employed in the business, where the capital is from and what it's being used to fund in the business. It is like a snapshot of the company and relates to a **single point in time.**

By contrast the **P&L account** records the business's income and expenses **over a period** and tells you whether it's made a profit or loss – there's an accounting convention that a loss is stated in brackets like this: (loss).

BALANCE SHEET

A simple balance sheet tells you:

1. Where the company's funding comes from:
   ■ Shareholders
   ■ Lenders (bank)
   ■ Money owed to suppliers (creditors)

2. What it is being used to fund:
   ■ Land and buildings
   ■ Machinery and equipment
   ■ Raw materials
   ■ Finished products
   ■ Money owed by customers (current debtors)
   ■ Money at the bank

Note that creditors are people you owe money to (they are giving you 'credit') and debtors are people who owe money to you (they have debts to you).

I hope that, looked at like this, it's beginning to make sense. Can you see that:
   ■ Land and buildings
   ■ Machinery and equipment
are needed in the business long-term so are 'fixed assets' while the rest are used up and replaced so are called 'current assets'?

On the next page I have set out a traditional balance sheet. You will see that the left-hand side (capital and liabilities – 'liabilities' means what the company owes) and the right-hand side (assets) 'balance' – they both add up to the same. If they didn't, it wouldn't be a balance sheet. And just to make it absolutely complete we would need to give it a title specifying the date on which it is accurate (businesses are always dynamic and changing so the balance sheet relates to one specific date) such as:

Balance sheet of ABC Ltd
as at 31 December 2006

Capital and liabilities		Assets	
Issued share capital	£15	**Fixed assets**	
		Land / buildings	£9
		Machinery / equipment	£6
Loan from bank	£5	**Current assets**	
Current liabilities		Raw materials	£2
Creditors	£2	Finished products	£3
		Current debtors	£1
		Cash	£1
	£22		£22

P&L

Now let's turn to the profit and loss account. Here you total up your expenses and your income to see whether you have made a profit or loss:

Expenditure
- Rent
- Rates
- Interest paid to bank for the loan
- Salaries
- Raw materials
- Electricity
- Phone bill

Then you add up your revenue from sales to give you your income, and set this out, like the balance sheet so one is opposite the other. Can you see that some costs are 'fixed' – the business has them however busy it is and they tend to be long-term (often called 'overheads'); whereas others vary in line with how busy the business is and are 'variable'? Hence what follows:

Expenditure		Income	
Fixed costs		**Revenue from sales**	**£??**
Rates	£1		
Salaries	£8		
Interest paid to bank	£2		
Variable costs			
Raw materials	£15		
Electricity	£2		
Phone bill	£1		
	£29		**£??**

You'll see that it isn't complete. We know the outgoings for the period were £29. If the revenue was more than that, we have made a profit; if less, a loss.

A profit...

Expenditure		Income	
Fixed costs		**Revenue from sales**	**£32**
Rates	£1		
Salaries	£8		
Interest paid to bank	£2		
Variable costs			
Raw materials	£15		
Electricity	£2		
Phone bill	£1		
Net profit	£3		
	£32		**£32**

... or a loss

Expenditure		Income	
Fixed costs		**Revenue from sales**	**£29**
Rates	£1		
Salaries	£8		
Interest paid to bank	£2		
Variable costs			
Raw materials	£15		
Electricity	£2		
Phone bill	£1	*Net loss*	£3
	£32		£32

We put the profit or loss figure on the side it needs to go to make the two columns add up.

And just for completeness we need to specify the period to which it relates:

Profit & loss account for ABC Ltd
1 January–31 December 2006

And that's all there is to it. Actually I've lied a little bit. You may see two things that I haven't included here. One is a balance sheet item, the other is a P&L entry.

The first is **goodwill**. This appears in balance sheets on the right-hand side as a fixed asset and generally means that bit of a business which represents why customers come to it (its reputation) that isn't just a matter of its fixed assets. Goodwill appears under the 'fixed assets' heading and is used to make the company's capital side and assets side balance. It is often used where a company is taken over and what is paid for it is more than its actual assets are worth. The excess represents goodwill – i.e. the worth of the company over and above the assets it owns. If you didn't understand that, don't worry about it. Here's an illustration.

Balance sheet of ABC Ltd
as at 31 December 2006

Capital and liabilities		Assets	
Issued share capital	£15	Fixed assets	
		Land / buildings	£9
		Machinery / equipment	£6
		Goodwill	£3
Loan from bank	£5	Current assets	
Current liabilities		Raw materials	£2
Creditors	£5	Finished products	£3
		Current debtors	£1
		Cash	£1
	£25		£25

To provide a need for goodwill I've increased the figure for creditors on the left-hand side. Note also, while we're on balance sheets, that any previous profits that aren't paid out to shareholders by way of dividend are called **retained earnings** and become part of a company's capital and liabilities.

The other, the P&L item, is **depreciation**. This is a figure that accountants put in to allow for the 'wear and tear' that the assets in a business incur as they are being used, which means that in due course they will need to be replaced. So each year the company allows a bit for depreciation to reflect the fact that sooner or later the equipment will wear out and money will need to be spent replacing it. This is an expense of the business so it appears on the left-hand side and reduces the profit or increases the loss:

Profit & loss account for ABC Ltd
1 January–31 December 2006

Expenditure		Income	
Fixed costs		**Revenue from sales**	**£32**
Rates	£1		
Salaries	£8		
Interest paid to bank	£2		
Depreciation allowance	£1		
Variable costs			
Raw materials	£15		
Electricity	£2		
Phone bill	£1		
Net profit	£2		
	£32		**£32**

If you are still puzzling over goodwill and company takeovers, all will be explained in the next chapter.

A word of warning about accounts

Accountants will understand what I am about to say. It's easy for the rest of us, especially if we are not especially numerate or financially literate, to assume that numbers never lie and are black and white in terms of the information they convey.

Numbers aren't like this at all. In the way that mathematics is a language, so numbers can mean a multitude of things. The pejorative term 'creative accounting' is a tautology: all accounting is creative to a greater or lesser extent. Which is why I often feel a twinge of sympathy for accountants who get sued by shareholders for auditing a company which then goes bust, or for vetting an acquisition which proves to have been worth less than the acquiring company thought.

Different companies present their accounts in different ways and use different conventions and financial ratios. International accounting standards differ markedly, not just in terminology and presentation, but in the treatment of many activities such as mergers, pensions, reserves, finance leases and the value of financial instruments. These differences result from different philosophies (e.g. in terms of the purpose of accounts: to inform shareholders or to protect creditors?) in different countries.

Chapter 3

GROW OR DIE: GOING PUBLIC AND DOING M&A DEALS

SPEED-READ SUMMARY

- Venture capitalists realise their investment by selling the shares – their exit routes include trade sales and flotations

- Franchising is a way of building market presence quickly – and reducing start-up risk

- A flotation is when a private company lists its shares on the Stock Exchange – and is known as 'listing' or 'floating' or 'going public' or 'doing an Initial Public Offering'

- Shares in public companies are held by institutional investors – pension funds, insurance companies and fund managers

- A public company can use its shares to buy a target – this is called a takeover or M&A (merger & acquisition)

- A bid is recommended or hostile – depending on whether the target's directors accept it or not

- Competition authorities prevent companies from building up market-dominant positions, for instance through M&A

- Companies sell off non-core assets, often through MBOs (management buy-outs)

- Private equity is the use of institutional investors' money in order to take public companies private

- Businesses can never stand still – they grow or die and their CEOs worry about competitors

- The price/earning ratio is the most commonly used means of comparing companies' financial performance

The most dramatic development in a company's life is when it goes **public**, also known as **floating**, **listing**, doing an **Initial Public Offering (IPO)** or a **flotation**. This is when its shares are listed on the Stock Exchange for the public to buy and trade (hence 'going public'). There are three reasons for doing this:

- To allow the venture capitalists to realise their investment (this is known as their **exit route**) so they can reinvest in other small businesses, grow them, sell them and so on
- As a mark of maturity – to show the world that the business has arrived and is a major player
- To raise more equity finance by issuing fresh shares to new shareholders

It's a bit like a football club being promoted. Public companies have the letters 'PLC' after their name.

LISTING REQUIREMENTS

In order to float on the London Stock Exchange, the company has to meet an extensive list of requirements. These are designed to ensure (1) the company is properly organised and managed, (2) prospective investors have as much information as they need to make an informed decision over whether to buy shares in the company and (3) the information is correct.

The company issues a **prospectus** which is like a brochure, in which it tells the world about itself, its products, its history, its management, its prospects and its financial standing. You'll be pleased to hear that the prospectus must contain an 18-month cashflow forecast.

The company will appoint a number of advisers to help it, including a **broker** (a Stock Exchange member firm) to **sponsor** it. The sponsor plays a central role in advising the company, e.g. on what it needs to do to meet the Stock Exchange's **listing requirements**. The broker acts as an interface between company and potential investors. It markets the shares to them and puts in place any **underwriting arrangements**. Underwriting is a form of insurance that on the day the company goes public its shares will be bought. The underwriters (banks and financial institutions) guarantee to take up any of the shares that aren't sold.

If the flotation is a big success then investors may not get as many shares as they apply for, in which case it is said to be **over-subscribed** and **share allocations** are scaled back. If it is **under-subscribed**, the underwriters pick up the unallocated shares. Once the shares do trade, if they rise above the issue price, they are said to **trade at a premium**; if below the issue price, they are said to trade at a **discount**.

WHO BUYS THE SHARES?

It's easy to assume that the shares are bought by individual investors. In fact, under a fifth of all shares in the UK are owned by individuals. The rest are held by **institutional investors**. There are three types of institutional investor:

- **Pension funds** – most large companies have a pension fund for their employees so that they have a retirement income to live on
- **Insurance companies** – they invest the premiums people pay and meet claims out of their investment returns, so insurance companies are big buyers of shares
- **Fund managers** (also called **asset**, **wealth**, **money** or **portfolio** managers) who manage investment funds (see box on the next page) for **retail investors** (i.e. individuals) as well as managing **wholesale money** (for institutions such as pension funds and insurance companies)

Once the company has gone public, it has to meet ongoing requirements laid down by the Stock Exchange, otherwise its listing could be **suspended**. The company must:

- publish financial information regularly
- notify the Stock Exchange as soon as anything major happens in its business that may affect its share price
- send **circulars** to its shareholders whenever it wants their consent to do anything significant with its business

This is because the London Stock Exchange is keen to maintain an orderly market in which (1) all shareholders are treated equally and (2) all **price sensitive information** is in the public domain. Buying or selling shares on information that isn't public is called **insider dealing** or **insider trading** and is illegal (i.e. it is a criminal offence).

Investment funds

An investment fund is simply a pile of money that investors entrust to a fund manager to invest for them. The less colloquial name is collective investment scheme. The best way to understand them is by looking at the two most well-known and traditional types of collective investment scheme in the UK: investment trusts and unit trusts.

Investment trusts

In the 1860s, canny Scottish solicitors created investment trusts as a way in which clients with only a small amount of money could invest safely in the stock market. Let's say I have £5 to invest and company shares cost roughly £5 each. I can buy one share in one company. This is risky because that company could go bust and I will lose all my money. So that I can diversify my risk, wouldn't it be great if I could buy a share in a company whose job it is to invest in lots of other companies? And that is what an investment trust is. They are called trusts because that was their original legal structure but nowadays they are public companies that invest in the shares of other companies. The most famous in the UK is Foreign & Colonial: I can buy a share in F&C and through that investment get indirect exposure to about 400 companies – the companies that F&C invests in around the world.

Unit trusts

The other form of collective investment scheme is the unit trust (this really is a trust). Here, a fund manager creates a fund and sells units in it. If I sell 20 units at £1 each I have £20 to invest. If over, say, a year I invest wisely and double the fund's value from £20 to £40, each unit is now worth £2. If a unit holder wants to get their money out, they come to me and I cancel or redeem their unit and give them their £2. And if someone, seeing my success, wants to invest in my fund, they can buy as many units from me as they like but each will cost £2, not the £1 that units cost at the beginning. Note that the value of any fund can go down just as easily as it may go up, depending on what markets are doing.

Closed-end and open-ended

With a unit trust, the fund manager can issue as many units as there are investors who want to buy them so for this reason these funds are known as open-ended. By contrast, an investment trust is a company so the number of shares in issue at any one time is finite, which is why they are called closed-ended schemes. Nowadays there are funds that are companies but which behave like unit trusts. They are called OEICs (open-ended investment companies) or companies with variable capital.

Hedge funds

Hedge funds are collective investment schemes which take big speculative risks in order to generate big returns. In doing so they can lose their investors' money quickly, so they are not for the faint-hearted. Four things you need to know about them:

- They use financial instruments called **derivatives** (such as futures) which can be very risky (**hedging** – see next chapter – normally means the use of derivatives to guard against risk, whereas hedge funds use derivatives to incur risk, so their name is itself misleading)
- They often sell investments they don't have in the hope those investments will go down and they can buy them more cheaply later – this is known as **going short** or **shorting the market**, and is also risky (by contrast, ordinary funds are 'long' funds: they buy)

- They are often structured as **limited partnerships** for legal and tax reasons and investors may be required to stay in for several years
- The fund manager is paid a **performance fee** which may be as much as 50% of any gain (by contrast, most fund managers earn an annual fee which is a tiny percentage of the funds under management)

SECONDARY ISSUES/RIGHTS ISSUES

Although companies tend to raise fresh equity capital when they float, this isn't their only opportunity to expand their share capital. At any point they can come back to the market and raise more funds by issuing fresh shares. These are called **secondary issues** and in the US are called **seasoned equity offerings**.

Whenever a UK public company issues fresh shares it has to offer them to existing shareholders in the same proportions as their existing shareholdings. So if I own 10% of a listed company and it wants to issue fresh shares it has to offer 10% of that fresh share issue to me. I am said to have a **right of pre-emption** in respect of them, i.e. I have first option to buy them. This is why secondary offerings are sometimes called **rights issues**. Of course, I don't have to buy them. I can pass up the opportunity and they can be offered for sale to others. The reason existing shareholders have this right of pre-emption is to ensure that their percentage of the company is not **diluted**. I would be pretty annoyed if I owned a chunk of a company and suddenly found that in percentage terms my shareholding had just shrunk because the company had issued fresh shares without offering some to me.

The franchise idea

I mentioned McDonald's in the previous chapter. McDonald's is a franchise. Franchising is a fascinating form of business – and not to be sniffed at. Essentially it addresses a number of business issues and tackles them simultaneously. It is particularly prevalent in retail markets (e.g. shops, retail outlets; and services sold directly to the consumer).

People like consistency of product and service so they are suckers for the brand. When you buy a tin of Heinz Baked Beans you know exactly what you are getting. When you go into a Burger King you know exactly what you are getting. It's a promise or guarantee to the consumer that implies consistency of quality and process. So it makes sense to establish a brand. (A lot of brands are illusory – we kid ourselves that we are getting an identical product each time, but we find it reassuring.)

However, you need to establish a brand quickly – before it's copied by others – and so that it gains market presence and consumer recognition. But small businesses usually lack enough money (capital) to establish this degree of market penetration and presence quickly.

So, instead of trying to expand rapidly on its own, a business may become a **franchisor**. It encourages others (**franchisees**) to set up using its brand. They use the logo, they sell the same products or services and provide the product or service in the same well-defined way. In return they pay the franchisor for use of the brand and also for support which may include everything from providing the goods themselves to offering training to the franchisee's staff – all to achieve consistency so customers think they are dealing with the same organisation no matter which outlet they go to. The franchisor is usually entitled to a percentage of the franchisees' profits.

This degree of market impact lodges the name in consumers' minds and leads to far more customers-per-outlet than either the franchisor or franchisees could achieve on their own, without the franchisor having to provide all of the upfront capital (the franchisees usually borrow what they need from a bank). The rate of growth is far faster so everyone benefits: franchisor and franchisees.

It isn't just franchisors who can get rich through franchising. McDonald's has made many people round the world millionaires through enabling them to become master franchisees (having several outlets) in new markets.

M&As (MERGERS & ACQUISITIONS)

Once a company has floated, it can start to do **M&A** deals – taking over other companies. Companies take over other companies to:

■ knock out a competitor (but if this is likely to lead to a monopoly, government **competition authorities** may step in to stop it or impose conditions)
■ enter new markets quickly

In short, to achieve their strategy.

M&A is the takeover of one company (the **target**) by another (the **bidder**). Private companies can take each other over but it can be easier for a public company to take over another public company because:

■ the bidder can use its own shares (which, being traded on a stock exchange, have an immediate value) instead of cash to buy the target's shares, and
■ the target's shareholders aren't its directors so they are more likely to agree to a bid even if the directors will (as is usually the case) lose their jobs once the bidder is in charge

However, as in all things, Cash is King in business, so a bidder offering cash will always be more welcome than a bidder offering its own shares.

This brings us back to cashflow. All businesses are in the food chain: they buy from suppliers and sell to customers. What matters is: (1) when your customers pay you and (2) when you pay your suppliers. The first thing corporate raiders and acquisitive companies do when buying a business is to bully its suppliers into extending credit for payment. So instead of paying in say 30 days, they will insist on paying in 60 days – and then find any and every excuse not to pay. This may drive some suppliers to the wall because of the disruption to their cashflow.

This is how people put together huge conglomerates – by acquiring companies, stripping out all except crucial costs and then doing the same again before the cost-cutting catches up with them. The question they always ask is: is a particular process worth the cost? If not, they cut it. This generates huge short-term profits. The trick is to keep on doing it before the lack of investment shows, or to sell off the business as soon as possible. Going back to the tale

Competition

Governments in developed economies are concerned to ensure **competition** so that consumers benefit from choice and competitive prices and **new entrants** are able to enter the market.

In the US, competition regulation is called **anti-trust** from its origins in fighting the early railroad and oil trusts ('trust' in those days meaning 'big business'). In Europe, competition regulation happens at a national and EU level to ensure open markets.

In general, competition regulation focuses on:

- **Monopolies** (from the Greek meaning *monos* = one and *polein* = sell) which are about a single provider having a dominant position in the market so it can set prices and undercut new entrants, preventing them from becoming established. A **horizontal monopoly** occurs when a company takes control of others offering products to the same markets and may even maintain their separate brands to sustain an appearance of competition. A **vertical monopoly** occurs when a company controls the various steps in the supply chain from creation of the product or service through to its sale and delivery to the customer

- **Cartels** which are centralised organisations set up to coordinate several independent providers which can lead to **quotas** (restricted production to maintain high prices), **price fixing** between them and **restrictive practices** to prevent newcomers from entering the market

- **Mergers** which may lead to market dominance in a sector

The result of a regulatory investigation can range from those involved agreeing to restructure their businesses (e.g. a merger may be allowed to proceed provided the acquiring company sells off certain operations of the target) to court cases, fines which can be a significant percentage of turnover and even prison for implicated executives. Much of the analysis is economic, looking at the impact on markets, and much of the legal argument centres on defining markets and interpreting data.

of sardines in the last chapter, this is very much 'buying and selling' rather than 'eating' and a lot of people (including professionals, by acting as advisers) can make a lot of money out of it.

The bidder makes an offer to the target's shareholders to buy their shares in the target for a price that is higher than the market price (in other words for a **premium**). If the bid succeeds, the target will be wholly owned by the bidder and will become its **subsidiary**. A subsidiary is a company that is owned by another company. Big businesses may consist of many companies with a **parent** or **holding company** at the top of the **group** and all the rest being known as **group companies**.

Business terminology

B2C (business-to-consumer) – This term applies to companies that make and sell products and services that people buy and use, also known as **retail**.

B2B (business-to-business) – applies to companies that sell goods or services to other companies, also known as **wholesale**.

Channels to market – the ways in which a company reaches its customers.

Sectors – different companies do different things. If two do roughly the same they are said to be in the same **industry** or **sector** – and are likely to be competitors. Sectors fall broadly into three:

- **Primary** – extraction of natural resources (including oil, minerals and agriculture)
- **Secondary** – conversion of natural resources into products (manufacturing)
- **Tertiary** – the service sector (intangible goods and services) ranging from insurance to tourism

Some argue that there is a fourth (quaternary) sector which is about exploitation of know-how: information, research and education.

Multinationals – companies that operate in several markets (and which may therefore decide to list on several stock exchanges) are called multinationals or **MNCs** (multinational companies). They have internationally recognised names or brands such as Coca-Cola, McDonald's, Microsoft, Ford and Nike.

RECOMMENDED BIDS AND HOSTILE TAKEOVERS

Some targets are happy to be taken over if the price is right –
because all directors have a duty to do what is in the best interests
of their shareholders. These are called **agreed** or **recommended
bids**, because the directors of the target recommend the bid to
their shareholders, i.e. they advise their shareholders to accept the
bidder's offer. But many are not – especially if the target's directors
are likely to be sacked. They **reject** the bid which then becomes
hostile (or **contested**).

The bidder then has a choice. It can withdraw its offer, in which
case that's the end of the matter. Or it can persist in its attempts to
persuade the target's shareholders to sell their shares to it. For
instance, it may argue that the target's management are a bunch of
incompetents and that it would make a better fist of running the target
than its existing management. For these reasons passions can run high.

The bidder will be advised by a **bank** that coordinates activities
and issues the **offer document** on behalf of the bidder. In banking
circles, advising on M&As is one aspect of what is called
corporate finance.

So that bids don't get out of hand and don't go on too long
(because of the uncertainty they cause), there are detailed rules
about how such bids are conducted. Takeovers are policed by the
Takeover Panel which has a rule-book called the **City Code on
Takeovers and Mergers**. The Takeover Panel isn't a government
body. It is in fact a committee with a full-time secretariat but with
experts seconded from banks, law firms and accountants in the City.

In particular, the Panel polices the **bid timetable**. Hostile bids create
enormous uncertainty for both companies and so the sooner the
outcome of the bid is known the better; and both sides need to enjoy
equal treatment to put their case and counter the other side's. There
are also rules to ensure that when the bidder has majority control
(more than 50%) of the target, it is required to buy out any minority
interests at a favourable price: it's no fun owning 10% of a company
that is being run by someone else for their benefit.

Old CEOs never die – they just pop up elsewhere

When a company is taken over, it can be traumatic for the CEO: you may be sacked and your reputation suffers.

But some CEOs (chief executive officers), labelled **captains of industry** by the press, seem to go from one large company to another getting massive **golden hellos** (a sum for signing on), big salaries and grants of **share options** (together known as the **remuneration package**) and huge **golden parachutes** (compensation for being sacked, for instance if the company is taken over) plus enormous contributions to their **pension funds**.

They are often the CEO of one major company and on the boards of several others. Often they seem to be rewarded for failure, then pop up heading another big company.

It's to stop these excesses that **corporate governance** – the relationship between the people running a company (the board) and those who own it (institutional investors) – has become a big issue. See Chapter 5.

A **reverse takeover** is when a smaller company takes over a larger one.

SELLING OFF NON-CORE ASSETS

Apart from buying other businesses, companies also sell off bits of their business that are no longer relevant to their strategy. These are called 'non-core' assets. Such sales often follow a successful acquisition when the bidder starts to integrate the target and realises that some bits of the acquired business are of no interest to it.

The bits not wanted can be sold off piecemeal in what are called **asset sales**. Or they can be injected into new, separate companies whose shares are then sold off. Doing this is called a **hive-down**. Payment can be in cash or shares (if the buyer is listed, in which case it is called a **share-for-share exchange**) and can be paid immediately on completion or postponed till a future date (called **deferred**) or based on the earnings of the business under new ownership (called an **earn-out**). If a buyer just wants some of the assets, this is called **cherry picking**.

MBOs

Often these sales are to the managers of the business being sold. This is called a **management buy-out** (MBO). The managers know the business better than anyone else so want to buy it; and by owning it they will put real effort into making it successful – and ultimately hope to sell it off, perhaps by going public in due course. But in order to buy the business they will need outside funding and this is usually provided by venture capitalists – another example of how these things all connect. So venture capital providers don't just fund start-ups; they also fund MBOs of established businesses.

Not all MBOs are small. Some can be big deals that depend on a high degree of borrowing and are called **LBOs** (leveraged buy-out – leveraged means highly borrowed or **highly geared**).

PRIVATE EQUITY

Some takeovers of public companies are done specifically to **take those companies private**. These deals are often funded by institutional investors. They put money into a fund and that fund is used to mount the takeover. The target is then dismembered and the components merged with other businesses and then sold off or listed. These deals are led by private equity boutiques. These are like venture capitalists but they specialise in **public-to-private deals**, as these types of M&A are called. One of the most well known is KKR (Kohlberg Kravis Roberts). Venture capital is itself now regarded as part of private equity: **upstream private equity** is the act of raising the money from institutional investors; **downstream private equity** is the act of spending it, either on public-to-private deals or on start-ups (which is the traditional venture capital activity).

I've dealt with bids in some detail because they involve many sets of different professional advisers – so you may become involved in one. Also because your clients – if they are senior people in a public company – will be constantly thinking about whether to make bids or (more worryingly) whether they may be on the receiving end of one.

Who determines whether a company is taken over? Their shareholders, i.e. the **institutional investors** mentioned earlier – which is why big companies have **investor relations units** that liaise with shareholders. CEOs worry constantly about the share price of their company: if it dips it may be vulnerable to a takeover; if it goes up unexpectedly, someone may be building a stake prior to announcing a bid; in either case the CEO is likely to be out of a job if the bid succeeds.

GROW OR DIE

Shareholders in a company will stand by the management and won't sell out to a bidder if they feel the company is going forward and expanding – i.e. if it has a strategy. **Businesses never stand still**. If they are not going forward, they are going backward, stagnating and, in relation to their competitors, shrinking. So all businesses must expand to survive or else risk being overtaken (and maybe taken over) by their competitors.

This is why businesses are forever changing. They take each other over, get rid of bits that are considered non-core, move into new markets, develop new products, change their names and branding, reinvent themselves – and they do this on an ongoing basis, in pursuit of strategies (much of this is 'buying and selling' from the sardine tale). In business, if you do stand still, your competitors will copy your ideas, undercut your prices, improve on your goods or services and steal your customers.

I hope by now that you are beginning to see business as a dynamic, endlessly changing landscape – which is what makes it interesting. Over any 10-year period, 40 of the 100 companies that make up the FTSE 100 (the 100 largest companies by market capitalisation listed on the London Stock Exchange) disappear from it: they are taken over or shrink. Over the 40 years from 1957 to 1997, 85% of the S&P 500 (the equivalent US index) disappeared. GE (which used to be General Electric) is the only original member left of the Dow Jones 30 (another US index) and its business has changed out of all recognition.

READING THE FINANCIAL PAGES

People get freaked when they see pages of tightly-clustered columns of figures in the financial pages of the press. But what these figures tell you is really quite straightforward.

First you have to realise that the financial pages cover all sorts of different markets from shares and bonds to bills (short-term bonds), commodities ('soft' ones like coffee and cocoa and 'hard' ones like gold), investment funds, foreign exchange (the relative values of different currencies) as well as interest rates.

Here we will focus on shares. Each share market has a number of indices – these represent an average of the prices of the companies whose shares are in the index. In the UK the most well known is the FTSE 100 mentioned above. You also get the FTSE 250, the FTSE 350 and the FTSE-All Share.

Typically, you may come across some or all of the following information about a company's shares:

- **Market price** – the share's value at the market close the previous day (usually an average of all the quotes provided by the various market makers)
- **Price change** – yesterday's closing price compared to the day before
- **Price movements** – the highest and lowest over the previous 12 months: this shows you how **volatile** (up and down) a company's share price is
- **Market capitalisation** – how much the company is worth (arrived at by multiplying the number of shares in issue by the share price): this tells you how big the company is
- **Gross dividend yield** – the dividend divided by the share price expressed as a percentage: this tells you how much income return you are getting for your capital investment in the company's shares (see the next chapter for more on yields). Investors wanting income (dividends) will go for a high yield
- **Price/earnings ratio** – the p/e ratio is the share price divided by the earnings per share (EPS) with EPS being the net profit over the company's most recent trading year divided by the

number of shares in issue. The p/e ratio is used as a measure to compare how much dividend you get for the price of the share between companies in the same sector (p/e ratios differ between sectors). Another way of looking at it is that the resulting figure tells you how many years it will take on the basis of the current dividend stream to get back the cost of the share. The p/e ratio is the single most commonly used way of assessing company performance. Investors looking for growth (increase in share value over time) will look for high price/earnings

- **Dividend cover** – the ratio of profits to dividends, i.e. the extent to which the current dividend is 'covered' by current profit: the better the cover the more cautious the company is being in not paying out all of its profits to shareholders but retaining earnings to fund expansion

READING AN ANNUAL REPORT

All public companies produce annual reports for their shareholders, but anyone can get a copy just by asking the company or looking at its website. UK companies are obliged to file their annual accounts at Companies House where they are available for public inspection.

An annual report contains two types of information:

- **Soft** – details of the management's background together with their views of the company's prospects and future market conditions; and
- **Hard** – financial data (but remember my warning towards the end of the last chapter)

The sorts of hard, financial information to look out for include:

- **Gearing** – the ratio of shareholders' funds (equity) to liabilities (debt); a high level of gearing is riskier because borrowings are high relative to equity, but may also indicate that the business is expanding fast by maximising the capital available to it
- **Income gearing** – the ratio of interest payable on the company's debt to the profits out of which that interest is paid (this is similar to the role of dividend cover – see above – in relation to the company's equity base); again, the higher the

ratio the more the company may be stretched to service its debt if profits fall, but it may also be a positive indication of a company straining at the leash to expand as fast as possible

- **Pre-tax profit margin** – this measures the profits earned per pound sterling of sales. Profit margin indicates how efficient a company is, how sustainable its competitive advantage (see below) is and how resilient it is likely to be if faced with adverse market conditions
- **Return on capital employed (ROCE)** – this is a key performance measure of what economists call 'economic rent' (sustainable return) and is indicative of a company's efficiency in using its assets funded by its capital, and its ability to generate earnings that will provide future dividends – a reflection of its sustainable competitive advantage

ROCE, however it is measured, connects with strategy. In Chapter 1, I said that the point of strategy was to create sustainable competitive advantage. To couch this in economic terms, a company is expected to generate returns that are consistently greater than its **cost of capital** (i.e. the money invested in it). These returns are called **economic rent** by economists who say that a sustainable competitive advantage leads to above-normal rent. Of course, such rents will attract new entrants who drive down economic rents. Which takes us back to Porter's Five Forces.

INTERNAL WAYS OF ASSESSING ROCE

Since the primary role of a company is to create value for its shareholders, the managers of the business apply a variety of ways that measure the return on the shareholders' funds, including:

- **Total business return** – which captures changes in the value of a business over a period and the cashflows generated by it during that period
- **CFROI (cashflow return on investment)** – which compares the cumulative cash invested in a business with the cash the business is producing, while allowing for the ageing of assets employed in the business as well as inflation
- **Free cashflow** – operating cash less interest on loans, taxes and investment (this is in many respects the same as earnings)

- **Discounted cashflow** – which is used to evaluate possible projects by assessing how much the capital required to fund the project would generate if invested elsewhere, and then comparing that return to the project's expected return: if that return is less than the alternative, the project should not be undertaken (the reference to 'discounted' is because the future return has to be turned into today's money by subtracting the intervening return to get back to 'net present value' – but the key question is what discount to apply)
- **EVA (economic value added)** – a measure invented by consultants Stern Stewart which seeks to calculate the value of a business activity that is left over by subtracting the cost of executing that activity and the opportunity cost (i.e. what could have been generated by an alternative activity)

For their part, shareholders may consider:

- **Market value added** – which is the difference between the current market value of a company (i.e. its stock market value) and the capital contributed by shareholders. If it is positive, then the company has added value; if not, it has destroyed shareholder value (true of many M&A deals)
- **Total shareholder return** – which measures three cashflows associated with a share: purchase price (cash out); dividend stream (cash in); and value realised on sale (cash in)

The point of all of these measures is that different ones are appropriate at different times and for different purposes. Like the slipperiness of accounts (mentioned in the last chapter) all these measures have their limitations. Unless you are an accountant or management consultant, you don't need to understand these measures fully. You just need to recognise what business people are talking about when they mention them – which takes us to the next chapter: the international financial markets generally.

Chapter 4

BONDS, LOANS AND THE FINANCIAL MARKETS

SPEED-READ SUMMARY

- Bonds are issued by public companies and governments

- The majority of bonds are bearer instruments that pay a fixed rate of interest and are called fixed-income securities

- The rate of interest (the coupon) is stated in hundredths of a per cent, called basis points

- Bonds that are rated below investment grade are called high-yield or junk bonds

- The principal types of bank are commercial (lending), investment (securities underwriting and trading) and bundled (both)

- Asset finance (finance leasing) is a form of loan-based funding where the bank buys the asset (plant and machinery, including ships and planes) and leases it to the borrower as lessee for the asset's useful economic life

- The foreign exchange (forex) market is where currencies are traded for immediate (spot) or future delivery, crucial for direct and indirect overseas investment

- Interest rates are used to control inflation – when interest rates go up, so does the currency, but exports and company profits go down as do stock and bond markets (bond values go down but yields go up)

- Companies hedge against financial risk using derivatives such as swaps, options and futures

- The shipping and insurance markets are huge – but are not part of the financial markets

So far we have looked at equity raising through listing on the Stock Exchange. But being a public company opens up another avenue of finance, this time on the debt side. We already know that debt consists of loans. There is another type of debt: **bonds**.

A bond is basically an IOU which can be sold to someone else. This is why bonds are said to be tradable. The word 'bond' also means guarantee (my word is my bond) – as in 'posting a bond' to guarantee that something happens or someone behaves in a certain way. But in the financial markets it means a tradable 'I owe you'.

Shares and bonds are called **securities** – not to be confused with a bank 'taking security' as in Chapter 2.

Only public companies can issue bonds. Private companies in the UK aren't allowed to issue bonds and, in any case, aren't big enough to raise the sort of amounts to make a bond issue worthwhile or to have the name recognition to make an issue successful. But public companies can and do.

A company that wants to raise, say, £100 million (bond issues are only worth doing for substantial amounts) will issue an IOU that says something like: 'I will pay you £100 million in 10 years' time and in the meantime I will pay you interest of 5%.' Whoever buys the bond will hand over £100 million to the company and in return the bondholder will receive £5 million (which is 5% of £100 million) every year for 10 years.

At the end of the 10 years the bond is redeemed (it expires) and the holder gets the £100 million back again. It's as simple as that, except that instead of one bondholder providing £100 million, there will be hundreds of institutional investors buying smaller amounts which total £100 million.

INTERNATIONAL BOND MARKET

Unlike loans (which are provided by banks), bonds are **tradable**, which means that institutional investors can buy and sell them – which is why the international bond market is global and huge, one of the biggest financial markets in the world.

Companies aren't the only issuers. Governments are big issuers of bonds. In fact the biggest borrower in the world is the US government. Its bonds are called US treasuries because they are issued by the Treasury Department. UK government bonds are called gilts because they used to have a gilt edge as a mark of distinction.

Companies can usually borrow more cheaply by issuing a bond than by getting a loan from a bank, because a bondholder can simply sell the bond to get its money back whereas it is trickier for a bank to sell a loan (loans aren't designed to be bought and sold in quite the same way).

CORPORATE BONDS

UK listed companies issue **debentures** which are registered bonds issued in the UK in sterling and listed on the London Stock Exchange as debt instruments. Debentures are often secured over the company's assets so that if the company defaults on the debenture, the holder can seize company assets and sell them to recover what it is owed (this is what lawyers call security but don't confuse it with **securities** which is the term used in the financial markets to mean bonds and shares). But the debenture market is domestic and relatively small.

By contrast, international bonds are **bearer instruments** (whoever holds a bond is treated as owning it). In the old days when they were issued as bits of card, they would have **coupons** attached that the holder would clip and return to the issuer in order to get the interest owed (that was the only proof required that you were the rightful recipient of the interest). This is why the interest payable on a bond is often called the coupon. The majority of bonds pay a fixed rate of interest throughout their life (e.g. 5%) which is why bonds are often called **fixed income instruments**. Because the amounts in question are so large, the rate of interest is expressed in hundredths of a percentage, called **basis points**.

An international bond is issued by a company outside its home market and is often denominated in dollars (the currency of international finance and trade). Although bonds have been issued internationally for centuries, the current market dates from the 1960s when issues were made to tap dollars held on deposit in European banks – hence the term 'Eurodollar' and 'Eurobond' (which does not, yet, mean a bond denominated in euros).

CREDIT RATINGS

In order to issue an international bond, a company has to get the issue **rated** by a **credit rating agency** (such as Standard & Poor's, Moody's or Fitch). The rating agency will vet the company's financial position and 'rate' the issue in terms of the company's ability to service the debt (pay interest on it) and repay the principal. The rating agency (to which the issuer pays an annual fee as well as activity-based fees in relation to each rated issue) will continue to monitor the company's ability to meet the interest payments and repay the principal on maturity. Ratings range from 'triple A' (written 'AAA' or 'Aaa' depending on the rating agency) to 'below investment grade' ('Ba1' or 'BB+' or 'BB') and if the issuer's financial condition deteriorates or – in the language – its ability to service or repay becomes 'impaired', it may be immediately **downrated**.

The reason for this is that traders in the bond markets buy and sell at a moment's notice and want to know quickly whether the issuer is likely to default. They don't have time to undertake extensive credit analysis, unlike a lending bank which will pore over a company and its accounts before making a loan to it.

JUNK OR HIGH-YIELD BONDS

If the rating goes 'below investment grade', many of the institutional investors that hold the issue will have to sell (pension funds in particular are usually forbidden by their trust deeds to hold securities that are below investment grade). The market value of the bonds will go down as fewer institutions will want, or are able, to hold them. A more pejorative term for 'below investment grade' is **junk bond** or **high-yield bond**. There are banks and traders that specialise in buying junk bonds cheaply and holding them in the hope that the issuer's fortunes will recover and the bonds will be repaid in full.

But junk bonds are not bad in themselves. For example, a company may deliberately issue a short-term, high-yield bond (paying a high rate of interest) to fund an M&A deal – then if the takeover is successful, it will refinance the issue on more preferential terms when the takeover has been completed (this is called **acquisition finance** – see page 58).

DIFFERENT MATURITIES

Bonds can have maturities ranging from 90 days to up to and beyond 20 years.

Bonds of very short duration are called **commercial paper.** These issues are made by large, listed companies to fund a short-term working capital requirement (you see, it all connects). They usually have a maturity of just 90 days and don't pay interest. Instead they are issued at a discount to their face value: at the end of the 90 days the holder is paid the full face value. So if CP with a face value of 100 is issued at 99, the company receives 99 and in three months' time pays back 100. So for three months' money the company is paying 1%, which equates to an annualised rate of 4%.

What tends to happen at the end of the 90 days is that the CP is **rolled over** – the amount owing is repaid by a fresh issue of paper made to replace the paper that has expired. Commercial paper is bought by banks to park short-term deposits, but mainly by other large companies to invest short-term revenues that aren't immediately needed but will be soon.

Bonds with maturities over five years are called **medium term notes** or MTNs. They are often issued as part of an **MTN programme** where the company has a panel of three or four banks that have agreed to meet all of the company's debt requirements including loans and MTNs. The company decides at any point what it needs, tells the panel and the one offering the cheapest rate gets the business.

Any bond over 10–12 years is called a **long bond**. As a general rule, the longer the tenor, the higher the rate of interest the company will pay to offset its **credit risk** because the longer the

What's a 'bank'?

Possibly the trickiest term in the financial markets is the word 'bank'. It covers a multitude of different financial institutions which do different things. Banks are the source of debt funding.

A bank that makes loans is called a **commercial bank.** Commercial banks take deposits from people like you and me (our monthly salary cheque for example) and they lend us money (e.g. by way of overdraft). They pay us measly amounts of interest on money we deposit with them and charge us usurious rates of interest on any money we borrow. They keep the difference (this is called the **margin** or **turn**). Lending to you or me is called **retail banking** (it's the consumer market). Lending to companies is business-to-business or **wholesale banking**. Commercial banks also fund themselves by borrowing from each other on what is called the inter-bank market and the rate of interest they charge each other is LIBOR (London inter-bank offered rate).

Then there are **investment banks**. These don't lend or invest. What they do is help companies and governments issue **bonds**: they advise them on how to issue bonds and at what price (this is called **origination**) and they underwrite the issue of those bonds. They also **distribute** those bonds to institutional investors. All of that activity is called primary market activity. Investment banks also buy and sell 'second-hand' bonds in what are called the **secondary markets** – where they act as market-makers (being prepared to buy from or sell to investors, so providing a market for those bonds) and **dealers** (buying bonds for their own account).

Investment banks now do the same for **shares** (for instance in arranging, underwriting and distributing the shares in IPOs), but they didn't always do this. In the UK this was traditionally done by **merchant banks**, which helped businesses trade internationally by providing **letters of credit** and **trade finance**. This knowledge of their corporate clients enabled merchant banks to advise them on raising equity finance and M&A deals (together called **corporate finance**) and on investing their profits and pension funds (called **fund management**).

Merchant banks have now all but disappeared – taken over by commercial and investment banks. In fact the biggest banks in the world combine all these activities – commercial, merchant and investment banking – and are called **bundled, conglomerate** or **universal banks**. Occasionally banks' credit ratings dip below those of their corporate customers – for instance, if the industry is in a periodic downturn. Then companies can tap institutional investors for funds directly, bypassing banks. This is **disintermediation** and banks hate it.

maturity, the less easy it is to predict what state the company is likely to be in when the bond expires.

Zero coupon bonds (also known as **deep discount bonds**) are issued without a coupon: they don't pay interest but are issued at a discount to their par or face value; on maturity the holder receives the face value. So, for example, a 5-year bond with a face value of 100 that is issued at 80 will reward the holder by paying an additional 20 on redemption, which is a 25% return over five years on the initial investment, or 5% a year.

SYNDICATED LOANS

You still get loans in the international financial markets but these tend to be huge and because they are so big will be beyond a single bank to provide. So a company's bank will put together a **syndicate** of banks which between them will lend the company the money that it wants but on identical terms using a single **syndicated loan agreement**.

Each bank will go through its internal **credit approval** process, involving **due diligence** (examining the company's financial standing – due diligence also occurs in M&A deals). Once the loan agreement has been negotiated and signed (this is called **completion**) the company can **draw down** the money provided it satisfies some conditions precedent (various **legal opinions** and **certificates** ensuring the documents are duly signed and the borrower is legally capable of borrowing).

Other types of bank

Central banks are government-owned regulators of banks and they act as the **lender of last resort** to stop any individual bank from going bust.

Supranational banks are part of the International Monetary Fund and their job is to channel funds into parts of the world that need them to develop their economies and industries. Examples include the **World Bank**, the **European Investment Bank** (which is a lending bank rather than an investment bank), the **EBRD** (European Bank for Reconstruction and Development), the **Asian Development Bank**, the **African Development Bank** and so on.

During the life of the loan the company must comply with **covenants** (promises) in the loan agreement. Any breach by the company of the terms of the loan agreement is an **event of default** which allows the banks to **accelerate** the loan (ask for the money back early).

Acquisition finance

One of the growth areas for syndicated loans is in M&A transactions, where bank lending is called acquisition finance. As you now know, acquisitions are traditionally funded by the buyer's equity ('paper') in a share-for-share acquisition. But debt finance is often more attractive to:

- the target's shareholders (they get money not the buyer's shares)
- the buyer, since the costs are tax-deductible (whereas dividends are paid out of after-tax income)
- the buyer's shareholders, since any additional issue of equity may depress the buyer's earnings-per-share (since there are more shares in issue) which is a key profitability figure

The debt can be provided as a loan. But **high-yield bonds** (see earlier) are also used in acquisition finance to fund an M&A deal for a short period until it is refinanced with a loan or bond at a lower rate of interest.

Acquisition finance is also used to fund MBOs and LBOs (see previous chapter). Sometimes a bank may want the option of turning its loan (or part of the loan) into shares if the bought-out business does well, in which case that debt is called **mezzanine finance** (mezzanine is a floor that's mid-way between two others; so this type of debt is mid-way between debt and equity). It is **convertible** from debt into equity, which is what convertible bonds are.

ASSET FINANCE (ALSO KNOWN AS FINANCE LEASING)

A lot of businesses don't actually own the assets they use. Whereas you and I might want to own the place we live in or the car we drive, businesses aren't interested in ownership provided they have the **economic use** of the asset. So instead of borrowing money to buy an asset (such as an aircraft in the case of an airline or an oil rig if you're an oil company), they get the bank to buy it and then **lease** it to them. This is like renting a flat rather than buying it with a mortgage – you never end up owning it.

This can actually be cheaper than borrowing and buying, for two reasons. The first is that the bank actually owns the asset so it feels more secure, which means it is exposed to less risk (if the company defaults, the bank owns the asset so can easily grab it back). This in turn means that it will charge less by way of **rental** under the lease than it would have by way of interest under a loan. The second is that the government gives tax advantages for capital investment (as buying big assets for use in business is called) – in order to encourage business to invest in itself and remain competitive internationally. These tax advantages are passed on, in part, by the bank – in effect reducing the rental payable under the lease.

What happens is that the company enters into the lease with the bank. The lease term (length) is for the useful economic life of the asset (say 15 years). By the end of that primary term (as the lease period is called) the bank has been paid out – in other words the company's payments of rental (usually quarterly) have paid back the bank the cost of the asset and the interest on the principal over the 15 years (in this sense the payments work just like a mortgage – the further along you get, the greater the part of the payments that is paying off the principal cost of the asset).

So after 15 years the asset is either sold in the second-hand market and the company leases a new one; or it can continue to lease the asset but at a peppercorn rent (i.e. next-to-nothing since the bank has already been repaid). During the course of the lease, the company is required to **maintain** and **insure** the asset (almost as if it owned it) and is prevented from **selling** or **charging** the asset to anyone else (since the bank is the owner).

You'd be surprised how many things are leased: most airlines lease rather than own their planes; most train companies lease their carriages. Virtually anything can be leased provided it is used in a business context. This includes oil rigs and ships on the one hand and audio recordings and films on the other.

Finance leasing should not be confused with **operating leases**. If you rent a car when you go on holiday, that is an operating lease: it's not for the car's useful economic life and you certainly don't expect to maintain it or insure it. The hire company does that.

By the way, **hire-purchase** and **conditional sale**, which were mentioned in Chapter 2, are similar to finance leasing but they are different from it in that legal title to the asset does pass so the company does end up owning the asset.

You may come across **sale-and-leaseback** transactions. These are a form of asset finance in that a company which, say, owns its office may sell the office to a bank and then rent it back, in order to realise its capital investment in the office – i.e. get a lump sum out of the office. The idea here is that unless a company's core business is property ownership, it should not be a land owner but should instead use that capital in its main business.

FOREIGN EXCHANGE

The single biggest financial market in the world is the foreign exchange or **forex** market, which is where currencies are bought and sold (by the way, there's no physical marketplace for forex – it's all conducted between banks by telephone and on-screen).

When you go on holiday you need to change pounds (sterling) into the currency of the place where you are going. When you come back you change back whatever is left over. Usually you do this by going to a bank or a currency changer like Thomas Cook. In exactly the same way, companies, banks and institutional investors need to change currencies.

Companies need to do so when they do business overseas. They may get paid in a local currency and need to translate that back

---

Trade finance

International trade is financed by something called **trade finance**. A bank issues a **letter of credit** on behalf of its customer which can then be used by that customer to pay for goods it is importing. The letter of credit is given to the seller in return for the goods.

The seller can either present it to the bank for payment (there is usually a three-month period before the letter of credit can be presented) or sell it for immediate payment (this is a bit like factoring; the seller won't get all the money represented by the letter of credit but most of it). This international second-hand market in bank letters of credit is huge and is called the **à forfait market**.

into pounds sterling. Companies may also build factories abroad or set up trading subsidiaries. Doing this in another country is called **direct investment**. Institutional investors that invest in the shares of companies around the world use the forex market to convert sterling into local currencies to buy those shares on local stock exchanges. This is called **indirect investment**.

There may well be local regulations on the extent to which foreigners can own local businesses – some countries are worried that important companies may fall into foreigners' hands. This sort of attitude is called **protectionism**, where countries try to protect their businesses and markets by controlling access to them (although history shows that open markets generally prosper more quickly because they are forced to become competitive by educating their workforce, dismantling restrictive practices and harnessing technology). There may also be regulations on the extent to which you can export local profits and **exchange controls** on transfers of currencies.

The forex market doesn't exist as a single, physical market. It is a virtual market that is made up of banks, institutional investors and the treasury operations of governments and big companies, all dealing with each other. There are also specialist currency brokers who act as intermediaries. The forex market is open all the time. When Europe is open it is centred in the leading financial capitals with London ahead of the pack. Then as New York opens, it switches across to Wall Street and then follows the sun across to East Asia – Tokyo, Hong Kong and Singapore. It is also an unregulated market in the sense that no single government or regulator is responsible for it. The only condition of being able to trade in it is whether anyone else will trade with you and that depends on your 'name' or credit rating. If you are a big bank, financial institution or company with a good credit rating, you can trade. Otherwise, forget it.

There are two markets in the forex market: the **spot** market (buying currency for immediate use) and the **future** market for delivery at a later date. Going back to the holiday example, if you buy the currency now because you are about to go on holiday, that is a spot market transaction for immediate delivery. But if you are going on holiday in the US in six months' time and are worried that the dollar will increase against sterling over that period, you might buy dollars at today's rate for delivery in six months' time. That is a **forward contract**, also known as a **future**.

Treasury

Big companies that do a lot of business overseas often have a treasury department. For example, they may be using the foreign exchange (forex) market so much that they need in-house forex dealers who can get the best prices. And if they are handling incoming and outgoing flows of money in large volume, they may need to invest incoming flows in the **overnight money markets** to get a good rate of return or buy other companies' commercial paper as a short-term investment (you see how it all connects!). The treasury department is often responsible for working out the best and cheapest ways of raising and managing the company's short- and long-term funding.

THE IMPACT OF INTEREST RATES ON THE CORPORATE WORLD

As companies expand internationally, they come into increasing contact with the world's financial markets. Foreign exchange, bonds, shares, loans are all part of the financial markets where companies and governments raise money. And they are all highly sensitive to interest rates – which are of great concern to companies which are big users of debt. So if you are talking to the finance director of a client company or someone who works in a company's treasury department, you can discuss interest rates. What follows is a simple explanation of how these things are all interlinked.

In the UK, interest rates are set by the **Monetary Policy Committee** of the Bank of England. The MPC is required to keep **inflation** within limits that are set by the Chancellor.

In an **inflationary environment**, prices go up (i.e. demand for goods and services outstrips supply) so the value of money is eroded because it buys you less. Governments don't like inflation because it erodes the value of people's savings (which they don't like) and makes them spend rather than save. If they don't save for retirement or rainy days, the government ultimately has to help them and it can only do this by raising taxes, which is unpopular with the electorate. So the MPC has to maintain interest rates at a level that keeps inflation under control. A little inflation is all right. It has the effect of gradually increasing asset values (e.g. house prices) which increases the feel-good factor. The opposite of inflation – **deflation** – is worse: consumers don't spend because they know the price of goods and services will be cheaper tomorrow – but then they don't buy them tomorrow either, because prices will be lower still the following day, so demand dries up. Industry falters and the economy grinds to a halt. So if the MPC is too cautious and keeps interest rates too high, the economy can grind to a halt and tip into deflation.

In the UK, the speed with which house prices rise is a strong indication of inflation. If people move house a lot, they buy new white goods, furnishings, and so on, and all of this feeds into industry. If house prices are increasing fast, people feel wealthier and spend more on going out and holidays. This is why the MPC gets worried if house prices go up too quickly.

WHAT HAPPENS IF INTEREST RATES GO UP

If interest rates go up, the cost of borrowing to companies increases. This reduces their profitability. This is one reason why their share price tends to go down (the other is that investors take their money out of the stock market and put it on deposit at banks to get the benefit of the increased rate of interest, so pushing the stock market down).

An increase in interest rates also reduces the value of corporate bonds because, in relative terms, the rate of interest those bonds pay is now less attractive because interest rates have gone up.

Companies are also hit in another way. As foreign institutional investors bring money into the UK to get the benefit of the increased interest rate, they convert their cash into sterling in order to deposit it with banks. This has the effect of driving up the price of the pound in the forex market. This has the effect of making the cost of UK exports to overseas buyers more expensive since those buyers now have to spend more in their local currency since it has gone down in value in relation to sterling. So UK exports decline. This, too, has the effect of reducing the profitability of those UK companies which export overseas, which in turn will reduce their share price.

If the MPC reduces interest rates because the economy is faltering, then everything I've said above is reversed.

	Interest rates ↑	Interest rates ↓
Value of pound sterling	↑	↓
Impact on UK exports	↓	↑
Cost of corporate borrowing	↑	↓
Company profits	↓	↑
Company share prices	↓	↑
Value of corporate bonds	↓	↑

MARKETS LOOK TO THE FUTURE – THE PRESENT IS DISCOUNTED IN THE PRICE

Note that this doesn't always happen. The markets don't like interest rates going up. But they like it even less if the economy is out of control. So if the MPC fails to increase interest rates when the markets think it should, the stock market may react by going down anyway. Equally, if the MPC signals that interest rates are going up, the markets may reward it by failing to react at all – because they feel the economy is under control. In fact, what this shows is that markets are always looking to the future, hence the expression that 'the bad news is already in the price' (in other words, it has been discounted).

This is also why a company's share price often goes down when its annual profits figures are good (because investors think they have seen the best of it and assume that profits will go down) and why the share price of companies that produce bad results often goes up – because investors buy in the hope that things can only get better.

Bond yields

A bond's yield is the rate of interest it pays expressed as a percentage in relation to its market value. This is driven by interest rates.

Take a triple-A rated company (i.e. very credit-worthy) which has issued a £100 million bond paying 5%. At the time interest rates are 4.5% so this is attractive to institutional investors. But if interest rates move up, the 5% coupon (coupon is market slang for rate of interest) will be less attractive. So the market value of the bond will fall until the coupon in relation to the market value looks attractive again when compared to current interest rates.

For example, if interest rates rise to 10%, the bond's market value will have to fall until it is in effect paying at least 10%. To do that, its market value must fall to £50 million, because a bond that costs £50 million and pays £5 million a year in interest has an effective yield of 10%. Of course, the bond is still a £100 million bond (that is its **face value** or **par value**, also called its **nominal value**) and on maturity it will still pay back £100 million. Only it will now cost just £50 million to buy, which is its **market value**.

RISK MANAGEMENT

Interest rates are a risk. ORM (operational risk management) is about managing all such risks. These include:

- **Internal fraud** – by an employee (e.g. embezzlement)
- **External fraud** – by an external person (e.g. computer hacking; theft of industrial know-how)
- **Health and safety** – the risk of employees being injured or suffering discrimination
- **Clients, products and business practices** – this can range from giving a client negligent advice to producing a faulty product (product liability)
- **Damage to physical assets** – ranging from weather disruption to terrorist acts
- **Systems failures** – through computer or telecoms mishaps or breakdowns in power supplies

There are other risks:

- **Regulatory risk** – if an organisation is in a regulated industry (e.g. banking) then one of the biggest single risks is that of losing your licence to operate

- **Legal risk** – the risk of being sued
- **Political risk** – especially if a company has subsidiaries operating in unstable economies
- **Funding risk** – the risk that a company may be unable to borrow or raise equity finance at a critical time

The financial markets include:

- **Interest rate risk** – that interest rates will go up (for companies that are borrowers) or down (for institutional investors that have money in bonds or on deposit)
- **Currency risk** – that your currency will go down in value or that a currency you want to raise funds in will go up
- **Counterparty risk** – that the party on the other side of your deal or transaction goes bust or refuses to fulfil their obligations
- **Specific risk** – that a particular investment (e.g. shares in a specific company) will go down in value
- **Market or systemic risk** – the risk that a whole market (possibly the entire market in which a company does business) will go down in value or disappear

In addition there is **aggregation risk**, from two separate risks coming together, and **concentration risk**, from greater-than-expected exposure to a particular risk.

Risk isn't bad. It is the lifeblood of business in the sense that the greater the risk incurred, the greater the return should be – provided it is managed. Companies manage risk through a variety of ways. They guard against operational risk through:

- Planning (e.g. disaster recovery and business continuity plans to ensure the business can carry on; and alternative sources of raw materials or power)
- Security procedures (e.g. vetting employees by taking up references; preventing access to premises without security swipe cards)

They guard against financial risk through hedging and insurance.

Arbitrage

Financial markets are these days closely correlated (they move up and down together).

That's because if there are pricing anomalies between markets (the same bond costs more in the US than it does in Europe), **arbitrageurs** will exploit the pricing difference. They will buy the instrument where it is cheapest and sell it where it commands the highest price and pocket the difference.

The act of doing this drives up the price where they buy it (increased demand) and drives down the price where they sell it (increased supply). Arbitrage activity helps to keep markets in equilibrium.

Banks, brokers, even individuals, are involved in arbitrage across all markets in all assets (shares, bonds, derivatives, forex, commodities).

HEDGING

Companies guard against rises in interest rates and in foreign exchange by **hedging** using **derivatives**. These are known as **risk management** instruments. Companies buy standard, tradable derivatives on futures and options exchanges. They also buy customised ones directly from banks in what is called the **OTC (over the counter market)**. Derivatives can be either debt-based or equity-based (they are called derivatives because they are derived from other instruments).

Institutional investors and banks use **VAR (value-at-risk)** measures to assess the maximum loss that a portfolio is likely to sustain. They measure the beta of particular stocks and shares – beta is a measure of how closely correlated to an index a security is. The less correlated, the more volatile it is in relation to the market as a whole and so the riskier it is. They too use derivatives.

Examples of derivatives include:

- **Swaps** – these can be interest-rate or currency swaps. Interest-rate swaps are used by companies to switch borrowings from fixed-rate to floating or vice versa depending on which way they think interest rates are going to go. Currency swaps are used by companies to switch funding from one currency (say sterling) into another (say dollars) because they want the latter to invest (e.g.

to build a factory in the US)

- **Options** – these enable a company to buy something at a future date at a fixed price if it wants to
- **Futures** or **forward contracts** – these are agreements to buy something at a future date at a particular price. If on that date the actual price is lower, the company must pay the difference. If the actual price is higher, it receives the difference. These can be dangerous instruments if not properly understood

RISK MANAGEMENT THROUGH INSURANCE

Companies also protect themselves against risks by taking out **insurance** cover. Insurance and shipping – still the way most businesses transport goods around the world – are intimately linked, though not, strictly speaking, regarded as part of the financial markets.

SHIPPING, THE BALTIC EXCHANGE AND LLOYD'S OF LONDON

It's still hard to grasp – given the number of aircraft in the sky at any one moment – that the bulk of the world's trade (at least four-fifths) moves by ship. The shipping industry is huge in its own right (as is **ship finance** – the maritime application of asset finance discussed earlier).

Greece – especially Piraeus – is traditionally the home to many ship-owners and there are international ship registries all over the world. But London remains a centre of international shipping. It has the **Baltic Exchange** where ship cargo-carrying capacity is traded (the contract to hire a ship to carry a cargo is called a **charter party** and if the length of the charter is exceeded, the ship-owner charges **demurrage**). The forward market in charters is a good indication of expected economic activity around the world. Of course, taking cargoes across oceans is a risky business, which is how Lloyd's of London developed.

Insurance and shipping are intimately connected. The one was spawned by the other: people with maritime interests – captains, shipowners and merchants with cargoes – would gather in Edward

Lloyd's coffee shop in the 1690s to make deals and share information about the fates of vessels and their cargoes. Wealthy individuals would share the risk of insuring a ship and its cargo. They became known as **underwriters** and had unlimited liability: they had to meet a claim even if it bankrupted them. Eventually the insurance market outgrew the coffee shop and moved, taking the name with it.

MANAGING AGENTS, MEMBERS' AGENTS AND NAMES

Lloyd's was therefore a club – like the Stock Exchange – and made its own rules. The Stock Exchange had jobbers and brokers; Lloyd's had **managing agents, members' agents** and **Names** (always written with a capital 'N'). Managing agents ran **syndicates** (not to be confused with syndicated loans) and were the modern-day underwriters. Each syndicate had capacity to underwrite risk. This capacity was provided by Names. Names were not active members of the market (although most managing agents were also Names and were called **working Names**); they were individuals who were essentially investors. Members' agents acted for Names, putting them on syndicates and managing their affairs.

SYNDICATES AND BROKERS

Each of the syndicates specialised in certain types of risk: marine, motor, aviation and non-marine (everything else). The managing agent would accept risk on behalf of the syndicate. His expertise lay in pricing risks, the price being the **premium** paid to the syndicate for underwriting the risk. Brokers, acting for clients with risks, placed those risks with syndicates by going round managing agents who would accept a slice of the risk, which went on the underwriter's **slip** (bit of paper).

WHAT HAS HAPPENED TO LLOYD'S

It used to be considered a great honour to be invited to become a Name at Lloyd's because, provided you had a certain level of wealth, you could keep that money invested elsewhere, earning a return, and would only need to invest it in Lloyd's to meet losses. But in the 1980s, three developments devastated the market: (1) a series of heavy losses through big natural disasters, coupled with (2) internal fraud and (3) liability imposed by the US courts for asbestosis illness which retired workers in America were only now developing but which was covered by policies written at Lloyd's several decades before.

Lloyd's kept going but only by making capital calls on Names, many of whom lost all their money and were bankrupted. Nowadays, Names have all but disappeared and have been replaced by corporate capital (companies acting like investment trusts which provide Lloyd's with its underwriting capacity).

Nowadays many ship-owners belong to clubs in which they insure each other – these are mutual risk-sharing associations and are called **P&I Clubs** (protection & indemnity).

This chapter has looked at the international financial markets open to companies and the macro-economic factors affecting those markets. At this global level, big business also has other Big Issues to worry about – as we shall see.

Joint ventures and alliances

One way of expanding – especially overseas – is by entering into joint ventures and alliances with other companies to exploit new markets together.

At its simplest, a joint venture can be an agreement just to cooperate, share information and expenses and develop joint opportunities. At its grandest, a new company (NewCo, as it's often codenamed before being launched with a proper name) may be created (jointly owned by the joint venture parties) which then undertakes a whole new business, with the two shareholders contributing capital, know-how and people.

In both types there are complex formulae for sharing and paying out profits; in the case of NewCo there will be provisions allowing each party to buy out the other and mechanisms for fixing the price at which that is done, depending on NewCo's performance.

Joint ventures, alliances and federations are some of the ways in which big business is tackling big issues – see the next chapter.

Chapter 5

BIG ISSUES FOR BIG BUSINESS

SPEED-READ SUMMARY

- The speed of change is accelerating – companies need to innovate or die

- We live in a knowledge economy where know-how is more important than the traditional means of production

- Technology is a major driver – forcing a convergence of platforms and content which is becoming interactive and distributed

- The web has provided additional channels to market but traditional businesses (such as information publishers and some retailers) are being disintermediated

- Technology is enabling different approaches to customers through data mining and data warehousing – methods of detecting and collating customer buying patterns and preferences leading to mass customisation, micromarketing, markets of one – which encourage churn

- This in turn means that niche markets are flourishing – the longtail effect

- Businesses are always looking for efficiencies through business process re-engineering (BPR), continuous improvement, outsourcing, offshoring, supply chain management, just-in-time fulfilment and quality systems

- The world has gone consumer – shopping used to be a tedious way of buying essentials but is now a major leisure activity – and global, which is posing multinational companies enormous challenges

- Individual entrepreneurs are as aware of these forces as multinational corporates

---

 W e are now entering the world of the big **multinational companies** (MNCs) that are active around the world, listed on several exchanges and have a globally recognised name or brand. They are exposed not just to the vagaries of the financial markets but to huge changes in the way we live: these are what management consultants call **paradigm**, **seismic** or **tectonic shifts** (the **secular trends** I referred to in Chapter 1). The biggest single change is that the speed of change is itself accelerating: with each passing year the world is a higher-velocity place.

In this chapter I'm going to discuss some of these shifts because this will complete the picture of what concerns client companies and bring us full circle to strategy. This also affects finance because companies that are perceived to have the best strategies for dealing with these issues will be more desirable to banks and investors, making it cheaper for them to raise finance, which in turn enables them to undercut the competition. Each supports the next in a virtuous circle.

INFORMATION AND COMMUNICATIONS TECHNOLOGY (ICT)

Applying the PEST model from Chapter 1, you will be aware that technology is possibly the single biggest catalyst in the business world at the moment, prompted by the growth of the personal computer and the internet on the one hand and mobile telephony on the other. What we are seeing is a **convergence of platforms** covering phones, television, the internet and gaming consoles. This is also prompting a **convergence of content** (music, film, digital data) and the idea of **networked distribution** which allows us to access content online on a pay-to-play basis instead of buying CDs, DVDs and applications software on disk. Soon software will be provided over the internet (this is called 'software as a service') rather than bought in shops.

Businesses are having to adapt to the additional **channel to market** which the internet offers. A small number of companies – such as Amazon and Google – are entirely internet-based and were amongst the few survivors of the first dot.com boom in the late

1990s. At first, many conventional businesses feared that the internet would put them out of business. But in fact this hasn't happened: many traditional businesses have adapted to a **brick 'n' click** environment, combining on the one hand the bricks and mortar of traditional retail outlets with, on the other, internet ordering (a mouse click away).

In finance, companies sometimes access institutional investors, by-passing banks when companies' credit standing is better than that of banks. This is called **disintermediation**. This bypassing effect is happening in the wider world as a result of the web, allowing **blogging** and **podcasting**. Traditional 'publishers' ranging from newspapers to radio stations and record companies are being disintermediated. Wikis (web pages that allow anyone to log into them and change them) allow collaboration and sharing of knowledge on a mass level with few attendant costs. Wikipedia, the free online encyclopaedia, is hitting traditional encyclopaedia publishers hard. It's thought that the last newspaper will cease publication around 2040. Long before then a book like this will be available online, free, and won't be produced in hard-copy form. People are no longer passive consumers of information: they are active in its creation.

But one lesson of the dot.com bubble is that many things don't change as quickly or as radically as one might think, or in the most expected way. In fact, some traditional businesses have benefited the most: postal services and vans providing home delivery have benefited from online shopping. Remember IBM's prediction that the world would be run by a handful of huge mainframe computers – and the reality that we now all have one.

BPR AND ERP

The impact of technology has also been felt by companies in the back office (the back office is the admin part of a business) through **business process re-engineering** (BPR) where companies have replaced idiosyncratic, and often manual, administration systems with software packages like SAP which enable companies to move to industry-wide standards of administration. This is an example of **enterprise resource planning** (ERP).

The idea here is that no matter what a business does in terms of its goods or services, its customer base, its markets and geographical location, there are certain basics that it will have in common with all other businesses. All businesses need to have financial controls. All businesses have employees whose payroll and other details need to be maintained. All businesses have basic administrative functions, such as having an inventory of their assets. The idea behind ERP is that you can buy a software suite that will do all of this for you in a way that reflects **best practice** (often called **best-in-class**). Why create your own when you can copy the best bits of what everybody else does? Big organisations have been spending a lot of time and money over the last 10 years installing ERP systems and migrating their existing data and processes to them.

OUTSOURCING

Key to ERP are the strategic questions: what are we really in business to do and what are we best at? As a result, two other trends have also taken root over the last decade: **outsourcing** – getting rid of non-core activities and getting a third party to do them (e.g. getting a third party to run 'your' call centre); and **offshoring** – getting routine tasks done elsewhere (e.g. word processing sent to India where it can be done overnight at a fraction of the cost).

Outsourcing (or **BPO – business process outsourcing** as it is also known) is a way of removing cost by transferring the service to a third party which can do it more cheaply because they are doing it for others too. They tend to be more specialist and more innovative in their own core business, so outsourcing deals can become strategic partnerships where the supplier identifies and passes on improvements and economies. Outsourcing enables the buyer to transfer to the supplier systems and functions it would otherwise take too long to change. Outsourcing is also risk sharing: changes in technology are borne by the supplier (though part or all of the cost may be passed on).

Outsourcing actually becomes a way of analysing what a business does: what it is actually in the business of doing, and what it should leave to others to do. Nike, the sports shoemaker, analysed its theory of the business and realised that it was a brand not a shoemaker, so Nike doesn't make any of its products. It outsources the manufacturing and simply brands the product. Most airlines have outsourced the provision of on-board catering. Their theory of the business tells them to focus on flying. EDS, the US technology provider, is responsible now for running much of the UK government's IT requirements on an outsourced basis, while the government focuses on the job of governing.

In this way the issue of outsourcing becomes an ongoing dynamic question allowing organisations to manage outsourced services as dynamic portfolios, modifying them as their strategic importance changes and retaining the management capability and a core portfolio in-house. They use outsourcing to manage risk, like a financial option or insurance product.

Put the two together – outsource to a provider in another time zone – and you've got **offshore BPO**. US company GE did this in 1997, setting up Genpact, a back-office captive (i.e. subsidiary) in India to service its businesses in India, China, Hungary and Mexico. In 2004 it then sold a 60% stake in Genpact to a private equity firm. Genpact is now expecting to generate as much from other companies (third-party customers for which it will do what it does for GE).

USING THE DATA PROVIDED BY ICT

ICT has had a particular impact on retailers, such as supermarkets. Supermarkets now routinely collect and keep a lot of information about our individual buying patterns (e.g. through loyalty cards). They can develop profiles of particular types of customer and their preferences. They now look at individuals in terms of their **lifetime value** to the business rather than just in terms of individual transactions. This approach is called **customer value management** (turning each interaction with a customer into an opportunity to learn more about, and sell more to, that customer). It is informed by trawling through vast amounts of data in databases to detect patterns of behaviour, an activity called **data mining**.

Data mining is the extraction of implicit, previously unknown and potentially useful information from large sets of data. It is done

Ideas from the East

Fifty years ago, Japan was derided for producing 'knock-offs' – copy-cat products that it was able to replicate by **reverse-engineering**: taking products originally manufactured in the US or Europe, stripping them down to their components and working out what they consisted of and how they were assembled.

With the expertise it gathered, Japan then led the way in manufacturing. It has since been overtaken by South Korea and now China where labour is cheaper, and China may in due course be overtaken by India. But Japanese engineers introduced many innovative ways of thinking about industrial production including:

■ **Just-in-time production** where you don't hold big inventories of stock – instead you have only what you need immediately to hand. All businesses now do this. Dell, for instance, only makes computers to order. It does not have to warehouse large stocks of PCs in the hope that customers will (eventually) buy them.

■ **Continuous improvement** or *kaizen* which means that you never stand still but constantly question how and why you do things. Again, all companies are committed to this these days. Southwest Airlines in the US famously studied the way Formula 1 cars make pit stops to improve the speed with which it turns around planes on the ground.

In fact the Japanese have had the last laugh: a Ford car made in the US now has more foreign parts inside it than a Toyota sold in the States – because these days Toyotas are made locally.

using mathematical tools called genetic algorithms (sets of statements organised to solve a problem in a given number of steps), neural networks (computer programs modelled on the human brain and trained to recognise patterns in data) and other tests such as rule induction (which identifies the rules inherent in a conclusion in order to reproduce it and provides similar answers elsewhere) which can determine, for example, whether a direct marketing sample is statistically valid.

Data warehousing is where you keep data that can be mined or, to be more technical, it is a 'subject-oriented, integrated, time-variant, non-volatile collection of data in support of management's decision-making process' (quoting Bill Inmon, the guru on the subject).

This means the data is organised by subject or entity (e.g. customer) not by application (e.g. sales or stock control), it is held in a consistent form, it is not only current (as on a database) but also historic and time-stamped as such and, once stored, does not change nor is it updated as it would be on a database.

Of course it's much harder to do than it sounds. One of the issues that businesses face is how to deal with **legacy systems** (previous generations of information technology) and the data these systems contain. Often it is a laborious and expensive task to get different ICT systems within a business to function properly together and to **migrate** data from old systems to new ones.

Examples of data mining applications

- Government forecasting of toxic hazards arising from human or animal exposure to chemicals, making predictions by analogy with other chemicals known to be toxic which share a common structure
- Banks identifying the level of risk contained in loan portfolios by detecting trends in defaults and bad debts for different customer types
- Credit card companies segmenting their customers by profitability so enabling them to run targeted retention programmes
- Markets that publish information of recent trades weeding out human errors in price information by flagging up deviations from expected price movements
- Mail order retailers segmenting customers by buying habits and patterns ('micromarketing')
- A car manufacturer using a data warehouse of yield management problems (previous faulty vehicles removed from production, so causing a gap) to decide how to deal in seconds with a current halt of the train (production line)
- Armies detecting enemy units from previous patterns of behaviour when visual and radar confirmation of identity aren't foolproof (e.g. tanks on a skyline)

The US retailer Wal-Mart (which owns Asda in the UK) is a famous pioneer of the use of this type of data. That's how it started putting babies' nappies alongside beer on its shelves, so boosting sales of both, because it saw that men are often sent to buy nappies by their wives but buy beer as well or instead (as Homer Simpson would attest). Now it encourages them to do so. Such sophisticated use of data and stock control means that Wal-Mart can move, overnight, all of its stocks of a certain product across the US. So, when snow was once unexpectedly forecast on the east coast, Wal-Mart managed to get all its stocks of gloves shifted overnight from around America to east-coast stores ready for open-of-business the next day. This takes incredibly sophisticated, technology-enabled **supply chain management systems** (also called **logistics**).

SUPPLY CHAIN MANAGEMENT

It's no good having your manufacturing working at full capacity if it's simply creating inventory that needs to be stored somewhere and is ageing so may never be sold (all of which represents a cash investment). Estimating how many to make to meet expected demand, taking into account seasonal fluctuations and the transportation time can lead to massive over- or under-production which in turn can make a business go bust. It's mission-critical stuff.

Supply chain management brings together the processes linking marketing and sales with production, the physical facilities involved (factories, warehouses, truck fleets), the technology that helps to plan, manage and predict demand, and the allocation of roles and responsibilities.

All these things involve trade-offs – between manufacturing flexibility and location, distribution cost and inventory holding. For example, having fewer warehouses may lead to increased transport costs. And this at a time when product lifecycles (remember them?) are shortening so that the speed with which products are invented, manufactured, brought to market and superseded is accelerating.

Swedish carmaker Volvo turned itself inside out when it redesigned its supply chain so that it only makes a car once that car has been ordered – but has to do so to a tight delivery schedule with a wide array of possible specifications on offer (an example of 'mass customisation'). The same with Dell which famously only makes each computer in response to an order yet is able to deliver it within days.

BUSINESS EFFICIENCY

Technology is having a massive impact on cost-control, itself a

> ## Sales force automation
>
> Even the traditional door-to-door salesman has been turned into a superman with sales force automation which enables him (or her) with laptop, PDA and mobile to offer immediate customised order fulfilment.
>
> Through SFA, the history of interaction between the company and the customer is updated in real time and made available at all contact points (salesforce, call centre, local branch, head office, after-sales service, complaints) simultaneously giving the company a so-called 360-degree view of each customer. This means that whenever you call and whoever you speak to at a company, they can have instant access to your up-to-date consumer profile.

perennial theme of business (making more for less). Businesses are having to become more efficient all the time: customers are sensitive to price and the leanest competitors offer the best prices. Companies are forever examining what is **core** and **non-core** (which is an issue of strategy). Is it best to be highly specialist (but run the risk that your expertise becomes redundant) or to be diversified (doing a number of things but without being a market leader at any of them)? These things go in fads as businesses move from one to the other.

QUALITY SYSTEMS

Over the last 20 years the **quality movement** has taken off – the Japanese examples of just-in-time production and continuous improvement are examples of this. It can be traced back to Edwards Deming, an American who 50 years ago studied manufacturing in its early days and was committed to driving out faulty products. For him, even if only one widget in a thousand was badly made, that statistically insignificant figure was too high. This is what people in business mean by quality. Yes, they use the term when marketing 'quality' products and services, but don't be surprised if you come across quality in a different sense, meaning a systematic approach to achieving perfect repetition. It leads to refining and documenting processes. The modern form is called **Six Sigma** – a productivity-enhancement programme pioneered by General Electric (now known as GE). Incidentally it has its artistic equivalent in Robert Pirsig's *Zen And The Art Of Motorcycle Maintenance* which is a semi-autobiographical account of a philosopher driven to insanity by his quest for the meaning of quality (and if you can work that into a conversation with a client, you're doing well).

CONSUMERISM

Supermarkets are symbolic of the rise of consumerism. Shopping used to be a boring means of getting food and clothes. Now it's a **leisure activity**. A shopping mall is where you spend the whole day; look how many shops have cafés and even restaurants. Take a look at opening hours. In the old pre-consumer days, shops would have early closing days (usually Wednesdays and Saturdays) and wouldn't open at all on Sunday (that was for going to church). Now they are open every day, on some days till as late as 10pm. Some supermarkets even claim to be 24/7.

As a result, **the world has gone retail**. The consumer is king. And whoever controls access to the consumer is market-dominant. And that is retailers. So important is the retail space that publishers have to pay to get their books in window displays. If manufacturers don't deliver goods in packaging that fits directly on supermarkets' shelves, those goods are turned away. So strong is the retail channel to market that supermarkets drive hard bargains with suppliers and require them to manufacture own-label goods (i.e.

Churn

Businesses try to create customer 'loyalty' (a lot of car advertising is designed to reassure recent purchasers that they made the right choice). But a contrary pressure is 'churn'.

Companies now spend a lot of time and resource luring customers from each other: mortgage lenders, credit card companies and mobile phone operators are just some of those forever chasing the same customer base, leading to a rapid merry-go-round as consumers go from one to the next to exploit the latest offer.

The speed with which customers move is called churn. It's an increasing cost to companies as they cannibalise each other's customer loyalty. They end up chasing their own tails.

By the way, a key weapon in combating churn is data mining (see elsewhere in this chapter) which enables telcos (telecom companies) to predict from a drop-off in traffic when a customer is about to defect.

---

bearing the supermarket's logo, not the manufacturer's).
Look at how many supermarkets have gone into lending, insurance, investment and other financial services. Even the basics of selling groceries has changed: because people travel they have much wider tastes and want greater and more exotic choice. They expect food to be fresh and available all-year round – just imagine the impact on a supermarket's supply chain: how quickly food needs to get to the shops and from how far afield. With online shopping and home deliveries, customers don't even have to come to the store.

And when we do, it's easy to overlook that supermarkets have increasingly got us to do their job for them, all in the name of choice!

In the days of the corner shop, the man behind the counter got what you wanted down from the shelves and wrapped it for you. Now we do that; we push our trolley round, fill it ourselves, queue at the cash-till, put our purchases in bags and take them out to the car. In supermarkets that have automated tills you can do the check-out staff's job yourself. All of this saves supermarkets huge amounts of money. Soon they'll have us stacking the shelves...

SERVICE ECONOMY

In an economy where the consumer experience is paramount, service becomes key. This, too, is having interesting side-effects. I know of one professional service firm where they get their

---

Focus on the core client base

Many of these developments are in the retail or B2C (business-to-consumer) market.

But in the wholesale market, also known as B2B (business-to-business), there has been increasing reliance on the core client base – the idea that 20% of your clients produce 80% of your income (this 80/20 rule is known as the **Pareto Principle** and applies in all sorts of different situations).

One development of this is an emphasis on **client relationship management** (CRM) where businesses try to get close to their biggest corporate customers, forging close contacts at different organisational levels, understanding their clients' strategies and where power lies – which provides opportunities for young professionals like you to develop key relationships with people your age in client organisations.

---

associates working in teams changing the wheels on Formula 1 cars; and another where the front-of-house staff (receptionists, caterers) all have a background in five-star hotels. It's about speed, consistency and the whole wrap-around client experience, which is why effective training and systems become crucial.

GLOBALISATION

All of this presupposes a further move to **mass markets**, the same good being manufactured in huge bulk to achieve **economies of scale** and then being sold into all major markets around the world. This is one aspect of **globalisation** – where major companies pursue business outside their home country, in search of new markets and more consumers.

That's why they are often called **multinational companies** or MNCs. The most obvious examples are those companies whose brands are known the world over – such as Coke (or The Coca-Cola Company as it likes to be called), McDonald's and Nike. Take car manufacture. Car making is a global industry. More than 140 countries exported car parts in 2000. Cars built by Ford Motor Company in the US now have a higher proportion of foreign-made components than cars made by Toyota in the US, making Toyota's arguably more 'American' – whatever that means.

International trade: grey markets and parallel imports

A big issue in global business is that of parallel imports and grey markets. Everyone has heard of the 'black market' which is illegal trading activity, often in counterfeit goods, usually kept covert to avoid tax.

By contrast, the **grey market** is legitimate. It is the sale of goods through distribution channels other than those used by the manufacturer and by third parties not connected with the manufacturer.

Grey market activity happens when the same goods are sold at significantly different prices in different markets. It makes sense for third parties to buy the goods in the cheaper market and sell them in markets where they command a higher price (an example of arbitrage).

Examples of goods traded in grey markets include cigarettes, electronics, clothing and food. Goods which are sold in grey markets are called **parallel imports**.

Tobacco companies that have found their products increasingly legislated against in the developed world have turned to emerging markets in search of new consumers – with enormous success: when you're poor, a smoke is the cheapest form of relaxation and recreation you can find; and in parts of the world where life is still cheap, who cares about the health risks?

As you can imagine, there's a lot of politics involved in this, from people who object to the homogenisation of life and protest against globalisation, to those who see that until the world is a level playing field, smaller exporting countries (often Third World) will be crushed by larger ones (hence the role of the World Trade Organisation and movements like Fairtrade), and environmentalists who see big oil companies as wreckers of natural habitats and supermarkets as carbon polluters because they airlift produce overnight from far-flung corners of the world enabling consumers to get year-long access to produce that used to be seasonal.

At the same time there are anti-trust and competition authorities trying to ensure that businesses do not exploit unfair monopolies, and trading blocs like the European Union that try to encourage free trade and movement of labour within their boundaries to create level playing fields for all (see Chapter 3).

Besides, there is a contrary pressure (fuelled by developments like customer value management and internet retailers like Amazon and eBay) to 'mass markets of one' where products and services with small markets are increasingly viable. This is called the **longtail effect**, a name purloined by the publisher of this book: it is nowadays viable to produce a book that will have a limited readership because digital on-demand printing means that you don't have to print 10,000 copies in one go and store them, and the internet means that a small but significant number of likely readers can be reached. This was not possible 20 years ago. So as globalisation creates a bigger market for a narrower, blander range of goods and services, so small markets for idiosyncratic products spring up in globalisation's shadow.

Corporate governance (and corporate social responsibility)

Public companies are required to make their management more transparent through adherence to voluntary **corporate governance** codes which set out how they should be run and the use of **non-executive** directors and chairmen to check up on what the directors are doing and how much they are being paid ('non-executive' simply means you don't have a day-to-day role in running the business, which is why non-executive appointments tend to be part-time – but often well rewarded, a controversy in its own right). These issues matter to the institutional investors that hold their shares.

Some argue that a company's role is not simply to make profit for its shareholders. It has duties to all its **stakeholders** and these include employees, customers, pensioners (past employees) and – in the case of big businesses with extensive operations that affect the local community – those who live nearby. Environmental concerns, in particular, have been a driver in the development of the idea that companies need to be good corporate citizens too. This is called **corporate social responsibility** or CSR.

THE KNOWLEDGE ECONOMY

Another big theme is the move to what Peter Drucker termed the knowledge economy – the idea that what businesses know (for instance about their customers – see earlier) is more important than what they make. The pillars of capitalism used to be money (capital), the means of production (equipment) and an abundance of cheap labour (employees). But nowadays people recognise that technology has reduced the cost of production and that competitive advantage depends not on how much you make and at what price but on **what you know**. Your employees are no longer just muscle and brawn needed to operate machines; they are now **knowledge workers**.

Take something as basic as getting coal or oil out of the ground: what matters is knowing where to dig or drill. The same with farming: knowing about soil and crop rotation is what makes the difference. And these are all examples of **primary industries** (meaning that they are basic and involve basic commodities found in the ground or earth).

Now a business's most important assets have feet – and they walk out of the door every evening. Companies recognise that what their employees carry round in their heads is critical to the business. If what matters is what you know, it follows that businesses need to try to record, store and codify this information and make it available organisation-wide.

This is all part of what is called **knowledge management**. Companies have appointed chief information officers (CIOs) and know-how managers to capture and organise it and have focused on how they record, store and share it.

There is greater concern about how they protect it, with increasing reliance on legal rights. A visible example of knowledge is the **portfolio of patents** that big companies have: a patent protects your rights to an invention. Companies also protect their names and slogans by registering them as **trademarks** to protect their brands (**brand management** is about how you communicate and project your goods and services to the market). These collections of patents and trademarks are referred to collectively as **intellectual property rights** or IPR or just intellectual property (IP). A company's IP can be its single most important asset. It's the licence fee for using Windows that has made Bill Gates as rich as he is. As the developed world becomes less of a **manufacturing economy** and more of a **service economy**, what a company knows becomes its biggest source of competitive advantage. And knowledge of your customers can be the most important type of know-how you have (see earlier).

IMPACT ON WORK

This shift from production to knowledge has changed the relationship between employers and employees. People used to stay in the same job all their lives. But business is too changeable for companies to offer that guarantee. The deal used to be: 'Give me your lifetime and when you retire I will pay you a pension.' Now employees want opportunities to develop their skills and expertise. So the deal now is: 'Let me use your talents and I will enhance them.'

This is what a Harvard professor called Alfie Kohn calls the **psychological contract** between employer and employee. It means that those employers best at retaining talent do so by making their people marketable through giving them opportunities, experience and training. People now expect to be able to work flexibly (e.g. from home by accessing the workplace remotely) and to achieve a better work/life balance.

The downside is that individuals are now expected to acquire new skills, in order to remain relevant to the skills market, throughout their lives. This is **lifelong learning** and is a reflection of the fact that we will all have to work longer and retire later. This is a **demographic** issue: as we live longer, so the burden of pensioners on those in work is increasing and risks becoming too heavy a load for younger generations to carry unless individuals save more for their pensions or work longer. But as Charles Handy points out, more people are becoming self-employed **portfolio workers**, doing a number of different things, some of which are paid and others not.

PRIVATE V. PUBLIC SECTOR

A final theme in this far-from-comprehensive survey is that of the blurring distinction between the private sector (i.e. business) and the public sector (the state or government). The last 20 years have seen private-sector methods imported into the public sector and people now move increasingly freely between the two.

In the 1980s the UK pioneered **privatisation**, the selling-off of state enterprises – often monopolies such as telecommunications, utilities (water, electricity, gas) and transport (ports, airlines, airports, railways, bus companies, toll roads, bridges and tunnels). By attracting private-sector investment, these old state enterprises could modernise more quickly and improve the services they offered consumers, often in a newly-opened-up competitive market in which prices would be lower. The state would shrink and the cost of modernisation would be **kept off its balance sheet**. OBS (off balance sheet) funding is a way of enabling a company, bank or government to access funding without having to include it as a borrowing.

There are different types of privatisation. At its purest and grandest, it is about **selling off state-owned industries** often in their entirety. But less extreme versions include **commercialisation** (subjecting an activity to private-sector competition, which may include joint ventures between the state and the private sector) and **market liberalisation** (removing state monopolies so anyone can compete). An example of joint venturing which achieves OBS for the state is **public-private partnerships** (PPP) also known as the **private finance initiative** (PFI).

PPP/PFI

This is a bit like asset finance and project finance, in that the private sector build the required project (toll road or bridge, school or hospital) and then the state pays the builder/owner for the use of it over its useful economic life (say 30 years). There may also be an element of outsourcing because the private-sector contractor may also manage the school, looking after the premises, providing school meals, and so on.

This way the state keeps the capital cost OBS, which makes it look financially prudent, allowing the government to spend without officially exceeding its public-borrowing targets. In actual fact it is simply turning that capital cost (a balance sheet item) into expenditure (a profit & loss item) since over the 30 years the contractor will recoup the build cost of the project and the interest on that cost. Since the private sector never does anything except for profit (and its cost of borrowing is higher than the state's) the overall cost to the state is arguably much higher than if it had undertaken the project itself.

Aside from the political desire to look prudent by postponing the real cost and storing up trouble for a time when it is no longer in power, the only real advantage to the government of doing this is that it is able to bring many more projects on-stream than if it only had the money to build them one at a time. It's a bit like franchising: you can open a dozen shops rather than just one. This way you can build a score of schools or hospitals at a time rather than a handful. But the cost in the long run is greater.

Still, PPP and PFI have kept professionals of all types in lucrative work for some time now, so who are you and I to complain?

PRIVATISATION

The big daddy of all of this – privatisation itself – is a somewhat different beast. It has been used in virtually all sectors, from energy production and transmission (oil, gas and electricity, for example), utilities (such as water), transport (ranging from airlines and airports to roads, bridges and ports) to mineral and other resource extraction, industrial plant projects, waste treatment processes and financial services.

There is hardly a sector around the world that has not been subjected to privatisation of one form or another, from grand global initial public offerings to the grant of a franchise or concession. The methods of sale cover the spectrum, from trade sales to a single private-sector entity already in that business through to fully-fledged IPOs: BT, which was privatised in three tranches in the 1980s, was the first global IPO and encouraged the convergence between the underwriting of bond issues and share issues, now dominated by investment banks.

All privatisations have at least one aspect in common: the need to attract willing buyers or investors. Privatisation is about selling. The buyer (whether a company or institutional shareholders) will want to know what he is buying. This usually means that the industry in question has to be restructured to make it attractive to outside investors. The process may begin as a reorganisation, to separate the industrial activity from the rest of government, and so identify the revenue stream and cost basis attributable to it.

This will usually lead to **corporatisation**, under which informal trading arrangements – often with other public-sector entities – are formalised as arm's length contractual relationships, ownership of particular assets is established and state guarantees are removed. The enterprise is turned into one or more companies whose shares are owned by the government. Privatisation then consists of selling those shares to the private sector.

The next step is to create a **competitive environment**. Whilst investors may prefer to buy a privatised monopoly this is usually at odds with government aims which may include **raising levels of**

service, **driving down prices**, **modernising the infrastructure**, **encouraging a market**, **developing skills** and widening and deepening **share ownership** – many of which are strongly felt by governments in developing countries which is why privatisation has taken off around the world. It's a way of creating a modern economy where previously there wasn't one. But the key is to create competition. Restructuring an industry actually means creating a new one, creating a new market where none existed before.

This occurs at two levels. The first is structural, by breaking up an industry into a number of undertakings. In the case of power (gas or electricity) this can include the creation of more than one generator and vesting the national transmission network and local distribution systems, operating at lower levels of pressure or power, in several entities. The transmission network can be granted common-carrier status, so it is accessible to all generators on equal, non-discriminatory terms. Regional distribution companies' retail operations can be opened up to competition. This has happened all over the world.

The second level relates to the control and conduct of these entities in the private sector. The existing monopoly power or dominant position has to be controlled. In addition to the continuing regulatory role retained by the existing competition authorities, it may be necessary to appoint an independent agency with specific powers and duties to carry out this task. There's a balance to be achieved between encouraging competition while making the sector attractive to investors.

Once an industry has been privatised, government may wish to retain a degree of control, for instance through **a golden share**, which provides special rights of veto in certain circumstances. Where government retains a majority interest, investors will want protection from possible government action, ranging from dumping shares on the market to interfering in commercial decisions.

THE NEED FOR OIL

Much privatisation has been spurred by the collapse of communism. But possibly the single biggest geo-political factor at work is the industrialised world's need for oil. Oil is running out. The world's peak oil production (when half of the world's available source has been produced) is expected to be reached any year now. Spare capacity as a percentage of total production is at its smallest ever. Non-OPEC supplies are expected to start diminishing by 2010. The UK is no longer a net exporter of oil, having exploited its North Sea fields. Hence the US's interest in the Middle East.

INNOVATE OR DIE

What all of these changing and challenging factors mean is that business must 'innovate or die', as Christopher Freeman warned companies 20 years ago in *The Economics of Industrial Innovation*. It's what keeps CEOs awake at night. It's the golden goose of business.

Management writers draw a distinction between new product development (NPD) and innovation management (IM). NPD focuses on the process required to produce a single new product (NP). IM is concerned with creating and managing the organisational environment which turns one-off NPs into a sustainable stream or pipeline.

Innovation covers both new products and new ways of making existing products. At the birth of any industrial sector there is radical product innovation, followed by radical innovation in production processes, followed by widespread incremental innovation. So in a mature market innovation is around finding new ways of delivering the same product service but more efficiently. For this reason, it matters little whether or not an idea is objectively new as measured by the lapse of time since its first use or discovery; if the idea seems new and different to the consumer, it is an innovation.

Management writers have identified the different sources of NPD. There is the 'technology push' model where scientists make unexpected discoveries which are then manufactured and marketed (as in the pharmaceuticals industry) and the 'individualistic school', which holds that innovations are the result of unique individual talents and such innovators are born (with an important role played

Government, economics and statistics

Government looks closely at the country's **GDP (gross domestic product)** which measures annual output in goods and services. This is broken down into **private** and **government consumption**, **investment** and **exports (balance of payments** – if they are positive it means the country is exporting more than it's importing; if not, the country is consuming more than it's producing).

Government is a key component of the economy, as an employer (the NHS is the biggest single employer in Europe) and consumer (consumption taking the form of expenditure on everything from military equipment to schools). Government's own expenditure is funded by **taxation** and any shortfall is met by borrowing (**public-sector borrowing requirement**).

Government studies **output by sector** using a range of measures from manufacturing output and retail sales to housing starts. A key economic principle here is **supply and demand**. Supply is the quantity that producers are willing to sell at a given price. Demand is the quantity that consumers have the capacity and willingness to buy at a given price. When the price is lower, demand will increase; when the price is higher, producers will make more so supply will increase. The intersection is the **equilibrium point** when the **market** **'clears'** (supply and demand match). Although often described as the supply curve, supply and demand are straight lines that intersect on a graph where the vertical axis is quantity and the horizontal axis is price.

Supply and demand drive **inflation** (Chapter 4) which the government monitors through a variety of measures – including the **retail price index** which is based on a 'basket' of typical household spending – and **unemployment**. In the long run, economic performance can be enhanced only by increasing employment and, therefore, output. **Supply-side economics** is the use of incentives (e.g. lower tax) to increase the level of full employment.

Government has to pay for unemployment by providing benefit for those not in work so it is keen to see **full employment**. Unemployment has social and political implications (increased unemployment can lead to crime and an unemployed electorate is unlikely to vote a government back in). But full employment can be inflationary since any shortage in workers/skills will drive up wage demands. The **lump of labour fallacy** is an economic argument which says that reducing working hours will not increase employment (by spreading the work around). It is now used to label any economic argument that relies on the mistaken belief that something is a constant when it is in fact variable.

by serendipity or unexpected discovery, as happened with the Post-it which was a by-product of the search by 3M for strong, not weak, glue).

The 'market pull' model suggests that innovation is stimulated by the marketing function which initiates new ideas from close interaction with customers. The 'social deterministic school' argues that innovations are the result of a combination of external social factors and influences, such as demographic changes, economic influences and cultural changes and that when conditions are right, innovations will occur.

As you can guess, innovation is intimately connected to an organisation's knowledge and skills. There is a 'coupling model' which holds that innovation is the result of the simultaneous coupling of knowledge within manufacturing, R&D and marketing. The 'interactive model' suggests that innovation results from the interaction of the marketplace, the science base and the organisation's capabilities.

Innovation, then, is a combination of (1) theoretical conception, (2) technical invention and (3) commercial exploitation; the result of which is successful implementation within the organisation.

But enough of this. Here's a story about innovation to bring us back down to earth. The US NASA programme spent millions of dollars developing a pen that would write in space (upside down, zero gravity). The Russians didn't bother. They gave their astronauts pencils.

WHAT ALL THIS MEANS FOR SMES

Small and medium-sized enterprises (SMEs) are no strangers to innovation. In fact pharmaceutical companies are increasingly outsourcing their research and development into new drugs to external SMEs.

This chapter has looked at macro-economic factors affecting business and, in particular, big business. But if the businesses you advise are small, don't think for a minute that these issues aren't relevant. In fact, in my experience – and as a management consultant I have advised just as many SMEs as I have large businesses – SMEs make better and more interesting clients, for two reasons. First, the people in SMEs tend to own them and so they are completely immersed in the running of their businesses and are attuned to strategic ways of thinking and sensitive to their external environments. There is a sense of urgency about them and, as people, they tend to be quick-witted and don't have airs and graces. They get to the point and want you to do the same. This means they can be demanding clients and keep you on your toes, but that's what makes serving them so satisfying. They expect you to grasp what these sorts of issue mean for them.

Second, they are able to make and implement decisions quickly. Their businesses don't have much by way of hierarchy. Management tends to be concentrated in a small number of senior people. They don't have to build consensus or get buy-in (though the best always do). And once they've decided on a course of action they get on with it and expect everyone else to do so too.

So don't think for a moment that smaller corporates aren't just as interested in what these big issues mean for them too. Their markets may be more local, but, if anything, they feel change more quickly and if they don't adapt and respond they are likely to go out of business even more quickly than their bigger brethren.

WHAT THIS MEANS FOR YOU

You need to do two things, regardless of how big or small your clients are. First, you need to keep abreast of changes in the business world. This chapter hasn't been a comprehensive survey of big issues. It's just meant to get you thinking and provide you with some of the basic business vocabulary. What I suggest you do is scan the pages of *The Economist* magazine (it's a weekly that comes out on Fridays), especially the business and finance sections towards the back. And cast your eye from time to time down the contents list of the *Harvard Business Review* just to get a feel for what's hot.

Second, you need to be able to talk to clients in language they understand, and you need to be able to relate to them as people – which is what the next chapter is about.

PART 2: Understanding Clients as People

Chapter 6

IT'S A PEOPLE BUSINESS

SPEED-READ SUMMARY

- When dealing with clients you deal with people

- Professionals talk at clients too much – ask questions and listen instead

- Use open questions (which start with words like How, What, Why, Where or When) rather than closed questions which require only a Yes or No answer

- Listen actively by applying EARS (Engage, Ask, Reaffirm, use Silence)

- Be interested not interesting – use the follow-up question

- You have two ears and one mouth: use them in that proportion

- Think of clients as falling into different personality types – Commanders, Expressives, Amiables and Analysts – depending on whether they are task or people focused; and whether they ask or tell

- Some clients want to build a relationship based on your knowing each other as people – but others don't

- Ask clients about their role and their organisation's business. Find out a client organisation's structure and purpose

- Develop a sense of the roles within it

- Ask yourself (and your client) why they need a particular piece of advice and what they are going to do with it – then deliver it in a format that enables them to do so

- Get to know what other professionals do

- Clients like the professionals they use to work well together

I hope by now that you are getting a feel for what business is about. You know how businesses grow from private companies into public ones, the purpose of takeovers, the importance of strategy and the role of money as the lifeblood of business as well as being the measure of how well a business is doing. You've got a feel for the international nature of the financial markets and how companies access them, the impact of inflation and interest rates (**macro-economic** factors as they're called) and the big issues challenging big business.

This is all very interesting (and I hope I have managed to impart a sense of the wonder and excitement that I still feel about business). But it's not the most important thing.

The most important thing is: the people you encounter in business.

However big or small the clients that your firm or employer deals with, you will not be dealing with faceless organisations but with people. That, for me, is one of the most rewarding things about business: getting to know, and dealing with, different types of people. Clients of mine have over time become good friends and I hope you too will enjoy this gradual merging of work and life outside work. After all, we spend so much of our lives working we might as well use it to forge good and lasting personal relationships.

So the second half of this book looks at clients as people and how you can relate to them.

So why do you think I've told you all this stuff about business? What are you going to do with it when you meet clients?

PROFESSIONALS

I am assuming that, whatever your chosen professional field, you have the basic knowledge and competence required to succeed in it: in short, you know your subject (or are on the way to learning it). That's what all of your learning and training has equipped you with.

But you also need to develop your 'people skills'. All of the information I've given you about business will provide you with topics you can engage clients with, in order to find out more about them and their business, and how what you do for them helps their organisation achieve its aims. This is what commercial awareness is: the ability to contextualise the advice you give so that it is useful to clients because it helps them achieve their goals.

Having this business knowledge should give you the confidence to ask questions. It's only by asking questions that you will find out what your clients want you to do and why. And you need to know the 'why' without which you won't have a proper idea of the 'what'.

Professionals start off with one huge disadvantage. We think of ourselves as experts who give advice. And that means we think we only give value when we are imparting advice or information. And that means we talk either 'to' clients or, even worse, 'at' them (so severe is this trait that the French have coined the term *déformation professionnelle* for any walk of life that produces its own distinctive idiosyncracies – so I guess we should be flattered).

Think of the last date you went on. Who do you think enjoyed it the most? You or your date? Then ask yourself: who did most of the talking? When we talk we tend to enjoy ourselves. When someone is talking at us all the time it gets tiring – even if we find what they say interesting.

LISTENING AND ASKING QUESTIONS

The key to getting off on the right foot with a client is to listen and ask questions. As the saying goes, God gave you two ears and one mouth: use them in that proportion.

The more you understand what your client is trying to do and where the advice you give fits in that picture, the more you will be providing advice and assistance that your client really appreciates. And the funny thing about business is that clients don't value the professionals who know the most or who are the most expert; they value those advisers who enable them to get to where they want their business to be. So you don't have to be the most brilliant person in your year to be a hero to your clients. Usually the professionals with the best client skills aren't the most brainy or learned of advisers. They are the ones most closely attuned, and sensitive, to their clients and their needs. And anyone can develop the skills to do that.

So here's how to do it.

HOW TO CONDUCT A CONVERSATION

You might think this pretty obvious. But let me give you two tips. First, use **open questions**. An open question is one which begins with a word like How or What or Why or Where or When. It is 'open' because it allows the other person to fashion a reply in whatever style and to whatever length they like. It opens them up. A **closed question** is a direct question implying a yes or no answer. 'Do you feel OK?' is a closed question. 'How are you feeling?' is an open question. Closed questions are necessary sometimes, for instance to check your own understanding of what someone has said. Open questions are good when starting to get to know people.

Second, there's an acronym called **EARS** which I find helpful. It encourages what is called **active listening**:

E – *Engage*: look people in the eye, smile, nod

A – *Ask*: use questions (see above)

R – *Restate or reaffirm*: this is about checking understanding, especially when taking instructions from a client, by playing back to them what they have said – this is when closed questions can be useful ('Am I right in thinking that…?', 'So what you are saying is…?')

S – *Silence*: allow people time to think and respond; don't try to fill the space (journalists use this a lot, letting people blunder on to fill the space)

The key here is to let people speak. I am very bad at this. I get excited and start interrupting. Don't do that. Let people end their sentences. Otherwise they feel rushed and start to speed up. Let the conversation develop its own tempo. If, like me, you have a butterfly mind, try to train it and keep it under control.

BE INTERESTED NOT INTERESTING

One of the challenges young professionals face is that clients are often a lot older. It may be difficult to relate to them (especially if they are in their 50s, married with a family and heavily into football and you are in your early 20s and a single woman with no interest in sport whatsoever). But you're not trying to make an impression on them by showing how interesting you are. You are trying to impress upon them how interested (in them and their business) you are. By the way, older people naturally like talking to younger people and only a small minority are too driven or impatient to want to try to help you increase your understanding of business in general and theirs in particular.

So ask questions rather than talk at people. But be careful. I find I ask people too many questions. As a former journalist I find people interesting and try to find out as much about them as quickly as possible, often subjecting them to a barrage of inquiries. Friends complain that they feel 'on camera'. So don't interview people: it makes them uncomfortable and they suspect your motives.

Incidentally, one aspect of NLP (Neuro-Linguistic Programming – which has many good things to say about behaviour) with which I disagree is the suggestion that to build a relationship with someone you might mimic their body language. It is true that you can detect a lot from people's posture and the way they express themselves if you watch and listen closely enough. But if you consciously vary your behaviour in response to theirs, it can appear artificial and even manipulative. People see through it. The purpose of my suggestions here is to give you confidence to get off on the right foot with people, not to inveigle them into liking you.

ASK A SECOND QUESTION

When you first meet a client and are trying to find things in common, it is easy to seize on something they have said and kill the conversation stone dead:

Client: I've just got back from the England match.
You: Oh, are you a football fan?

Client: Yes.
You: So am I.

Instead, ask a supplementary, follow-up question:

Client: I've just got back from the England match.
You: Oh, are you a football fan?
Client: Yes.
You: Who do you follow?

It gives you more information to home in on and keeps the conversation opening outwards.

PERSONALITY TYPING

So what about the people you are conversing with? If you are going to make the best impression with a new client, then you need to make a quick assessment of the sort of person they are. As you can imagine, there is a lot of theory about how to do just this. The trouble with this theory is that it is at best superficial, people being the wonderfully complicated creatures they are, and at worst manipulative (see my comment above on NLP).

So the test of whether these theories or models are worthwhile is whether, on balance, they help rather than hinder, rather than whether they are comprehensive and always applicable. See what you think.

This one was devised by David Merril, a psychologist, who suggests that there are four types of managers (see box on next page).

The top two (Analyst and Commander) tend to be **task-oriented**, the bottom two (Amiable and Expressive) tend to be **people-focused**. Those on the left (Analyst and Amiable) tend to **ask questions**. Those on the right (Commander and Expressive) tend to issue orders and **tell** people what to do. Many professionals are Analyticals; many businessmen are Commanders or (like Richard Branson) Expressives.

Commanders (Task/Tell) are action-oriented. Typically they want options and solutions, succinctly expressed. Many corporate clients

The Analytical Type Thinking	**The Commander Type** Action
The Amiable Type Relationships	**The Expressive Type** Intuition

tend to be like this. Applying two rule-of-thumb tests – what do their offices look like and how do you do lunch with them – their offices tend to be sparsely furnished and uncluttered (Lord Weinstock of GEC was famous for having nothing on his desk and requiring proposals on a single sheet of paper) and you do lunch with them by asking them what they want to do, if anything (lunch often not being in their timetable, being for wimps). So, with them, be brief and to the point; stick to business and skip the chit-chat; and persuade them by citing objectives and results.

Expressives (People/Tell) are big picture people. They get bored by detail but like enthusiasm and energy. They want to know what the effect of something will be and they drive things along through sheer personality. Their offices have pictures on the wall of them meeting important people. You do lunch with them by making a booking at a flash restaurant where you are well known to the maître d' who shows you to your favourite table and, en route, you introduce your guest to other local worthies sitting at theirs. So, with Expressives, entertain, stimulate, be lively, ask them for their opinions and keep your eye on the big picture and don't flood them with technical detail.

Analysts (Task/Ask) arrive at decisions by asking questions and evaluating options. An Analyst wants lots of detail, so always go prepared. Their rooms tend to be untidy (although they know where everything is) and you do lunch by offering them the options (five minutes to get a sandwich, 15 to go to the staff canteen, 30 to have a pizza) so they can decide what suits them best. So, prepare your case in advance – attend to detail; be clear and avoid emotional argument; and draw up action plans.

Amiables (People/Ask) are badly named. In fact they are often the most important people in an organisation. They ensure the place holds together. Their concern is for the people in it and the impact of actions upon those people. They ask questions accordingly. They can be quiet but strong in their resolve. Their desks carry photos of family and friends. They use lunch to meet others and explore concerns. So they will like the opportunity to meet new people over a bite to eat. With Amiables, take your time and learn the whole story, ask 'how' questions to draw out their opinions and emphasise the people aspects.

Now, here's the crunch. Commanders and Amiables don't usually get on and Analysts and Expressives don't usually get on. But when occasionally they do, they get on famously. Let me explain. You can see that people who are Task/Tell are hardly going to tolerate those who are People/Ask; nor will those who are Task/Ask likely have much in common with those who are People/Tell. But just occasionally any one of these types may realise that the person they most need to rely on, to make up for their own orientation, is an opposite. Richard Branson (Expressive) famously surrounds himself with senior managers (Analysts) who actually run his businesses for him.

The purpose of this model is to enable you to make judgments (however superficial) about others. Actually, if that were all it did, it would have been discarded years ago (how accurate are such judgments?). What it actually does is to make you think what other people are like and at least to factor that into your thoughts and actions – and possibly to ask colleagues about them before you meet them.

The aim is to start to build a personal relationship. You don't have to become their friends exactly. Some clients don't want that. They have no small talk and have no interest in you. And any attempt by you to find out about them may risk being seen as intrusive and inappropriate. But you have to get on their wavelength. And one way of doing that is by asking them about their business and their role in it. People in business tend to like to talk about it. It takes up all of their time and it turns them on. So asking them about their business and their role in it is a good way in.

So, you're beginning to think about what a client may be like and how to approach him or her (which personality types do you think entrepreneurs might be?). You also need to know what they do.

Commercial conflicts

The more a PSF gets to know a client organisation, its business and strategy, the greater the risk of a commercial conflict with other, similar clients it serves. An actual conflict is where a PSF is barred from acting for two entities for regulatory reasons. For instance, a law firm acting for two parties suing each other or an investment bank acting for both the target and the bidder. There are usually regulatory bans on these things happening, laid down in law or in the regulations affecting a particular profession.

A commercial conflict is different. It's OK for a law firm to advise two companies which are head-to-head competitors but neither of them may like the law firm knowing its business while acting for the competitor. Nowadays clients are sensitive to commercial conflicts and will tell their professional advisers who they can and can't also act for. But there has to be some trade-off – for instance a guaranteed flow of work, otherwise the PSF may find itself locked into an exclusive relationship that doesn't reward it financially.

WHAT PEOPLE DO IN ORGANISATIONS

In the first part of the book I talked about organisations very much from the perspective of the person at the top – the CEO. One good reason for this is that in companies (as opposed to firms or partnerships) the lines of reporting tend to be clear-cut and hierarchical. So what the CEO wants done gets done: most people in senior and middle management know exactly what the CEO's priorities are because these are driving their day-to-day work (and if they don't they probably ought to, or else it may be a business that is on its way down).

But the CEO won't necessarily be the person you deal with the most or most of the time. The following is a list of the people you may encounter in terms of their **functions** (roles or jobs). It is not an exhaustive list and it works best when applied to a manufacturing company (rather than, say, a bank, charity or arm of government). Use it as a starting point and develop your own templates for the organisations you come across. Look at their **websites** and ask to see their **organograms** (diagrams showing structure): organisations only have people if they are fulfilling a necessary function so ask yourself what that role is. The key questions are:

- What is the function?
- What is its purpose? What does it do in furthering the organisation's goals?
- Who does it report to?
- Who reports to it?

Organisational politics (which, as a professional, you need to recognise and work round) generally turns on relations between functions and competition between them.

At the top of the tree you find the **CEO** who is charged with day-to-day responsibility for any- and every- thing in the company. The company will also have a **board of directors**, of whom the CEO (often called Managing Director) is the most important. The board runs the company and is the **executive** (it executes the company's plans). There may also be a **chairman** of the board who is senior to the CEO or MD. The chairman may be an executive chairman but is often non-executive (part-time). The chairman tends to have an outward-facing, strategic and ambassadorial role. But it is the chairman who tends to be instrumental in getting rid of the CEO or MD if the latter isn't doing the job well. An executive director is employed in the business day-to-day. A non-executive is part-time and is there in an advisory capacity. The functions most often represented at board level (executive directors) include:

- **Finance** – this is the second most senior role at board level after CEO/MD, for obvious reasons
- **Human Resources** – in a knowledge economy, people are the most important asset (after money, according to Dilbert)

The politics of organisations

Politics is almost a pejorative term ('He's playing politics') but in its original sense it just meant the affairs of the city ('polis' being Greek for 'city'). Whenever you bring people together, in either a city or a company, you get politics – different views on what should be done and how.

In any organisation you find politics caused by functional frictions (different bits of a business that are thrown into conflict) which may lead to personal animosity. As a professional you need to recognise this and work around it. You need to get to know client organisations in enough detail to know where the power lies and where the political cracks and fissures are to be found.

Professionals can be exposed to organisational politics in two ways:

Who is the client? The client is the institution but who at the client are you taking instructions from? If it is more than one person, what happens if those instructions contradict each other?

What is the role of the professional? Clients often complain that external advisers tell them what they already knew anyway – so why are advisers brought in? Often the answer is politics: the only way to get an organisation to change – even though everyone inside knows what is required – is to bring in a third party to implement that change. So you need to think closely about what is going on under the surface; what are the 'hidden agendas'; who's career is on the line; who can you really trust?

This is why you need to develop a wide network of contacts across a client organisation, so that you always know what is going on and so that if one contact is sidelined you have another to rely on. However, the fact is that, sooner or later, you and your firm may be out. A new broom may come in and decide to use another firm. Your contacts may be sidelined and leave.

But don't worry: your old contacts will turn up in new jobs elsewhere and bring their new employer to you as a new client – provided you stay in touch with them.

■ **Marketing & PR** – responsible for external issues such as customers, brand, image and public relations

Others include **risk management** (which may include legal, compliance and regulatory) to ensure the business is not going to be sunk by an unexpected exposure (**legal** may be represented separately). In a manufacturer, **production** may be represented along with **R&D** (research and development). In a know-how business, there may be a **CIO** (chief information officer). In an advertising agency, a **creative director** and so on. It depends on the particular industry. There may also be an **IT director** if systems are 'mission critical'. There may be a **director of administration** looking after premises, systems and so on. Increasingly companies have a **COO** (chief operating officer – a term which like CEO and CIO has come over from the US) who ensures the company is functioning smoothly and who is responsible for admin, systems, HR and some day-to-day financial management.

Examples of functions you may encounter further down the organisation include (alphabetically):

Accounts	Old name for the Finance function
Accounts Payable	Part of Finance – responsible for paying suppliers
Accounts Receivable	Part of Finance – receives money from customers
Administration	Elastic term that covers everything from the post room and towels in the washrooms to in-house catering, premises and systems
Back Office	New name for Administration – in a bank it often means the settlement function (settling trades)
Business Development	Same as Marketing
Buyer	Deals with suppliers
Company Secretary	Deals with record-keeping and filing to ensure the company is properly registered under company law plus the proper convening of shareholders meetings – in a large group may look after 300–400 companies
Compliance	Deals with regulatory issues – where an industry is closely controlled by law, this function ensures the company is abiding by the law (found in banks)
Credit Control	Chases customers who haven't paid their bills (debtors) – part of Finance
Estates Management	Responsible for the maintenance and legal aspects of the buildings and land the company occupies or owns
Facilities Management	New term for premises, print, mailroom and catering administration
Finance	Responsible for all aspects of money – from paying suppliers, getting paid by customers, working capital management and long-term funding of the business

Fleet	Responsible for any vehicles the company has or uses
Front Of House	Those parts of the business that interface with clients in person such as reception and catering in meeting rooms
H&S	Health & Safety – ensuring the company is compliant with applicable laws for the well-being of staff; often part of HR
HR	Human Resources – modern term for 'Personnel' – includes payroll, holidays and sickness records, recruitment, appraisal, performance, disciplinary issues and dismissal; responsible for staff handbooks and policies
ICT	Information and Communications Technology – computers, networks, telephones
Investor Relations	Dealing with shareholders, where the business is a public company
IP	Intellectual property – protects the company's copyrights, patents, brands
Know How	The company's 'soft' knowledge such as precedents and processes
Learning & Development	New term for Training – responsible for staff development, training courses
Legal	Responsible for all legal issues affecting the company, including contracts with suppliers, customer and employees and dealing with any claims brought by or against the company
Library & Information	Old term for Know How including published sources of external information
Logistics	Also known as supply chain management – responsible for getting the company's products to customers as quickly and cheaply as possible
Marketing	Responsible for the company's image and brand, identifying new markets for products and services
Middle Office	Found in banks and includes legal, compliance, regulatory and risk management – i.e. not client facing (front) and not purely admin (back) but necessary for the organisation's well-being
Pension Fund Trustees	A separate body, usually including the Finance Director, which looks after the company's pension

fund. Because pension funds are subject to increasingly complex regulations, the trustees (who are individuals drawn from the company's employees and management) often turn to professional external trustees to sit alongside them. There is another book in the *All You Need To Know* series about being a pension fund trustee

Petty Cash Part of Finance, dealing with the float of cash kept at the company, for instance for employee expenses

Planning Often part of Finance, plans the company's future needs for premises, people, funding and so on

Post Room Delivers internal and external mail. Also known as the mail room. In a multinational can be responsible for complex internal logistics issues

PR Public or press relations – responsible for communications with the world at large (as opposed to customers which is done by Marketing). May report to Marketing

Premises Old term for Estates Management

Procurement Same as Buyer but focuses on the process of selecting suppliers and the contracts negotiated with them – works closely with Legal

Production In manufacturing companies, responsible for the company's output (factories and production lines)

Public Affairs Sometimes part of PR or Marketing, this deals with government relations – for instance lobbying against changes in the law and dealing with any trade associations that represent the company's interests

Public Policy Same as Public Affairs

R&D Research & Development – in manufacturing companies, responsible for developing new products

Research Often part of Marketing or Library & Information – carries out research into subjects of use to the company, e.g. markets, buying patterns

Risk Management Identifies and mitigates risks that the business is exposed to – often includes insurance and legal

Sales Can be part of Marketing or a separate, related function – this is about making actual sales to customers and includes account management

Supply Chain Same as Logistics

Systems	Same as ICT
Tax	Deals with the company's tax position – can be a large department in big companies; often part of Finance or Legal
Training	Old term for Learning & Development
Treasury	Part of Finance, raises short- and long-term funding for the company, invests any surplus cash and deals in the foreign exchange market, converting overseas income into sterling

As you get to know people in a client organisation, ask them about their roles and the particular challenges they face.

Ask yourself what a client organisation's **service**, **product** or **purpose** is. Look at the relevant **trade publications** (every industry has at least one newspaper or magazine devoted to it) and get a feel for the issues which that industry faces. If you start to specialise in a sector, go to the relevant **industry conferences**.

Doing these things will enhance your understanding of what your clients are doing and why, and the issues they encounter. You will be able to engage them in interesting conversations which will increase their respect for you.

WORKING ALONGSIDE OTHER PROFESSIONALS

One thing that irritates clients enormously is having a set of professional advisers who don't get on but who try to score points off each other, jockeying for position, trying to out-compete each other. To avoid this, you need to know what other professionals do.

Accountants get involved with companies in many different ways. All public companies are required to have annual audits and accountants act as **auditors**, compiling the information that goes into the annual report and accounts. In the biggest companies, teams of external auditors are at work almost the whole year round. But accountants get involved in other ways. They may be **reporting accountants**, overseeing the financials of a bid, for example. Smaller companies may use accountants for **corporate finance** advice, on the raising of money. At one point the major accounting practices had management consulting arms, but these were regarded as causing a conflict of interest (it's difficult to report objectively on a company's financial position while you are advising it on how to improve that position).

There are different accounting bodies and qualifications. Chartered accountants belong to the ICAEW (Institute of Chartered Accountants in England & Wales) and they are the ones who make up the bulk of accountants in private practice (i.e. in firms). But management accountants who work inside companies may be members of CIMA (the Chartered Institute of Management Accountants) or ACCA (Association of Chartered Certified Accountants).

Examples: the biggest accounting practices are **PricewaterhouseCoopers** (PwC), **KPMG, Ernst & Young** and **Deloitte**. Andersen was the other major firm but was a casualty of the Enron scandal and fell apart.
Deal with: Finance Director, Finance, Accounts

Actuaries are statisticians who help pension funds work out what their future liabilities are likely to be and then advise them on how to manage their assets to generate a return to meet those liabilities. They do this by looking at the demographics of a group of people. So if, say, a pension fund has 4,000 retired workers and another 1,500 coming up to retirement in the next three years, the actuary can use information about that group (age profile, socio-economic mix, number of smokers, drinkers, those who have heart disease, etc) to work out the **incidence of mortality** – in other words, how many of them will, statistically, die when. Then the actuary can advise the pension fund on how much money it will be paying out to retired (but alive) workers and for how long. The pension fund then knows what investment return it needs to generate over, say, the next 5–10 years and can plan accordingly, hiring fund managers to deliver those returns.

Pensions used to be a boring backwater. No longer. People are living longer and are concerned about what they will live on. And companies have to account for future liabilities now, so they can't assume that future gains will fill any current funding gap. This means that the company (called the pension **plan sponsor** or **scheme sponsor**) must make up any shortfall. Pensions used to be based on your final salary – usually two-thirds of what you were earning when you retired – which was good because that was probably your maximum earnings level. These plans were called **defined benefits** (you knew what you were going to get). But they are expensive, especially if a company has to account on a present value basis. So many of these have been closed to new members and replaced by **defined contributions** schemes where you know how much you are required to put in but not what you will get at the end (that depends on investment returns in the meantime). Then, when you retire, the pot of money saved on your behalf is used to buy a contract (called an **annuity** because it pays out an annual amount, usually in monthly instalments) which supports you until you die.

Pension funds invest in a wide array of asset classes, including shares, bonds, foreign exchange and commercial property. Their extensive commercial property holdings mean that, in the UK, pension funds and insurance companies are the landlords of many businesses. It is partly for this reason that a peculiar convention of commercial leases is periodic rent reviews that are upwards-only (a tenant's rent can never go down, regardless of market demand).

Aside from actuaries there are all sorts of consultants who advise pension funds, for instance on fund manager selection and monitoring, benchmarking of investment returns and so on.

Examples of actuarial firms include **Hewitt, Tillinghast, Watson Wyatt, William M Mercer**
Deal with: Finance Director, Pension Fund Trustees

Architects are mainly involved in 'newbuilds' but may be brought in to help a company design additional space. One type are interior designers who don't just advise on the colour of furnishings but help companies get the best ergonomical use out of their premises. The trade and certifying body is the Royal Institute of British Architects.

Examples include: **Grimshaws, Richard Rogers, Skidmore Owings & Merrill**
Deal with: Estates Management

Advertising agencies Without advertising, most newspapers, TV and radio stations would fold. 'Controlled publications' are distributed free and depend entirely on their advertising revenue; but all publications – even news-stand and subscription publications – rely on advertising for some of their revenue. Advertising ranges from billboards and adverts on the sides of buses to product placement in films. Despite the onslaught of new media, traditional advertising is still a huge business. Agencies advise clients on campaigns, do the design work and buy the space (an industry in itself). Large design agencies also have **copywriters** who write the words ('copy' here means a piece of text).

Examples: **WPP**, **J Walter Thompson**, **Abbott Mead Vickers BBDO**, **McCann Erickson**, **Publicis**, **Ogilvy & Mather**, **Saatchi** (two separate firms)
Deal with: Marketing, Sales, PR, CEO, FD

Bankers You know from earlier chapters that these come in all shapes and sizes, but essentially divide between commercial bankers who lend money and investment bankers who arrange for the issue of shares and bonds. Bankers specialising in corporate finance advise on mergers and acquisitions and may also advise on the issue of shares (corporate finance is a traditional merchant banking activity now done by investment banks and to an extent commercial banks, especially when either is part of a conglomerate or bundled bank that does everything). Some possible areas of friction with bankers include:

- They like to be seen to be driving the transaction forward so may treat other professional advisers as lackeys
- As a professional adviser, you may be advising the bank as opposed to the bank's corporate client – be sure which of the two is your client
- Even where you are advising the bank, the corporate may be paying your bill
- The banker may only be paid on the successful completion of the transaction so if your advice is negative, this can annoy the banker

Examples: The top bundled banks include **Citigroup**, **JP Morgan**

Chase, **HSBC** and **Barclays**; the top commercial banks include **Deutsche**, **Royal Bank of Scotland** and **ING**; the top investment banks include **Goldman Sachs**, **Merrill Lynch**, **Morgan Stanley** and **Lehman Brothers**
Deal with: CEO, Finance Director, Treasury

Brand specialists advise companies on image and brand and are often involved at a strategic level in helping to define a business and its markets and what it says about itself. More routinely they develop new logos. Traditional graphics design and advertising work has been subsumed within this and there are large agencies that encompass advertising, brand management, design and PR.

Examples: **Interbrand**, **Wolff Olins**
Deal with: Marketing, Business Development, CEO

Brokers The term 'broker' means intermediary. A commodity broker sells commodities ('hard' ones include metals; 'soft' ones are agricultural produce). A futures broker sells futures (a contract to take delivery of a commodity or financial instrument in three months' time at a price agreed today). A stockbroker sells shares to retail investors. A corporate broker advises a company on share issues (and may be part of a bank). See the separate entry for 'insurance brokers'.

Examples include: **Collins Stewart Tullett**, **Killik**, **Numis**
Deal with: FD, Treasury, Pension Fund Trustees, Risk Management

Engineers build things, everything from industrial robots to computers, from chemicals to aircraft. They build and install equipment. Civil engineers construct buildings, bridges, roads, ports and airports. Structural engineers worry about foundations. Marine engineers specialise in ships, electrical engineers in power, highway engineers in roads, and so on.

Examples include: **WS Atkins**
Deal with: Estates Management, Systems, FD

Fund managers – also known as asset managers, investment

managers, money managers, portfolio managers, wealth managers –
manage money on behalf of a company's pension fund. If a pension
fund is big enough, it may have its own in-house fund managers,
employed by the fund to invest its money. But most pension funds
put at least some of their money out to external managers.

They can be stand-alone businesses started by the people who
work in them (**New Star**) or owned by banks (**Jupiter**, **Gartmore**,
Newton, **Mellon**). Fund managers specialise by:
- type of investment (e.g. shares, bonds, foreign exchange)
- geographic market (UK, Europe, US, emerging)
- type of security – shares or bonds

Those who invest equities (shares) specialise by:

- size of company (e.g. big cap – meaning large companies by
  capitalisation)
- investment style ('growth' – companies that don't produce much
  by way of dividend, 'income' – companies that do, and 'value' –
  companies whose shares are underpriced)

All of these are **active** managers, choosing investments based on
analysis. But since pension funds measure the performance of their
investments against the index (e.g. the FTSE 100), they are putting
an increasing amount of their money into **passive** or **index-
tracking** funds which simply match the index by investing in exactly
the same shares as the index contains. Active managers strive to
be **upper quartile** (in the top 25% of their universe of fund
managers) but it's a zero-sum game (for everyone above average
there is someone below average) with no guarantee that last year's
top performer will be this year's. Which is why passive investment
is increasingly popular, because it provides more consistent returns.

Fund managers report on a quarterly basis to a pension fund's
trustees. Those who persistently under-perform their benchmark
index are sacked and replacements are suggested by the advisers
to the fund (often actuaries or offshoots of them).

Examples include: **Fidelity** (the largest privately-owned one), those mentioned above and virtually every bank – usually with the bank's name followed by 'asset management' or 'investment management' in its title.

Deal with: Finance Director, Pension Fund Trustees

Graphic designers A lot of people who study at art school go into industrial or applied design rather than fine art and end up doing everything from designing consumer packaging to creating brochures. The American artist Edward Hopper illustrated adverts. Agencies can be small (I have known of one-man-bands working for huge companies) and are often departments within brand or advertising agencies.

Examples: Most are small boutiques; the largest are separate businesses in global advertising agencies.

Deal with: Marketing, R&D, Production, Business Development, PR

Insurance brokers act as intermediaries between insureds (companies) and insurers, helping companies buy insurance cover as cheaply as possible and advising on the sort of cover most appropriate. They also help with claims although large claims tend to be assessed by **loss adjusters** working for the insurer. Some big companies choose to 'self insure' – in other words they bear any loss themselves on the basis that this works out more cheaply over the longer term because they keep the premium they would otherwise be paying. Insurers can be extremely large and international in their own right.

Examples: Aon, Marsh & McLellan

Deal with: Risk Management, Finance Director

ITC consultants Information, Technology and Communications is the ungainly term used to cover specialists in everything from telephony to computer systems. These people vary from individuals helping customers on specific ITC issues to large firms advising banks on the installation of vast risk management systems. People may be the ITC equivalent of a plumber, installing wiring in below-floor ducts, to ITC strategists advising on the choice and installation of systems costing hundreds of millions.

Examples: Some of the major management consultants such as **Accenture**, **Capgemini** and **PA Consulting** do this; others include **Ovum**
Deal with: Systems, FD

Lawyers can be solicitors, barristers or legal executives but the distinctions are blurring. Barristers appear in court (but so can solicitors), solicitors advise clients (but so do barristers) and legal executives work in both firms and companies. Many large companies have legal departments.

Lawyers tend to be contentious (settling disputes, also known as 'litigation') or non-contentious (doing transactions and giving advice) and they specialise by expertise which can include: commercial (contracts), corporate (company law, listings and M&A), banking (lending), capital markets (bonds and shares), competition (dealing with regulators who strike down monopolies and market-dominant businesses in the UK and Europe), employment, intellectual property (copyright, trademarks, patents), pensions, real estate (property), shipping and tax.

Examples of top international firms include **Allen & Overy**, **Clifford Chance**, **Linklaters** and **Slaughter and May** (all UK) and **Cravath Swaine & Moore**, **Skadden Arps**, **White & Case** (US)
Deal with: Head of Legal, Compliance, Company Secretary, CEO, Finance Director

Lobbyist This profession is well established in the US but is new to the UK although there are several thousand – mainly ex-politicians and civil servants. Their job is to make sure their clients' concerns are raised at the right levels of government and the opposition (the term 'lobby' comes from the lobbies or hallways in Parliament). Industries that are likely to be affected by legislation and regulation use their trade bodies, advised by lobbyists, to press their case to ensure that they are not too adversely affected. In a sense, a democracy shouldn't need lobbyists to press the case of a few over the many. But modern life and government is so complex that you need to know people who know their way round the corridors of power.

Examples: Many PR agencies have lobbying departments. The most well-known lobbying organisations are charities, such as Amnesty International and Greenpeace.
Deal with: Public Affairs, CEO, Board, PR

Management consultants form the biggest pool of external advisers. The term can cover everything from strategy consulting to HR advice. Many are process consultants, advising a company on how it can achieve efficiencies (e.g. supply chain). Areas of growth include outsourcing and ERP (enterprise resource planning) which is the automation of back-office functions through technology. Here the barriers to entry are high with consultants such as **Accenture**, **EDS** and **Capita** often providing the outsource capability. But on the advisory side, the barriers to entry are low: many individuals set up as consultants having worked in a particular sector and are able to advise clients based on what they have learnt from advising others.

Examples include: **Accenture, Capgemini, Deloitte, KPMG, PA Consulting, PricewaterhouseCoopers** and strategy consultants such as **Bain & Company, Boston Consulting Group** and **McKinsey & Company**
Deal with: CEO, Finance Director, Board… everyone

Market analysts study companies and markets and make buy and sell recommendations for institutional investors to act on.

Examples: Analysts are found in banks and brokers
Deal with: FD, Investor Relations, Pension Fund Trustees

Market researchers provide detailed data on actual and potential markets. They are also sophisticated pollsters, carrying out telephone interviews with the same function in scores of companies to establish business attitudes to current developments of interest to companies. They often provide the raw data on the basis of which research reports are written.

Examples include: **Harris, Mori, Taylor Nelson Sofres**
Deal with: Marketing, Business Development, PR

Marketing consultants There are all sorts of marketing consultants, from those collecting data to do market segmentation (dividing the market up into types of customer to target) to those offering databases and systems to collate customer information. Others specialise in helping companies make tenders for big contracts. Still others provide training to staff in business development skills. Marketing specialists talk about 'above the line' and 'below the line'. Above the line includes advertising. Below the line includes sales promotion (encouraging buying at the point of sale, for instance through eye-catching displays, freebies and competitions).

Examples: **Omnicom**, **WPP**
Deal with: Marketing, Business Development

Patent attorneys are part-lawyers, part-scientists and deal with intellectual property. They help companies protect their know-how and inventions by filing for patent registration. Once you have a patent no one can infringe it. So patent registries do not accept applications without testing them rigorously, which is why being a patent attorney is extremely demanding (you have to be able to show why something is sufficiently different from what has come before to merit protection). It takes several years to qualify and join the Chartered Institute of Patent Agents. Big companies that do a lot of R&D have their own patent departments.

Examples include: **Marks & Clerk**, **Kilburn & Strode**, **Reddie & Grose**, **D Young** and **Boult Wade Tennant**
Deal with: IP, Patents, Legal

PR consultants have over the past 20 years become prominent advisers. The 'P' can stand for 'public' and/or 'press' and their expertise lies in dealing with the media. More 'news' gets into papers and on to TV through PR agents than you might like to think. Many TV and print journalists end up in PR. PR agencies put out press releases for clients, get articles 'placed' in the press, train clients in media skills (how to answer tricky questions, how to look good on TV), develop disaster plans and input to image and strategy. Financial PR is heavily involved in M&A activity where takeovers can be won or lost depending on press comment and public perception.

Examples include: **Brunswick, Citigate Dewe Rogerson, Financial Dynamics, Finsbury, Weber Shandwick**
Deal with: PR, CEO

Quantity surveyors These have nothing to do with surveyors (next entry) although many belong to RICS, the surveyors' body. They are intimately involved with construction projects and control the associated costs by undertaking feasibility studies, cost estimating, valuations and cost benefit analysis. They assess the cost of work, labour, materials and plant.

Examples: Arup, EC Harris, Cyril Sweett
Deal with: Estates Management

Recruitment consultants help companies find, select and employ people. Those that poach senior staff from other companies are called headhunters. They also advise newly appointed CEOs on how to settle in quickly (this is called 'onboarding').

Examples include **Michael Page** (recruiter), **Hays, Heidrick & Struggles** (headhunter)
Deal with: HR, CEO

Surveyors deal with land and premises. They have agency departments that broker deals (acquisition and disposal of land and buildings) and act on behalf of developers acquiring sites for development. They also have advisory practices that help with planning applications and the management of property on behalf of institutional landlords like pension funds and insurance companies. This includes dealing with corporate tenants, rent reviews and dilapidations (getting tenants to make good any wear and tear). Commercial property is a major asset class worldwide and the leading surveyors have merged internationally to form extensive networks of offices. Property professionals belong to the Royal Institute of Chartered Surveyors (RICS).

Examples include: **Jones Lang LaSalle, CBRE, DTZ Debenham Tie Leung, CB Hillier Parker, Drivers Jonas**
Deal with: Estates, Facilities, Finance Director

Tax consultants Tax is an interesting discipline that falls between accountancy and law. You don't, strictly speaking, have to be qualified to call yourself a tax adviser. But most tax advisers are either qualified accountants or lawyers or belong to the CIOT (Chartered Institute of Taxation) which offers qualifications to those who pass a set of demanding exams. Tax is regarded by people who don't know better as boring. It is actually an exciting discipline because HMRC (Her Majesty's Revenue & Customs) is forever dreaming up new ways of taxing individuals and companies, and tax advisers are forever findings ways round the regulations. So it is a dynamic field, constantly changing.

All companies are obsessed with tax and want to pay the minimum which, legally, they can. Tax avoidance (reducing your tax liability) is OK. Tax evasion (paying less than legally you should) is not. Multinationals structure their worldwide operations to minimise the tax-take which, since traditionally countries do not enforce each other's tax laws, can make for interesting corporate group structures involving subsidiaries in odd places of the world.

Other professionals as sources of new business

The professionals you encounter will become some of your most useful contacts. They won't necessarily become clients but they can refer clients to you. The marketing jargon for a referrer is a 'multiplier'.

A good professional contact can lead to a stream of new clients throughout your career but such relations are usually built on a degree of reciprocity (referring clients back in return). This can prove awkward because your duty is to act in the best interests of your client and refer them to the professional best suited to help them, rather than the one who refers clients to you.

The way round this is to give your client a choice of two or three professionals to choose from. Then it's up to your client to make his or her choice based on things like personal chemistry (so if the relationship doesn't work out it isn't your fault). You should tell each professional that you have given the client their name but be sure to tell them that theirs isn't the only name you have given. This is the most they can expect from you. Equally in return, yours may not be the only name they give their clients – so it will be up to you to make a presentation or pitch to win the client. For more on pitching see Chapter 10.

Top tax professionals tend to be very clever and very geeky. It takes a combination of rare skills – ability to analyse complex legislation and case law, and a facility with figures. People tend to be good at one or the other but not both. In practice, lawyers tend to worry about the law and accountants about the figures. But that's a gross generalisation.

Examples: Tax departments are found in **all the top accountancy and law firms**
Deal with: Finance Director, Finance, Accounts and any in-house tax advisers (the biggest companies have their own tax departments)

WATCHING THE PROFESSIONALS

Get to know what other professionals do in order to avoid friction with them. Observe the way they handle the client and build a relationship. Learn what to do (and, equally, what not to).

Now let's meet your first client.

Chapter 7

DOING THE WORK

SPEED-READ SUMMARY

- You won't be let loose on real clients immediately – your first client is your supervisor, but all of the previous lessons apply

- Learn how to be delegated to – and use that knowledge to help the person giving you work

- Seek feedback regularly, but not too frequently otherwise it bugs your supervisor and makes you seem unconfident

- Use appraisals to further your own development

- Much of the work we do today requires us to work in teams. If you can, find out your Belbin type(s)

- Become familiar with the principles of project management – clients expect it

- You need to be adept at managing your own use of time – this depends on your own preferred working style, how you manage what is on your desk and control what comes in through the door

- Managing client expectations is a key skill – the same piece of work delivered in the same way at the same time can generate satisfaction or complaint on the client's side depending entirely on how those expectations have been managed

- Key to handling complaints is showing empathy and rebuilding trust

- Keep checking with the client that what you are doing is what the client wants

- Clients like solutions, so become familiar with problem-solving techniques such as brainstorming, 'why, why, why' and fishbone

Here's the bad news. I've told you all about how to relate to clients. But, assuming you are a young professional in your first job, you are unlikely to be unleashed on a real client immediately. In fact your first 'client' will be your supervisor or boss.

YOUR BOSS IS YOUR FIRST CLIENT

Don't despair. Everything I've said so far about dealing with clients applies to your boss. Treat your boss as the chance to experiment and hone your client-facing skills. You want to build a relationship with her to ensure that you deliver what she wants. Some of the questions you would ask a client you won't need to ask your boss because (1) you know something about her business (since you are starting to work in it yourself) and (2) you know her function in it.

But you can usefully ask her about the clients she is trying to serve and what you can do to help her. In short, you want to be someone she can delegate work to. In order to do that, it helps to know how you should be delegated to: this is something that most senior professionals (your boss included) think they know how to do, but which they don't necessarily do that well. So you have to help them.

DELEGATION

This is how she should do it. She should select an appropriate task for the right developmental reasons (not just to shift something off her desk but because it will help in your development). She should also select you as an appropriate 'delegee' for good developmental reasons rather than because you happen to be available.

She should then **prepare the briefing** (see below), **carry out the briefing** with you and give you opportunities to allow her to **monitor how you are doing**. She should **liaise with others** – with the client so that they know you are doing the work; and colleagues so they know you are already busy – then, once you have done the job, **provide feedback** and, finally, find further opportunities to **reinforce your development** by giving you related tasks.

In the **briefing** itself, your boss should **identify the nature of the task and the client**, then **check your experience and**

availability, then she should **specify the output** she wants (note, draft letter, report – is it for her or the client? If the client, what will the client be using it for?) as well as **any constraints** (e.g. how much time to spend on it) and the **deadline**. She should then **check your understanding** by getting you to reiterate what she has said and to **check what your first few steps** will be.

She should also set up **an interim monitoring procedure** (specifying a midpoint when you can go back and report on progress) rather than just saying 'If you have any problems, come back' which makes you feel that if you do have to go back to her you have failed.

This is the theory. But busy professionals are often under too much pressure to delegate properly and, as a result, the job isn't done well. So next time they decide it's quicker to do it themselves. Your job is to ensure that does not happen. So you must make sure that you understand enough to be able to do the job properly. Do not be afraid to ask questions – if you fail to do so, your boss may not be available next time you need to. Be sure to establish:

- the required output (format/length) – what your boss needs it for and, if she is passing it to the client, what they need it for
- how much time it should take you
- when you need to have it done by (deadline)
- interim monitoring procedure (when you can go back, part-way through, to check that you are on the right lines)
- who else you can ask in her absence
- relevant background information on the client and task

Above all, think what you would want *if you were in her position*. In other words, put yourself in your client's (i.e. your boss's) shoes.

Sometimes your boss doesn't have time to do it like this at all. The theory says that her style in delegating to you will fall somewhere on a spectrum between an **asking/coaching style** (as outlined above) where she is trying to develop you and a **telling/directing** style where she is simply trying to get the job done. The latter is less risky and less time-consuming. If you develop a good relationship with her you can both agree which is most appropriate to the situation in hand (emergency = tell; less demanding timeframe = coaching).

By the way, Stephen Covey (author of *Seven Habits Of Highly Effective People*) encourages delegation: it takes more time initially to train someone up to do a job, correcting their mistakes, giving them a chance to try again on a different task, and so on; but he says it saves time in the long run. A job that a supervisor can do in an hour but will take her three hours to delegate and supervise properly may be one she is tempted to do herself. But if she does delegate, she is saving time after the third recurrence of that particular task. The best managers keep their desk clear by delegating. This allows them to spend their time on developing people (by delegating, then 'managing by walking about', supporting those they have delegated to) and being available to deal with crises.

FEEDBACK

The other thing you want is – once you've done the job – some feedback on how you have done. If professionals are bad at delegation, they are even worse at feedback. No one likes to criticise a colleague. So you must make it easy for them:

- Ask them to fix a time convenient to them
- Say you're not expecting more than 5–10 minutes of their time
- Be prepared to help them provide feedback by going prepared with two or three areas you can prompt them for feedback on (e.g. structure of output, depth of research, etc)
- If you can't think of anything, then (1) ask them what they had to change before acting on your work or sending it to the client and, failing that (if they seem happy with everything), then (2) ask 'If there was one single thing I could have done better, what would it be?'
- Whatever you do, don't try to argue against them or justify what you did – this is about learning for the future
- Make the process easy and enjoyable for them – then they are more likely to do it again – and don't ask too often: it can be annoying and smack of a lack of self-confidence

Just so you know, there are several accepted models for the giving of feedback. Here are two.

BOOST stands for Balanced, Objective, Observed, Specific and Timely. **Balanced** means setting the bad in the context of the good – sometimes called a 'praise sandwich' (good/bad/good).
Objective means that feedback should be based on behaviour, not personality ('You were late today' not 'You've got a slack attitude about getting to work on time'). This is because there's no point in criticising someone because of who they are (which they can't change). It's what they do that feedback is meant to try to change. **Observed** means that comments should be based on behaviour that has actually been observed, not on hearsay. **Specific** means that comments are restricted to one particular item (more than one can be overload). **Timely** means that it is done as soon after the behaviour in question as possible.

NITA feedback (NITA stands for the National Institute of Trial Advocacy, the body in the US that trains lawyers in courtroom skills) is more directive and, in some respects, easier to apply. There are four stages: **Headline**, **Replay**, **Rationale** and **Prescription**.

> **Headline** means that the person is told what it is about ('Chris, I'd like to talk to you about your presentation skills').

> **Replay** means – as with BOOST – the person being told precisely (as if being played back on video) the behaviour that is being commented on ('This morning, when you were presenting at the client seminar, you jangled the keys in your trouser pocket all the way through').

> **Rationale**: 'The trouble with this is that it distracted the audience from the very useful and interesting points that you were making, so they learnt less and came away with an impaired impression of the true level of your expertise.'

> **Prescription**: 'Next time, please try taking keys and coins out of your pockets so that, if you have to put your hands in your pockets, there won't be anything in them to jangle.'

The best supervisors use these and other models to give positive as well as negative feedback. Everyone likes to be praised but it helps to know exactly what you have done right, so you can replicate it, rather than being told in general terms that you were 'fine' or 'really good.'

Feedback should be given reasonably regularly – it may just be a few words in the lift or taxi on the way back from a client meeting. By contrast, appraisal tends to be more formal and may only occur once a year. The problem with appraisals is that they often occur too far away from the aspects of performance that are being appraised. Effective feedback overcomes this problem. Effective feedback at frequent intervals should support the appraisal process. Now you know that, see if you can get regular feedback.

APPRAISAL

In many organisations appraisals are done either poorly or not at all. Most supervisors hate giving appraisals because of the implication that they are required to be critical. Again, make their task easy: it's your job to get an effective appraisal so that you know where and how you can improve your performance. Only by doing that will you increase your prospects. Be a willing appraisee.

One way of doing this is to change the appraisal from being retrospective (backward-looking at the previous year) into a prospective process (something that is forward-looking). Ask your supervisor what the department or team's plans for the next year are and how you can play your part in helping meet those objectives. This is a good way of showing enthusiasm and of being able to discuss what sort of work you want to receive. By asking you are more likely to get. But you also need to explore with your supervisor where you need to improve your skills in order to take on the work that you would like.

Cast in this more positive, forward-looking light, the appraisal becomes more of a two-way discussion. Your supervisor is more likely to relax and give you an honest assessment of the areas on which you need to work. You can then ask for development opportunities and/or training to be able to develop these skills. And you can be sure that what you are doing is in line with the team or department's plans and strategy so you are more likely to be doing what your boss wants.

By the way, **upwards-only appraisals** are where your appraisal is informed by the views of your subordinates; and **360-degree appraisals** take into account the views of your subordinates, your colleagues (peers) and your seniors, as well as clients.

Of course, there may come a time when your appraisals seem negative. Don't take it personally. It may simply be time for you to move on to another organisation where your skills fit more readily with their strategy. In short, don't be afraid of appraisals: far better to know what people really think of you than to be kept in the dark and to be unaware of views being expressed behind your back. Ultimately your goal is to be a successful professional. And you can only do that in an organisation where your skills fit. So you owe it to yourself to be sure that they do. If you are in an organisation where appraisals are done badly or not at all and you aren't getting any encouragement or decent responses to questions about the team's plans, you may be in the wrong place.

For more on this, try reading the chapter entitled 'How's your asset?' in David Maister's book *Managing The Professional Service Firm*. Also, for a weird but wonderful approach to managing people, have a look at the book *Maverick* by Ricardo Semler. Both are mentioned in the bibliography.

GETTING THE WORK DONE

So, you're now involved in client work, either being delegated to or as part of a team or both. Now you need to get the work done. I am assuming that whatever your particular professional vocation, whether it's accountancy, the law, surveying, etc – you know the technical aspects of the job; in other words, you know the content.

However, being an expert isn't necessarily the only thing clients value you for.

The first thing you need to show is not just that you can do the work but that you can manage it. **Project management** is a buzzword amongst clients. But many professionals (other than management consultants and construction engineers) are poor at project management. They tend to think of it as requiring software like Microsoft Project which generates spreadsheets and Gantt charts. And they don't like it because it constrains their autonomy. Many professionals consider that their experience comes from having done things before so they plan how they are going to staff and run a client job on a mental back-of-an-envelope. Anyone needing anything more than that obviously lacks experience.

Teamworking: Belbin

As the world becomes more complex, tasks can no longer be entrusted to one person to carry out. Instead, work is increasingly team-based with different members bringing their own expertise to bear on the project. Crucial to a project's success is the way the team itself functions. A lot has been written about teams. A leading writer is R M Belbin.

Belbin studied the way groups of people work together in teams. From his studies over several years he drew a number of conclusions. These were (1) that teams need a certain distribution of types in order to succeed and (2) that each team member had a principal and secondary type that he could deploy. The principal was dominant but the secondary could be consciously asserted if necessary for the team's composition.

There are eight types altogether (although Belbin subsequently added a ninth: the specialist, in the team for his/her task-specific expertise).

They include:

- resource investigator – looks outside the team for help and ideas
- plant – creative thinker
- completer/finisher – ensures the job is completed to specification and on time
- chairman – often mistaken for somebody who takes charge; rather, someone who coordinates
- shaper – gets the team moving
- monitor-evaluator – analytical; weighs up options; prone to being conservative (many professionals are like this)
- team worker – ensures everyone is involved and listened to
- co-worker – practical organiser who turns a project into separate tasks.

All have their pluses and minuses. Belbin's point is that the more balanced a team is in terms of its make-up, the more effective it will be. Although Belbin is regarded now as old hat, the model's still a good starting point for establishing individual strengths and weaknesses. Take the Belbin test yourself. You can find sources on the web.

However, clients expect it and, indeed, think they are already paying for it. Many clients themselves use project management techniques. So should their advisers. A project plan is a good way of showing a client that you know what you are doing (that you have done it before). It instils confidence.

At its most basic it includes:

- A breakdown of a piece of work into stages
- A resource plan (who will do what when with an indication of how many professionals and their level of seniority/experience)
- Timescales
- Costs
- Contingencies (what may go wrong and how to tackle it)
- Cushion (allowance in time and costs for contingencies)

None of this requires a spreadsheet.

A classic bit of project management theory is the **trade-off triangle**. The three corners are **Time**, **Cost** and **Quality**. Improve Quality and the job may take longer and/or cost more. Shrink the deadline and Quality will suffer or costs will go up as more people are thrown at it; and so on. Professionals will say, 'This doesn't apply to us. We never – and can never – compromise on quality. Otherwise we'd be negligent.' Not so. Quality here doesn't mean technical skill. It means quality of service. You can compromise on quality – with the client's approval. For instance, you can give an oral piece of advice that you don't back up in writing. It saves time by providing a different level of service (quality).

This trade-off triangle can be a useful basis for having such discussions with clients. We'll be coming back to this when we talk about pricing and billing in Chapter 9.

TIME MANAGEMENT

There's some project management you need to apply to yourself. As a junior professional, you will find there are many demands on your time and you need to start prioritising. It may be tempting to read a book or two on time management (if you can find the time). They tend to cover three things, which I label: Head, Desk, Door.

Using a flipchart

If you are in a client meeting, even with only two or three other people, try using a flipchart instead of each person keeping their own notes (or, worse still, your acting as 'secretary'). Using a flipchart creates a focal point and concentrates energy. It means people don't spend their time writing things down, but can contribute instead. Tips include:

- Putting flip sheets up on the walls as you complete them

- Saying you will type them up after and circulate them
- Encouraging (1) only one person to speak at a time and (2) no side conversations
- Writing clearly and large enough for everyone to see – use capitals if necessary
- Writing alternate lines in a different colour (e.g. blue and black) to break the page up

How you manage time depends on what is in your head, what is on your desk and what (and who) comes in through the door.

What's in your head This is about how you work, what your working patterns are and what your aims are. It reflects how you are as a person. Things which also go under this heading (please pardon the pun) include: how you prioritise (different types of To Do list), decision-making models, creative thinking, breaking jobs into chunks (e.g. whether you read documents the night before to let the brain process them overnight), your peak working time (biorhythms), physical exercise and stress management and knowing your own working style (e.g. Belbin).

It's also about how to set goals: 'I want to lose weight' = hope; 'I want to lose 11 pounds by 1 December so I can wear my frock to the office party' = goal. It's also about planning your time – how to reduce the time you spend on jobs (e.g. always set deadlines otherwise the task expands to fill the available time) – and how to maximise the benefit of the time you do spend.

What's on your desk This is about the actual work you have on your desk, how you manage it and how you do it. This is where most of the tips come in. They're basically about reading, writing, communicating and binning. For instance: never pick up a piece of paper more than once without actioning it; always use the bin in preference to any other type of file; when to use email and how to use it; save time by replying by hand on the incoming note and keep a photocopy if necessary; how to read (reduce the volume you read and only skim read what you keep); and so on.

What (and who) comes in through the door This is about controlling the incoming flow of work and people. This is difficult to do when you are junior. You feel you have to do whatever anyone senior wants, even if you are already too busy or are not the right person. To answer this you need to understand the value of your function in the eyes of the organisation and what you should and should not be doing if the firm is to get the best out of you. It's also about preventing people from dumping needlessly on you. I know of one relatively junior person in an organisation who manages this brilliantly. A senior person comes in and asks her to copy something. She immediately does it with a smile but adds, 'Next time, the right person to go to is X because I'm actually supposed to be doing Y.' Because she does it charmingly she tends not to get repeat offenders. As you will, by now, be guessing, this is all about interpersonal skills: being assertive; saying no; negotiating; and so on. There are loads of books on each of these.

MANAGING CLIENT EXPECTATIONS

This is perhaps the single most important aspect to being a successful professional.

A client rings up. They need a document in a hurry. You ask when. They say tomorrow by midday. It's going to be a stretch for you to do it. You want to please them, so you agree. Next day you manage to get the document finished but later than you had hoped. You've still done an amazing job to get it out – you had to work till midnight to do so. But the client still only gets it mid-afternoon at 3.30. The client is disappointed – because you **over-promised** and **under-delivered**.

Rewind. A client rings up. They need a document in a hurry. You ask when. They say tomorrow by midday. You ask why. They say they need it to put in a pack which will go to the board of directors. When is it going, you ask. First thing the day after tomorrow, which is why they need to have everything ready by end of business tomorrow which is why they said midday. You ask a bit more about the form of document. They say it has to be short, no more than a page (that's good, you think, you were going to write 10 pages). You promise them they will have it by no later than 5pm tomorrow in the format they wanted. You do the job (without having to stay late, because it's shorter than you would otherwise have made it if you hadn't asked) and get it round to them by 3.30 the next day. They are delighted. You have **under-promised** and **over-delivered**.

Yet in each case you got it to them at the same time. But in this case, most importantly, you have earned their trust as somebody who not only meets his or her promise but exceeds it. So next time they will be a bit more relaxed and give you a more realistic deadline – without your having to negotiate it.

What matters isn't what actually happens. It's what *actually happens* set against what the client *expected to happen*. You can still do the same thing and deliver it at the same time but how the client reacts has nothing to do with that, but with what you led the client to expect. The old adage has it that:

Expectation of what will happen

LESS

Client perception of what does happen

EQUALS

Client satisfaction

In other words, client satisfaction is a relative, not an absolute, and it depends on what was promised to the client when compared to the client's perception of what was actually delivered.

Professionals who are good with clients grasp this: they probe the client's concerns; they get to the bottom of deadlines. They make their own lives easier as a result, impress the client each time and create

How to generate solutions

The buzzword now is 'solution'. Clients want solutions, not problems: 'Don't tell me what I can't do. Just tell me how I can do what I want to.' And everything is packaged as a solution these days: just look at what's written on the sides of trucks. So how can you come up with solutions? Here's a tip: it's not by sitting on your own at your desk with a hot towel wrapped round your head. You need to get together with your colleagues and even the client to get things going.

Brainstorm

This term is much abused. Strictly speaking it means getting a group of people to generate ideas, writing those ideas down verbatim without any editing or comment from anyone else, then once you have done this in two separate sessions, sorting the suggestions into categories and reviewing them to come up with a handful of workable solutions. A variation is 'wildest idea' brainstorm where only extreme or silly ideas are allowed – the purpose being that you can work back from the extreme to work out the underlying thought and turn it into something of practical application. It's fun to do and generates energy.

Why, why, why

Here, you start of with a problem and ask 'why' – for instance, why it occurred. Then you ask the same question of the cause, and so on, working back until you have the original cause. For example, a client complains that they left you a message but you didn't get it. Why? It didn't reach you. Why? It was taken down by someone in another part of the firm. Why? Because the switchboard was closed so the call was routed there. Possible solution: keep the switchboard open later. And so on.

Fishbone/mind maps

This is a pictorial equivalent to why, why, why where you illustrate the problem as a cloud in the middle of a flip sheet and draw lines out from it with each line representing a cause or contributor and then lines out from those as you probe more deeply. With a fishbone, the problem is the fish-head and you create a spine from which separate factors radiate out like bones. Mind maps are a visual way of showing and storing linked information. Again, professionals often tend not to be as visual as business people so these can be useful techniques to use with the right audience.

terrific client relations. All of that builds up a bank of trust so that when something does go genuinely wrong, the client is more forgiving.

DEALING WITH COMPLAINTS

There is a marketing maxim that one satisfied client may tell three others whereas a dissatisfied one will tell a dozen – which can undo the best business development efforts.

If you get an angry client on the phone, try the following:

- Apologise – say you are sorry that they are having this trouble and feel this way (even if the client is in the wrong, what you are apologising for is the fact that *they* are upset)
- Empathise – try to feel what it is they are feeling and try to show that you share their point of view
- Don't blame other parts of your firm – it never sounds good when someone in a service organisation blames another part of it or another colleague
- Take a full note of the complaint and say you will investigate
- Start to rebuild trust – make a promise you can keep. Don't promise to look into it and get back to them – because if you are unable to find anything out immediately you might not feel you can call them until you do, which may be a day or two later. Instead, tell them you will see what you can find out and will call at a certain time later that day. Then make sure you do so, even if you have nothing to report – that way you start to rebuild trust
- Tell your supervisor – and tell the client you will/have done so
- Identify whether the complaint is a result of a service issue (the way in which the firm does something) and suggest internal remedies and, if adopted, tell the client
- Try to find creative ways of resolving the issue

KEEP CHECKING

My final suggestion is to contextualise your advice so that you are really helping clients to achieve their goals. Ask yourself (and them):

- What is prompting my client to ask me for this help?
- What are my client's aims and goals – generally and in relation to this in particular?
- How will what I do help my client achieve those goals?
- How is my client going to use or act on my advice?
- How best can I present this advice for my client to use most effectively?
- How can I check all along the way that what I am doing is what my client wants?

Telephone technique

You will spend more time on the phone to clients than doing anything else, especially the more senior you get. Here are some tips:

- If you are sharing a room with someone else (more senior) don't get self-conscious when making your first client call – we've all had to do it, we've all been there
- Write out a brief agenda of what you want to cover in the call
- Call the client – but expect to find yourself talking to a switchboard or the client's secretary or his voicemail
- If you get voicemail, do leave a message saying who you are, where you're from (firm), what you are calling in connection with, when you are leaving this message and the number for him to call you back on
- When leaving your own phone number always say it slowly – just because you know it well enough to rattle off doesn't make it easy for someone else to hear it or write it down
- If you get through to a real, live person, always say who you are, which firm you are from and which project you are calling about
- Be ready to get the brush-off (e.g. the client saying they are too busy to talk) – do not take this personally even though it may sound rude and feel like a slap in the face
- When you do get to have a conversation, use your agenda to tell the client the points you want to cover – and ask the client whether this is a good time to talk; the client may prefer to fix an alternative time
- As you go through the conversation, tell the client which point you have just finished and which you want to move on to
- Single most important point: leave space for the client to talk and don't talk over them – maintain an easy tempo so you are not constantly interrupting each other. This is especially so in conference calls where lots of people can be trying to listen and speak at the same time
- If the conversation is a long one, end up with a quick round-up of the points discussed and agreed or follow up with an email confirming them
- Final point: when your phone rings, always say who you are when you pick it up

- What should I do by way of follow-up once I have completed doing what my client has asked me to?

A final suggestion: if the client assures you that everything is fine, then after the project ask the client: 'If there was one thing we could have done differently, what would it be?' (the same question I suggested you ask when getting feedback). But only ask this if you can be sure of being able to act upon the suggestion – and that anyone who deals with the client in the future does so too. Otherwise you are setting expectations you can't meet.

So far we've focused on the sorts of things you'll be saying to clients. Now we need to look at how you'll be writing to them.

Chapter 8

GET TO THE POINT

SPEED-READ SUMMARY

- Get to the point – say upfront what you are writing about and why – use a headline if it helps the client, and put the conclusion first

- Write the way you speak – use simple language and short sentences

- We read faster than we write so a lot of the 'scaffolding' we use when writing is unnecessary

- Clients (being busy people) are always trying to find reasons to stop reading – what they want to know is what they need to do next

- A client will, at best, read what you have written once – make sure they get the point by the end even if you need limited repetition

- Be personal but avoid humour

- Try not to hedge your bets – give your answer and then say how confident you are about it

- Put supporting material in an appendix – use an executive summary if needed

- Use boxes and headings to break up the text

- Use graphics whenever possible

- Use bulleted lists (like this one)

- Don't write a conclusion – when you've finished, stop

Employers have got it into their heads that young people can't read or write any more. I don't know whether this is true and, frankly, I don't care. My job is to help you. One thing I am clear about is that people don't have the time to read long, complex reports or letters of advice that don't get to the point straight away. Ricardo Semler, the Brazilian steel tycoon mentioned earlier, insists that in his company (one of the most successful in South America) memos are no more than a page long with a big headline, such as:

NEW SMELTING PROCESS WILL SAVE $200m

That way you are in no doubt what the memo is going to be about.

So in this chapter I am going to help you focus on the written language that you use when writing to clients. Most important advice is either given or confirmed in writing so you need to know how to do this. The good news is that you don't have to be a wordsmith (a great writer) to do it well.

1. WRITE THE WAY YOU SPEAK

Imagine that you are giving me advice orally ('orally' means 'by mouth' which means 'speaking'). Think of what you would say in the first two sentences. It would probably be something like this:

'You asked me to look into whether your company can [do something]. I have done the research and my answer is that you can't do it the way you originally proposed, but there is another way in which you may be able to.'

You would then go on to list the pitfalls of what I had originally wanted, and then set out a possible solution. So those first two sentences tell me in a snapshot what I need to know. They also provide the structure of what you are writing. If you follow that order, I can skip to the second part of what you have written to see what the possible solution is.

Various things flow from this:

- **Use simple words** – do not dress up your language to make it sound 'professional', the shorter the better
- **Use short sentences** – it's what you do when you speak. A sentence needs only a subject and a verb ('The man speaks') but can also have an object ('The company declared profits' – here the order is subject, verb, object). It's a good order to follow, one the brain takes in quickly
- **Use the active** not the passive ('The cat sat on the mat', not 'The mat was sat on by the cat' or 'The board passed the resolution' not 'The resolution was passed by the board')
- It's OK to **end sentences with prepositions** (words like 'to', 'in', 'on', 'at', 'from' – look how I ended the second sentence of my oral advice: 'be able to'. As Winston Churchill said: 'Having to avoid ending with a preposition is something up with which I will not put.'
- **Don't use technical language** unless you are sure the client will understand it – jargon can be a quick way of getting a point across but only if the client is also in the know

A quick test: read aloud anything that you have written. If you run out of breath before you reach the end of the sentence, the sentence is too long. Break it into two.

2. PUT THE CONCLUSION FIRST

I was taught at school to write essays (from the French word 'essayer' meaning 'to try'). In classical French composition, you start with an introduction ('Today I am going to write about') followed by a point or argument (called a 'thesis') followed by a counter-point or counter-argument ('antithesis') and so on until you pull it all together in a grand conclusion ('So on balance my view is…'). If this is the way you've been taught to write (or maybe you haven't if these employers are right), don't do it. Put your conclusion first. It's what newspapers do and these days it's the way most people are used to getting information.

Newspapers start off with a headline, then they amplify it in the first sentence. They provide more information in the first paragraph, and

Email

Be careful about emails. Here are things to watch:

- Has your firm got a rule about only sending emails that a supervisor has checked?
- If you are allowed to communicate directly with a client using email, treat it as you would a letter: check spelling and grammar before you send it
- It's better to be overly formal than too casual. A conventional beginning is to say 'Mr Stoakes' or 'Chris' and to end 'Regards' (which can sound a bit too cold) or 'Best regards'
- Watch out for 'strings' – this is where a string of exchanges is built up between you and a colleague internally and you then copy the latest one to the client – who is able to scroll down to see all of the earlier email correspondence. I have known several occasions when clients have been bad-mouthed in an internal exchange and the string has then been sent to the client without anyone checking
- Don't write long emails: readers hate scrolling down and complex emails aren't easy to read on-screen – they have to be printed out. So why not send a brief email with an attached memo instead?
- It is easy to get the tone of an email wrong: try to be straightforward, factual and don't use humour
- If you receive a nasty email, sleep on your reply overnight before sending it – you will want to tone down your own invective
- Before sending an email ask yourself whether it would be better to pick up the phone
- Manage client expectations: if you get into the habit of replying quickly to client emails, clients will soon build up an expectation of rapid turn-around all the time – sometimes it's better to be more considered; at the same time, emails carry their own inbuilt sense of speed – don't leave an email more than 24 hours before you reply

so on. The point is: you can stop reading whenever you like and you know what the story is.

This is the way to write: the client can stop anywhere and they know what your point is. This isn't always easy (it never is – I think it was Mark Twain who said: 'I'm sorry this letter is so long; I didn't have time to write a shorter one') but it's what clients want. Sometimes you have to 'show your working' – to show all the background research on which you have based your advice in order to cover your ass (technical expression meaning: to make sure you don't subsequently get into trouble if you've got it wrong). If so, stick that stuff in a separate appendix at the end.

Remember, clients don't have time to read. What is going through a client's mind when they are reading your words is:

- Why am I reading this?
- Can I stop reading this?
- What do I need to know?
- What do I need to do next?

There are only three reasons why people read, for:

1. Information
2. Decision and action
3. Entertainment and relaxation

Forget about 3 – that's about reading a thriller on the beach. Number 1 means the client needs to know what you are saying for information only (needs to be kept in the loop) but does not need to act on it. Number 2 is the real point of what you are writing: the client needs to take a decision and then implement it based on your advice. So give them what they need to know and tell them what they should do next. Sure, by all means point out the risks. But tell them first what to do then list the risks.

At this point I will say something contentious. Try not to qualify what you write. A qualification is: 'It seems to me that…' 'It appears to be the case that…' 'On balance…' 'On the one hand… but on the other…' Professionals do this to cover their backside. It's not what clients pay them for because it's of no real use. Tell the client what you think they should do. Tell them why it's not 100%. Tell them what the risks are and the likelihood of their arising. But be decisive. It's not easy but it's why professionals are paid so much. And, by the way, clients will appreciate this and, funnily enough, they won't sue you for getting it wrong when they know you are doing your very best to be as helpful to them as possible. Besides which, getting it wrong is not the same as being negligent.

Presentations

You may find yourself presenting to a roomful of clients. Remember that a presentation can be an inefficient way of getting information across:

- It is tiring listening to someone speak
- It is easy to be distracted whereas when people are reading they tend to concentrate on reading
- The acoustics may be bad and presenters often tend to have poor speaking voices

So you need to signpost every part of your talk: 'Today I am going to talk about [subject]. The single most important point I am going to make is [point]. But I will also be covering three other aspects. Please ask questions as I go along, but I will also allow time for questions at the end.'

The most important point is: do not read out your speech. At worst use notes. At best just speak to the slides (talk about each one as it comes up) – it's more natural, shows you know your stuff and engages the audience more.

Nowadays PowerPoint is almost expected – but only use it where necessary (audiences of more than 10).

Increasingly, professionals are using slides instead of writing reports. So if you do find yourself preparing a presentation:

- Plan to speak for no more than two-thirds of your allotted time
- Assume a maximum of one slide for every two minutes
- Have no more than six bullet points per slide
- Each bullet must be no more than two lines long
- Use visuals where possible

Like that.

- I prefer avoiding 'builds' (each bullet appearing separately) – I just put the whole slide up. Only use builds if you use a small number of slides and linger on each one (which I prefer not to do – people get bored).
- Don't read out your slides (the audience can do that for themselves) – just stress one or two of the bullets and illustrate them by giving examples and telling stories.
- Do say things like 'My final point' and 'To conclude' and 'Finally' when you are more than halfway through – it perks the audience up and they are more likely to listen.
- Make your last slide a blank one so that you know when you have finished without having to follow notes.
- If people do ask questions from the floor, repeat the question (it gives you time to think) so everyone hears it.
- If you don't know the answer, ask the audience what they think.

3. DON'T TRIP THE READER UP

At best your reader will read what you have written only once (though most will, as we have seen, stop or try to stop all along the way). So you need to get your point across. If it's a complex point, don't expect the reader to go back and go over it again until they get it. They won't. Once you've lost the reader, you've lost the reader for good.

This means two things: don't use language or words that will snag the reader's eye mid-flow and make them lose the plot; and if it's a complex point, you may have to make it more than once. A limited amount of repetition is all right to get a complex point across: find a different way of coming at it, of expressing it so that – assuming the reader does get to the end – they know clearly what it is you are trying to say.

Something else flows from this. It's what I call the speed of eye-to-brain transmission. We read quickly: the eye takes in the words and feeds them back to the brain. The brain processes them. Even if some sequences don't appear to make sense, the brain is saying, 'There's a logical point to this – the writer strung these words together in this order to make a point and that point will emerge soon.' In other words, the brain suspends disbelief and is prepared to make small jumps to keep the message flowing.

This means that you don't need the kind of linguistic scaffolding that most of us insert. Phrases like:

- It therefore follows that...
- In conclusion...
- You can see from the above that...
- As noted above...
- As a result...
- Consequently...
- For the avoidance of doubt...

We put these things in because we write much more slowly than we read, so, in writing, we assume it will take the reader as long to get down the page as it has taken us to write it. Wrong. The reader's eye is leaping down the page. What you wrote two pages back is still in the reader's mind. You don't need these explicit signposts referring back. It is still in the brain's memory cache. So leave these connecting phrases out. They are stodgy, unnecessary and slow the reader down.

It's for this reason that you don't even need to say things like: 'There are three reasons why...' You don't even need to number them. Just give them and the brain will work out that there are three. *The Economist* is splendid at this – at leaving out these stepping stones. It knows the reader's brain can make the leap unaided.

One other thing. If you read the newspapers, you also learn the following about anyone they mention: name, age, job, marital status, where they live. But you don't get all of this information in one place. Instead it's scattered throughout the piece, often in places which aren't especially logical: 'Joe Bloggs, 36, was sentenced to five years... Bloggs, a plumber, pleaded in his defence that...' The brain accepts this because it is an expert sorter of information. So you don't need to put everything up front: put the important point first and scatter the rest after. Some of the best-written pieces of professional advice I have seen adopt this approach. By the end – and you do read to the end with these – you've got all of the extraneous detail, but it hasn't clogged up the main points.

What George Orwell said

- Never use a long word where a short one will do
- If it is possible to cut out a word, always cut it out
- Never use a passive where you can use the active
- Never use a foreign phrase, a scientific word or a jargon word if you can think of an everyday English equivalent
- Break any of these rules sooner than saying anything outright barbarous

George Orwell *Politics and the English Language* 1946

---

4. USE VISUALS

Layout is important. It's a visual guide to the reader. Images make a bigger impression more quickly than words. Many business people are visual, many professionals are word- or number-driven.

So use short paragraphs (a paragraph can be just a sentence long but if you do this all the time, the page can look bitty).

USE HEADINGS

They break up the page and can provide structure. For instance if you make four points and give each a heading, you don't even need to number them, though that can also help.

Use bold to start a paragraph if you want to highlight a series of sub-points under a heading.

It can be stand-alone You can run the sentence on (see previous paragraph) or, as here, treat the bold bit as separate from the sentence (this one) which follows on from it.

Don't use narrative lists: they are tricky to read; they aren't visual; they use semi-colons which look Dickensian but which you should use after a colon (as here); and if you're using a colon you're meant to put 'and' after the last one (as here).

Use bullet points instead, because they:

- Look cleaner
- Are easier to read
- Avoid the need for semi-colons
- Attract the eye to the page

Sometimes in a long list the repetition of 'they' at the start of each point makes it easier to read: the reader may have forgotten that the list was prefaced by 'they' by the time she gets to the bottom. For example:

Use bullet points instead, because:

- They look cleaner
- They are easier to read
- They avoid the need for semi-colons
- They attract the eye to the page

> ## Boxes (with a tint)
>
> These are particularly useful, both for breaking up the page and making it look attractive; and for shoving in extraneous material that needs to go in your piece but breaks up the flow of what you are trying to say. So in the main body you can say: 'There are pros and cons of this approach (please see box) but my view is that...' Or if you need to refer to some research or a regulation, you can put it in here.
>
> The funny thing is that boxes make their contents eye-catching and interesting even when they're not (as you've probably noticed elsewhere in this book).

Do use charts, graphs and flow-diagrams if possible.

One final point about visuals. Instead of using brackets, use dashes (brackets can look introverted and have a habit of expanding so that by the time you get to the end you don't know what the sentence was saying) which tend to give a look of dynamism. Use dashes in the same way – to bracket off stuff which the sentence can live without – but with the benefit of that streamlined look on the page.

If you need any other proof about visuals, think about how you first looked through this book – scanning the pages, your eye caught by anything visual.

5. OTHER STUFF

Use punctuation and grammar to help the reader
The only rule you need to apply is: does my use of punctuation make it easier for the reader to read what I am writing?

Commas People feel strongly about commas. The English use commas in pairs, to bracket off a sub-clause, so the sentence reads equally well without that sub-clause (just like brackets – and dashes) as I've just done. Americans use commas to tell the reader when to pause for breath, even if there's no other reason for putting one in. So they will put a comma mid-sentence, and before the word 'and' (as I've just done). Don't worry about it. Both approaches are OK.

Important Try avoid using the word 'important'. If you're an expensive professional and I'm a busy client, you're only putting things in writing to me if they are important. So spare us both

Brochures and newsletters

As one of the younger members of the team, you may be asked to help with marketing it by writing a brochure or newsletter. Brochures give details about what the firm can do for clients. Newsletters are a regular way of keeping in touch by containing articles on topical subjects that might interest clients. Here are some tips:

- Use the brochure to tell stories about how the firm helped clients – and keep the stories anonymous: 'A company in the food industry needed to... we were able to assist by...' This is because clients are always wanting to know whether you have come across their issue before and how you dealt with it. Their eye will be caught by a story which relates even superficially to their own predicament.
- Don't use client lists – either the names are so well known that they are almost a 'so what' because they lack impact; or no one has heard of them. And mixing household names and nonentities can look bizarre. Besides, withholding client names shows you are discreet, which is what professionals are supposed to be

(this is not the majority view, but it is mine).

- Use ordinary language (as discussed in this chapter) not the stilted or technical language of professionals. If you want to communicate with clients, use their language.
- Write newsletter pieces like newspaper stories with a headline that says what it is about. Use diagrams and pictures if possible.
- Give the answer. Professionals worry that if they reveal what clients should do, the clients won't come to them for advice. Rubbish: if you can tell a client the answer in two sentences, it's not exactly advice you can charge much for anyway. In fact, all pieces should pass the 'recipe test' – it's so useful the reader tears it out and puts it on their wall at work.
- Recycle pieces: turn a client seminar into an article; get the article published in a trade publication; then run it again in the newsletter saying where it was first published – this always looks impressive, because it's a third-party endorsement (and if you do that, the original publisher will be satisfied since strictly speaking they may hold copyright).

telling me. And it's not just important, but it's very important to avoid using 'very important'. 'Very important' – for reasons I don't know – sounds even less 'important' than just 'important' does.

Be personal When I ask people what they like about writing style, they often say things like 'sense of humour'. Humour in business is dangerous. One man's joke is another's bad smell. But what I think

Writing for self-promotion – how to approach editors

Part of your career development is about building a personal reputation. A traditional way of promoting oneself is through writing articles. What follows is subject to your employer's rules – usually you will have to get a supervisor's approval and work with the PR or business development department.

- You don't have to be original or topical – there are perennial subjects that interest readers. Magazines like *What Mortgage*, *Bride* and *Golf* run the same articles in every issue (cheapest mortgage, how to arrange a wedding, how to cure your hook or slice).
- If you are writing about something topical, warn the editor as soon as you can so that (1) you get the editor's commitment to run it and (2) you beat your competitors to it. Editors usually respect embargoed information (information that they can't publish before a future date).
- Speak to the editor before writing the piece – you want to know whether the editor wants it and, if so, the word length and deadline.
- Never write more than the editor has asked for – it's always better to write less since the editor can make up the space with sub-headings and pull quotes (text extracted and inserted in a large font between quote marks – it breaks up the page). Otherwise the editor has to read, understand and shorten your piece. This is bound to cause mistakes. That's if the editor can be bothered. He may just spike it (scrap it).
- Never miss the deadline – editors are busy people and work to tight copy and press dates. As soon as you think you will be late, tell the editor and let him decide what to do.
- If the publication uses photos, send yours – editors like photos and readers like faces.
- If the article as published contains a mistake, don't blow up the editor or ask for a correction to be printed (if your piece is written according to the rules in this chapter, the reader will still understand anyway) – instead use it as an excuse to get the editor to agree to publish another piece; after all, you're trying to build up a relationship with the publication to get more pieces in.
- If the editor spikes your piece, don't get angry. Find out why: usually an advert came in late (adverts produce income so take priority). If the editor ran a piece by a competitor it's because that competitor has a prior relationship with the publication, which is what you want. So, as before, get the editor's commitment to run another piece next time.

they mean is a sense of personality. If you are trying to build a relationship with a client in order to become, in David Maister's memorable phrase, their 'trusted adviser', then it helps to be personal. I've written this book in a personal style as if I'm talking to you, to engage your interest and earn your trust. Yet many pieces of written advice from professionals to their clients are written in cold, stilted, old-fashioned, pompous language which tells the client that the professional is on a different planet and doesn't care a diddly about the client's problems.

Be patient Your supervisor is older than you. He or she was brought up differently. He or she will have particular writing preferences – we all do, and having anything you've written changed is like a slap in the face. So be patient. Write the way they want (they are, after all, your first client). And then when you get to be where they are, do your own thing and get your juniors to do it too.

Do what the client wants All of this chapter is irrelevant if it isn't what the client wants. If your client is a little old lady who expects 20 pages of closely-typed argument written in the sort of language that she expects professionals to use, give her what she wants – but make sure she pays for it (which brings us to the next chapter: making money).

Oh, and I hope you noticed that I haven't ended with a Conclusion.

Chapter 9

MAKIN' MONEY

SPEED-READ SUMMARY

- RULES are the levers of profitability for PSFs – Rates, Utilisation, Leverage, Expenses, Speed

- Speed is about the speed of collecting the cash in – the gap between money going out and coming in is the working capital requirement

- Working capital is provided by an overdraft (external) and/or partners' capital (internal) – often through partners' profits retained in the firm

- Pricing work depends on accurate scoping which in turn depends on a database of previous similar projects and their outcome

- Clients are asking a number of questions when they ask about price – the most important is: how many of these have you done before?

- There are many alternative pricing structures which allocate risk between the client and the PSF – the hourly rate rewards inefficiency and puts all of the risk on the client

- Clients don't buy on price – they buy on value for money

- Commoditisation of services moves every specialisation from 'expertise' to 'experience' to 'efficiency' at an accelerating rate

- Clients expect professionals to project manage

- Conduct post-completion reviews internally and with the client and use these to build a history of contingencies and outcomes that will make pricing more precise next time

- PSFs that do this build a strategic advantage – they portfolio-manage clients and work types, build market share and cross-subsidise below-cost entry into new markets

You already know about cashflow and profit, from Chapter 2. Now I'm going to give you an insight into how professional service firms make money. You don't need to know this now – after all, you won't (yet) be pricing jobs for clients or trying to manage those projects to a profit. But it's never too early to learn about these things. And those professionals who do best in their firms – who become partners, for instance – tend to be excellent at this stuff.

Let's get one thing straight. There's nothing inherently objectionable about wanting to make money. It's not an 'unprofessional' attitude to have. This is not about personal aggrandisement – it's not about fleecing clients and trying to become stinking rich. It's about being properly rewarded for your expertise, for the risks you run (for example the risk of being negligent) and for the benefits you provide your clients. It's about ensuring that the firm earns enough (1) to be able to stay in business day after day and (2) to support the lives of all of the people who work in the firm, and their families outside it. Besides, there's a psychological element to this: the more clients are prepared to pay for a service, the more they tend to value it – and you.

THE RULES OF HOW FIRMS MAKE MONEY

There are only five factors or levers that determine a PSF's profitability. They are:

- **R**ates
- **U**tilisation
- **L**everage
- **E**xpenses
- **S**peed

Their initial letters spell out the acronym RULES (which was invented by Professor Stephen Mayson, who is an expert on PSF management).

Imagine you are part of the team running a project for a client. It lasts six months and the basis of charging is the 'time charge' – how much time the team spends on the job. Each of the team members has their own hourly rate which reflects their seniority which in turn is meant to reflect the level of expertise they bring to the job.

RATES

The single most critical factor affecting the profitability of the job is Rates – the rate at which each team member is charged out at. Let's say your rate is £100 an hour. That is your **headline rate**. But in order to get the job, the team leader may negotiate a **reduced rate** with the client, which brings your rate down to £95. The team leader also agrees to a discount so that if over the length of the job your time amounts to more than £10,000, a further £5 an hour will come off your headline rate. That makes it £90.

Let's say that during the job you don't necessarily record all of the time you spend: sometimes you forget to put your time down; sometimes you under-record because you took an embarrassingly long time to do certain things. This is called **moral editing** (see box on the next page). Moral editing means that some time is simply not recorded, which again reduces the realised rate. Then, on top of all that, after the job is done, when the team leader comes to draw up the bill, he may decide to reduce the overall cost anyway because it looks too high. So he decides to **write off** some of the time recorded. If you recorded 10 hours on the job and he writes off an hour, that has just reduced your effective hourly rate by a tenth.

Then, when the team leader calls the client to agree the bill, the client may negotiate a further write-off. Finally, some clients don't pay on time and when they are chased they either pay very late or decide at that point to contest the bill. So that, too, can impact the profitability of the job. All of these things reduce the realised rate.

So what matters here is not your headline rate but the actual **realised rate** recovered when all of these factors are taken into account.

Here's a tip: the easiest way to improve the profitability of a job is by recovering, as nearly as possible, the original headline rate – and increasing it if possible (charging more for getting the job done sooner or for delivering a brilliant solution, for which you are able to charge a **premium** over and above the recorded time).

UTILISATION

This is a long word for saying how busy people are. If you have people assigned full time to a client project and some of them are twiddling their thumbs or are not kept fully occupied, the PSF is losing money, because it is paying for them without getting 100% productivity out of them. PSFs that are poor at keeping a pipeline of new work coming in, or have significant down time between client jobs, have a tough time managing utilisation.

In some professions, the joke goes the other way. In law firms, for example, young lawyers are often utilised 110–120% which is just

---

Time recording and moral editing

As a rough rule of thumb, most professionals find they can record one hour of chargeable time for every two hours they spend in the office. So if you are recording more than six chargeable hours a day, you are doing well (professionals who spend all of their time working on one lengthy project can often clock up much more chargeable time; those whose work is bitty and is spread amongst a number of jobs with constant interruptions may find time leaking away with only three or four hours properly recorded at the end of each day).

Often young professionals fail to record all of the time they spend on a job, because they forget or they feel embarrassed at how much time a simple task has taken. This deliberate under-recording is called moral editing and it is a nightmare for professional service firms whose billing basis is time-based where professionals are required to keep time sheets.

It means a PSF has no idea how long a project really took. This means that clients are being under-charged. It also means that the PSF does not have an accurate idea how long certain tasks take so that when it comes to price the next similar job for the next client, it quotes too low a figure. It also means that the PSF does not realise where training needs lie in the firm: it may think junior staff are finding certain tasks easier than they are; if it could identify this it could offer training in those tasks.

The decision whether or not to charge the client the full amount of what is 'on the clock' is best done by the team leader when finalising the bill. The way you can avoid the temptation of moral editing is by asking your supervisor (when you are being delegated to) how long the particular task should take. Then you can go back to them as soon as you know it is going to take longer: either you don't have the right skillset (a training issue) or they have underestimated the true nature of the job.

---

an arithmetic way of saying that they regularly work overtime (without being paid overtime, of course) which is why many lawyers seem to be in the office at all hours, nights and weekends included. Prolonged over-utilisation leads to individual burn-out and loss of morale so it's not an effective long-term management goal.

LEVERAGE

This is also known as 'gearing' and it's the ratio of profit-takers in a PSF (often called 'equity partner' or the equivalent) as against other fee-earners. In an accountancy firm it can be as high as 1:10 (one profit-taking partner to 10 fee-earners).

It differs between professions and is often mistaken to mean that the more footsoldiers a PSF has, the more money it will make. Not so. There's no point in having a lot of junior staff if the PSF hasn't the work to give them (utilisation) or if clients won't pay properly for them (rates).

What leverage really reminds a PSF is that it needs to be pushing the client work down to the most appropriate level of professional for the accomplishment of that work. It's no good having a senior person doing junior-level work (and only able to charge junior-level rates for it) because there is an **opportunity cost** in not being able to get that senior person doing senior-level work.

So on any client job, the team leader has to ensure that he has the right number of people at the right level to do the job as cost-effectively as possible – for the client and the firm.

EXPENSES

If a PSF is incurring a lot of third-party costs on a job (e.g. travel, cost of copying documents) and can't pass them on to the client, that will affect the job's profitability. In actual fact PSFs only have two types of expense: **fixed** and **variable**. Fixed is what they incur just to be in business – premises (rent and rates), people, systems. Variable are those expenses that go up or down in relation to how busy the firm is (e.g. telephone, stationery). There's nothing much a PSF can do about its fixed expenses in the short term – sacking staff and getting rid of premises take time and can have terrible long-term consequences for the PSF. And the variable ones are too slight to make much overall impact.

SPEED

You already know this one. It's our old friend cashflow. The quicker you get paid for a job, the more profitable it will be.

Let's assume that on this particular client project we agree not to bill until the job is done. It takes six months, so for that period the PSF is forking out to pay staff salaries, the rent and rates and so on. At the same time it has no money coming in on this job. In practice this cashflow 'gap' is met by other jobs that are completing in the meantime and being paid. But if you were to isolate this job from the rest, the cashflow gap could be large.

That's because the work done on the job remains **work in progress** (known as **WIP**) until it is billed. As soon as it is billed – and that may be some time after the job completes because professionals tend to put billing at the bottom of their in-tray – the WIP becomes what is known as **debtors** because the client now owes the firm money (see box on page 159).

Of course, the client doesn't pay as soon as it gets the bill: it too puts the bill at the bottom of its in-tray. So the PSF may have to use its credit control people to chase the client for payment. In some PSFs, this period – from billing to actual payment – can run into months and is counted in **debtor days**.

A PSF funds its cashflow gap (known as its **working capital requirement**) either by getting an overdraft from the bank or by getting partners to keep their profits in the firm. Either way, there's a cost to the firm: interest paid to the bank; or interest forgone by the partners on profit they could otherwise have taken out of the firm and invested elsewhere (basically they are lending this money to their firm). Either way, the actual or implicit cost is reducing the profitability of the particular job.

In some PSFs, the partners' capital account is vast: in short, they have a lot of their own profits left undrawn in the business to fund the working capital requirement. Sometimes this gives them a warm glow, like having a nest egg, especially if the PSF is paying them interest on those undrawn capital accounts. In reality, that money does not exist (i.e. it's not cash sitting in a till). It is enabling the PSF to be a banker to its clients by meeting the cost of the work done for them before they pay for it. It's much better to keep the working capital requirement tight, by keeping WIP low and debtor days low. Then partners can take their money out.

By the way, you can keep WIP low by agreeing with the client to bill them on an interim basis (known as **interim billing**) such as

Working capital requirement

There is always a gap in business between paying out money (for example to employees and suppliers) and getting paid (by clients). As soon as a client is billed, that client becomes a **debtor** because it owes the firm money. This may sound weird because customers are good things and debtors are bad. But the client now owes the firm money and the firm is its **creditor**.

Some people warn that if you give clients too much credit (the freedom to postpone payment for services) you are actually becoming their 'banker' because you're effectively lending them cashflow that should be yours. The **credit control** function has the job of policing this and ensuring that the PSF gets paid — even by threatening to sue customers who are bad debtors. Those that fail to pay — because, for example, they have become insolvent through poor cashflow — are called **bad debts**.

Debtor days tells you how long on average it takes the firm to be paid. This figure can be over 100 — in other words it is taking 100 days (well over three months) for the PSF to get paid from the time it sends out the bill. That is a three-month cashflow gap that the firm is having to fund.

You can begin to see why there can be a gap between the PSF paying money out and getting money in again. This gap is generally funded either by a bank overdraft (loan) or by **retained profits** (money that is paid out to equity partners) and this need to fund the gap is called the **working capital requirement**.

There are two strange things about this term. First it isn't a law or piece of government regulation even though it is called a 'requirement'. Even stranger, I think, is the use of the term 'capital'. I always think of capital as being a lump of money that you use to fund fixed assets in a business not to fund an income gap. So if you too find these terms odd and confusing, you're in good company.

every month for work done the previous month, rather than all in one go at the end. Clients actually prefer this: small but regular bills. It helps them keep a control on costs because if these bills start to rise it will trigger a reaction on the part of the client to review the work you are doing and how you are doing it. And commercial clients have quarterly (three-monthly) reporting systems so they like the work done in a quarter to be billed in that quarter. With new clients you can even ask for a **payment on account** – an upfront payment. This is great: getting paid before you've done any work.

Control of Speed (WIP and debtor days) is said to be a **one-off benefit**. If a firm gets them both down it suddenly gets flooded with cash which it can pass on to its partners to pay off their undrawn profits or reduce the overdraft. But if WIP and debtor days then start creeping back up, the working capital requirement goes up and either the PSF needs a loan from the bank or partners have to start leaving profits in the firm again.

So there you have it: you now know more about the finances of a PSF than many partners or owners who work in them. What you need to learn to do with this information is use it when pricing jobs for clients (something you won't have to do now but which you need to learn to do as your career progresses).

PRICING

Professionals are pants at talking to clients about money. We are embarrassed by it. And when we do we are often unclear. I think clients have six things going through their minds – consciously or unconsciously – when they ask us about price, not all at the same time or with the same emphasis.

1. How much will this cost? When buying anything, consumers want to know what the cost will be. Buying professional services is no different. Clients always have budgets they work to. Like anybody else they want to know how much something will cost before they commit to buying it (not least because with professional services it is so much harder switching advisers mid-stream; you can't just put it back in the box and return it to the shop). Ideally, PSFs should be able to quote clients fixed prices for particular jobs. Some can and do. Estate agents do. So do investment banks. They work on a 'swings-and-roundabouts' business model. Some deals never happen so they can't charge anything. So for those that do they need a large margin to cover those that don't. For many PSFs that charge by time this sounds a risky way of running a business – and it is. But like most risks, once you are used to it (especially if it is the industry norm), you become adept at doing it or you go bust.

2. How many of these have you done before? This is what clients want to know. It's like going to a doctor, dentist or surgeon. You want somebody who knows what he is doing, has had plenty of practice and knows how to deal with anything unusual. It's called experience or **track record**. Where a PSF charges by time and quotes various hourly rates, the client will press for a **fixed price** or at the very least an **estimate** or a **quote** (a quote is a binding estimate but falls short of being a fixed price; a fixed price is what the client will pay whether or not the job turns out to be larger or smaller than originally envisaged). But – and here's the point – a PSF's ability to give an accurate estimate will be seen by the client as a reflection of that PSF's track record. If you tell me you've done plenty of these before but can't then give me a quote or fixed fee, I may begin to wonder whether you've done quite as many as you are making out. The greater the track record, the more accurate and precise the figure should be, contingencies notwithstanding. Price as a proxy for track record is far more important to clients than PSFs realise.

3. What's the market rate? This is a price-check. It's the client saying: 'If I were to shop around, would the rates you are quoting me reflect the rates of other comparable PSFs?' (smaller, less specialist ones may quote less; larger PSFs with greater market presence, reputation and brand may quote more). Of course, one problem with hourly rates is that they only tell one side of the story. They fail to tell clients how long a job will take. In a sense, the less efficient a PSF, the longer the job will take and the higher the bill. So hourly rates are open-ended and reward inefficiency. Which, again, is a reason for quoting a price-per-job and not just a rate.

4. What's this worth to me? Whereas 3 is an objective test this is subjective. The same job may be worth completely different amounts depending on a client's own aims, goals and situation. For one client the project may be routine. For another it may be the key to a whole new strategy. Those professionals that know their clients well will have a good sense of this – and flex what they charge accordingly. For example, if getting the job done to a tight deadline is 'mission critical' to the client, ask for a success fee or premium for doing so.

5. How much of your inefficiency am I paying for?
Sophisticated clients are beginning to understand how inefficient and inconsistent PSFs are in service delivery. They know that juniors learn on-the-job and that much of their time is worthless. They know that some types of professional (e.g. lawyers) are only now adapting to large deals where they have to project manage big teams between time zones. Cute clients (i.e. street-smart) will negotiate hard on this.

6. If I pay you more, will you go the extra mile? This is the upside of 5. However hard clients can be with their advisers they do genuinely appreciate them. This is saying: 'I really want you and your PSF on this job because I know and trust you and am prepared to pay more to keep you. And if I have excessive demands that you meet (and I wouldn't be using you if you couldn't) I understand that I need to pay for that too, for going above and beyond the normal call of duty.' Professionals underestimate this factor – but the key is to negotiate it into the price at the outset, not wait in the hope of a reward at the end – which reminds me: there is a psychology about when to bill. Bill immediately after the project is complete – as soon as you can, while the client is feeling euphoric that (1) it's over and (2) they won't be seeing as much of you as they have done but (3) before the client forgets what a big deal it was. By the way, clients forget astonishingly quickly and often need reminding.

EXAMPLES OF PRICING STRUCTURES

Smart professionals have an array of pricing structures at their disposal, designed to allocate risk more fairly between them and the client. Hourly rates put all of the risk on the client; fixed price only payable on completion puts all of the risk on the PSF (it's the way estate agents work).

Structure	Explanation	Comment
Hourly rate	Rate per professional according to seniority	■ Open-ended ■ Places all risk on the client ■ Meaningless in terms of likely overall bill ■ Difficult for client to police
Estimate	Best guess at overall cost	■ Not binding – but a reputational commitment
Quote	As above but binding	■ Supposedly binding – but often breached
Fixed price	The price, fixed at the outset, that the professional will bill	■ Certain outcome – but will the professional build in too large a cushion to offset lack of project management skills?
Ceiling	Upper limit	■ In practice will be what the PSF charges, so is actually a fixed price
Fixed price with Override	PSF agrees fixed price (£250k) but charges that if time then goes beyond, say, £270k (override) – this protects the PSF against a big	■ Suggests professional has thought it through and has track record ■ But, once £250k is reached, PSF will

Structure	Explanation	Comment
Fixed price with Override (cont)	change in scope	race to ensure £270k is reached a.s.a.p. so it can start charging again
Discount	Reduction in hourly rate or overall bill to reflect volume of work	■ Discount from what? ■ Hours may be inflated to offset discount
Blended hourly rates	Rates of all professionals on the team are blended to result in a single hourly rate for all professionals involved	■ Encourages delegation at risk of partner being less involved than should be ■ Needs policing of team members ■ No way for client to check that the overall time spent is appropriate
Partner-based rates	All work is charged out at PSF's higher hourly rate	■ Disincentive for delegation – so guarantees partner involvement but often more expensive than is necessary
Value billing	Client pays PSF what client feels work is worth – after the event	■ Good in principle but PSFs are scared to offer this – requires trust between both parties ■ Needs definition of successful outcome ■ Ideal if it works because encourages efficiency and communication by the firm

Structure	Explanation	Comment
Incentive billing	Additional payment for meeting deadlines, achieving results – can be a mark-up from the hourly rate	■ Risk may be shifted too far on PSF if some outcomes are outside its control
Task-based billing	Specific elements of a project are fixed-price	■ Excellent way of discovering PSF's true knowledge of the type of work – encourages a dialogue at which specifics of the deal can be carved-out or made subject to caveats ■ Provides certainty ■ Requires PSF to be able to deconstruct types of project
Conditional fee	Payment only on result as percentage of hourly-based fee	■ Risk on PSF ■ PSF does not share in outcome – only gets a percentage mark-up
Contingency fee	As above but PSF gets a percentage of what client makes on the project	■ Risk on PSF but with negotiable upside
Abort fees	Fixed fee or 'no fee' arrangement with PSF if project does not complete	■ Risk on PSF ■ Effective in long-term relationship where PSF receives all of that client's work so can charge a premium for successful projects

COMMODITISATION OF PROFESSIONAL SERVICES

This is all very well but it fails to capture the dynamics of what is happening in PSF pricing. And that is that professional services are becoming commoditised at an accelerating rate. David Maister (he of 'trusted adviser') identified this when he coined the term the 'three Es'. All professional services start off as **expert**, like rocket science or brain surgery. Here you can charge what you like. But because this work is so specialist, there isn't much scope for leverage (remember leverage?) because you can't delegate much of the work. Some tax work is like this. It has to be done by senior professionals working on their own.

Most professionals think of what they do as being expert work. In actual fact it isn't. The bulk of it is what Maister calls **experience**. It's not cutting-edge, never-been-done-before. It's established, may be complex but isn't innovative. And provided the professional has done it before he or she will be able to do it again. It doesn't require hot towels round the head. It just requires track record. Most professional work falls into this category.

The 3 Es

Expertise	Experience	Efficiency
High diagnosis intensive	→→	High execution intensive
Highly customised	→→	Programmatic
High client risk	→→	Low client risk
Few qualified suppliers	→→	Many qualified suppliers
High fees	→→	High fee sensitivity
Brains	**Grey Hair**	**Procedure**

Source: David Maister

Finally there's **efficiency work**. This is routine, commoditised and doesn't even need a professional doing it. It can be systematised, with clerks using computer-driven processes (standard forms and steps, drop-down menus, flowcharts) to progress a project to completion. It needs a qualified professional to supervise it and deal with odd, tricky questions, but the bulk of it is commodity work, like a conveyor belt in a factory. So the leverage here can be really high.

Now – and this is where Maister's idea comes into its own – the whole point of the three Es is that all professional services move inexorably from Expert to Experience to Efficiency. It may take some longer than others but that's how they all evolve. And the more a service moves towards Efficiency the more clients expect it to be done for a fixed price. For instance, much of the legal work in buying and selling a house is Efficiency work and is now done by 'factories' with very few lawyers involved, for a fixed price of no more than a few hundred pounds.

IMPLICATIONS

As a young professional you may not think there is much you can do about any of this. I disagree. Look at the work you are involved in and:

- Ask yourself whether a project is being staffed as leanly as possible with the work pushed down to the lowest level of professional commensurate with the level of expertise required.
- Look at your team through a client's eyes.
- Consider whether you are making something out to be rocket science when a client sees it as routine.

No one wants to come across as overconfident and cocky but if you start raising these questions with your supervisor or team leader – asking questions rather than making observations – you will soon be regarded as a useful team member.

COST AS THE BASIS OF COMPLAINTS

Most arguments between clients and PSFs are over bills. But this is because clients don't really understand what professionals do (they understand the output but not necessarily what goes into it). So they find it hard to articulate any dissatisfaction with what they get other than by addressing the issue of price. If you encounter a client who is complaining about the price or a bill, probe gently to find out what is really bugging them. Remember complaints and managing expectations in Chapter 7.

VALUE FOR MONEY

No one really buys on price alone unless it is a commodity and the bulk of what PSFs provide is not commodity work (it's Experience rather than Efficiency). Most professional services are expensive. Clients know that. But what they really want to know is: what are they getting for what they are spending. In short they want **value for money**. You can be an investment bank or management consultant charging tens of millions of pounds. But if you are achieving a takeover or a new way of running the business for a client, your costs will pale into insignificance compared to the benefits you are providing: that is value for money (VFM).

One way of demonstrating VFM is showing the client what is involved. Draw up a **project plan** showing how the work will be **resourced**, which stages will be done when and which depend on others having been done first (**critical dependencies**). Show how you are allowing for contingencies – expected and unexpected. All of this demonstrates process (a sense of how things will be done) which implies track record. Services are intangible and can be hard for clients to grasp. Project plans help to make them visual.

PROJECT PLANNING, RESOURCING, MONITORING, REVIEWING AND PRICING

What follows is undoubtedly too sophisticated for your needs. But it may help if a team leader asks you to prepare a pricing proposal and project plan. Work through these steps before the project, to work out the price, and afterwards before finalising the bill.

1. THE CLIENT RELATIONSHIP

Ask yourself **how important this particular client relationship is**, in terms of:

- What is our previous experience with this client? How significant is this client to us? What is the nature of the relationship?
- What is the client's attitude to costs? How important are hourly rates or does the client prefer fixed fees? What is our previous history of fee quotes? What work have we given away in the past (general advice over the phone for which we haven't charged)?

Does the client appreciate this?

- How sophisticated is the client? Generally? In relation to this project? Does the client regard us as cheap or expensive? How sophisticated are the client's other advisers?
- How significant is this project to the client? What are the client's Critical Success Factors in relation to this project?
- If we are retained generally by the client, is it time to review the rates?
- If it's a pitch, why do we want this client? Which other firms does or might the client use?

Don't be too scientific: rate these as High, Medium or Low to get a feel for where the pressure points lie. You may not be able to get answers to all these questions, but they are still worth asking.

2. PRICING THIS PROJECT

Then consider **the particular project itself: how much will our bill be?** Try to arrive at an accurate estimate based on what I call triangulation (a number of methods which between them should narrow the range), such as:

- Total size/value of the project in £s (percentage fee)
- Initial gut-feel (finger in the air)
- Back-of-the-envelope time-cost calculation (how many people at what charge-out rate will spend how much of their time on it – total that up)

Then analyse the **risk factors**, their likelihood of arising and their cost impact (this is where a database of previous similar projects comes in handy).

These include the degree of (in)competence of any other advisers involved, whether on the client's side or on behalf of other parties, and which other advisers will do what in shouldering different aspects of the project.

Consider the number of meetings likely to be involved and the **complexity of issues** arising. If you have a **project template** which breaks the work down into costable stages, use that here. If you don't have all of the information you need, go back to the client and ask the client to get it – again, in my experience, this is where professionals let themselves down badly: they quote on **incomplete information** because they let the client off the hook. If the client can't provide as complete a picture as possible, neither can the PSF in terms of cost.

Consider how much of these you should express as **assumptions** in the client engagement letter. Some clients never look at the letter. For others, reliance on it will destroy the relationship. For other, trickier customers still, it's a useful Get-Out-Of-Jail to have up your sleeve.

To do this properly, you need (going back) historic data about similar transactions (which few firms have in any great detail). And (going forward) proper time recording, because if team members aren't recording all of their time on a matter – regardless of how much is written off – your historic data and current cost projections are flawed.

Then address **specialist input** from others in the firm and outside it. Who will do it, how efficient are they, what will you ask them specifically to do, what will the output be, have you asked them for an estimate, will you give them a budget, and will they give you an early warning of cost overruns? In many firms a state of guerrilla warfare exists between mainstream and specialist departments on these issues.

Finally, factor all of this into an amended figure, then pop up the corridor to bounce it off a colleague or two. Consider also whether the client has a **budget** for these costs – if you don't know, make a note to ask.

3. HOW FIRM IS THE DEADLINE?

Consider the timescale of the project. This has a greater significance on cost than you might think. Consider the impact of false dawns when the client posts a series of impossible deadlines. These rack up costs in repeated, unnecessary work.

Analyse the **commercial drivers** and likely **causes of delay** (if possible, do this with the client). How serious is the project's timescale? Consider a premium for accelerated completion.

4. CLIENT'S ATTITUDE TO CREATIVE PRICING

Also consider **creative pricing options** – fixed fees, capped fees, capped with overrides, success fees, etc. How receptive is the client? What possible structures can you suggest? What are the risks? What is the firm's previous experience? What cushion do you need to build in? Also consider regular interim billing: it focuses the mind, provides fewer surprises and is more welcomed by clients than professionals think.

5. INTERNAL MANAGEMENT/EXTERNAL REPORTING

Now consider **how the project will be managed internally**. How will work be delegated (by task, outcome, deadline or budget) and to whom? What allowances are you building in for contingencies, overlap, cascade, supervision, absence (illness, holiday)? How will the specialist input be managed? What warning bells are in place for overruns and contingencies?

Next, consider how these factors translate into **external client reporting**: frequency, exception, staged, by the time charge on the clock? How can progress be expressed in terms of client gains/critical success factors achieved? How will assumptions be reworked and checked against what the client requires?

At this point you can go back to the client, **get any further information about the project which the client hasn't yet provided**, and arrive at an estimate, informed by all of this preliminary work. Remember: in talking to the client about these things the firm is automatically addressing the six cost issues that are running through the client's mind detailed earlier.

If the project is subject to a competitive pitch or the client is threatening to give the work to another firm at a lower charge, hold your nerve. You need to consider:

- Do we want this work/client for strategic reasons other than profit? (Remember that if you quote a low fee to win the work you could be stuck with that rate.)

- Are we being inefficient or are we amongst the best and most cost-effective at this work? If the latter, tell the client (politely) to go hang. The firm is either up against a market leader who has deep pockets, in which case your firm will eventually have to withdraw from this type of work/client. Or (more likely) the other firm hasn't a clue and will get badly burnt, in which case always stay in touch with the client to pick up the pieces later.

Assuming the firm gets the work, everything mentioned so far needs to be harnessed to monitor the project as it progresses. Suggest setting up a **transaction log** in which to note unexpected contingencies, why they were unexpected, how they were dealt with, their impact on costs and how they were communicated to the client – this will feed into the database for future matters.

6. AFTER THE PROJECT IS OVER

Once the project is completed, there should be a **post-completion review**, an internal team debrief. What went right? Wrong? Why? Impact on fees? Lessons for the future? Talk to any other advisers involved on your side. Then, before calling the client, remind yourself (going back through the above) of:

- The client's critical success factors
- The initial fee quote v. what's on the clock
- Assumptions
- Timetable/deadline
- Contingencies and how addressed
- Overruns – if any, where and why?
- Client relationship – previous work/likely future work

All of the above steps should be considered at the outset of a project, before the fee has been agreed. Then all of this should be used to help manage the project. Once the project is finished, go back through all of these items to inform and justify the bill to the client in a **post-completion review with the client**.

Doing all of this preparatory work will help you speak to the client with more confidence and authority and help convince the client that the firm really knows how to run its business and is worth the price (VFM).

As I say, you won't be doing this sort of thing straight-off or even for a while, but learn how to do it and watch how others do it (well or badly) so that when your turn comes you are prepared and can shine.

PRICE AS A STRATEGIC ISSUE

As you can begin to see, a database of similar project plans with a record of outcomes and post-completion reviews (internally and with the client) can be an incredibly useful strategic tool for a firm. It can begin to see where it makes money, where it loses it, where projects run into trouble and how best to manage those contingencies.

This know-how can be used by the firm to price similar projects more precisely, **knowing how much of a cushion needs to be built in for contingencies**. Being able to price with precision means that quotes are more competitive so the firm builds market share in a particular type of work or project. This work then becomes part of the firm's core business and will be a major factor in attracting clients.

The firm can then use this core, profitable work to subsidise new areas of work (undercutting the competition to win work is called **low balling**) as it builds up similar databases around projects in those new fields, over time becoming more competitive.

Highly profitable types of work can be used to support new areas or less profitable work types that need to be done to keep clients happy. Sophisticated PSFs do this. They **portfolio-manage** their work types – firm-wide and department-wide – to develop a spread of work, and they portfolio-manage their client base. They quantify each client's lifetime value (heard that before?) not just in terms of profit but in terms of the PSF's overall strategic goals: acting for a certain client is worth a profitability trade-off if it brings other quantifiable benefits of strategic value, such as:

- trophy – it's good to be seen to be acting for client X in the market
- honing of expertise – client Y's work keeps us at the cutting edge
- using the whole firm – client A enables us to work across departments in the firm
- ambassadorial – client B does our business development for us:

they're forever telling people how good we are
- training – with client Z, their routine work is great for our juniors
- enjoyment – client M is great fun to work with

I remember bring horrified by one PSF which took on routine work from prestigious clients in the expectation of getting their best work too. This was the expectation but no one in the firm was managing it. In fact the most prestigious clients were taking the firm for a ride by giving their best work to competitors.

The two (work type and client) marry up. Sophisticated PSFs calculate which work types they have to do (at a loss) to retain their (strategically valuable) clients (and if a client isn't strategically valuable, why have it?), and which they can do at a super-profit because they are a market leader in certain clients' eyes for that type of work (and here the client's viewpoint is determinative).

FOOD CHAINS AND SNAKESKINS

Here – and this is where it gets interesting – sophisticated PSFs realise that they are managing a dynamic situation. They are constantly shedding their old client base and old work types like a snakeskin. As a firm moves up the food chain it manages out old clients and work types by becoming too expensive. It will be seen differently by different clients: by the new ones, as it moves into new markets, as at the cheap end; by older ones as reassuringly expensive. This is the art of **client base segmentation** and management.

So now you can begin to see how strategy, work type, client base and pricing all come together and how each affects the others. The PSFs that do this the best end up with the best work for the best clients and so attract the best people, which in turn leads to the best work for the best clients, and so on…

Have a look at the Boston Consulting Group matrix in Chapter 1 and try applying it to your firm's work types and client base. The lesson in all of this is that professionals are great at being activists.

We rush around getting the job done, then move on to the next. But we rarely sit down to analyse how we have done a piece of work or where we could have done better; or, at the start of a project, take the time to map out properly how it should best be done and what the risks are. So we have no way of monitoring our performance or improving upon it. How many post-completion reviews of projects are carried out in your firm? Increasingly, such reviews are being seen as critical to improvement in performance. Taking the time to look back on what has happened, drawing conclusions, deciding what to do differently next time and then actually doing it differently next time – this is how incremental improvement is achieved.

This is a theme I will return to in the final chapter. But for now let's focus on how you get clients and work.

Chapter 10

BUSINESS DEVELOPMENT

SPEED-READ SUMMARY

- Marketing is about 'meeting clients' needs profitably'

- Start building your own network of future clients and multipliers (referrers) – it's fun

- Participate in your firm's CRM (client relationship management) initiatives

- Get involved in pitches

- The pitching process is expensive (in time) so the firm needs to decide whether it should be appointed

- Identify the client's hot buttons by talking to the client before pitching

- Address these in the tender document but write it after deciding on the structure for the interview meeting

- Expect to be shortlisted

- Turn features into benefits by applying the 'so what' test and using 'which means that' to generate the client's perspective

- Emphasise 'you' not 'we'

- Treat every client inquiry as a pitch (analyse the hot buttons) even if you are going to get the work anyway

As I said at the very beginning of this book, doing a good job these days is no guarantee that the client will give you their next job, or that other clients will come to you. You also need to be involved in **business development** (BD). This used to be the preserve of partners in firms. Nowadays everyone is expected to play a role. If you want to get on in your career you need to know how to do this – especially if you, too, want to be a partner.

In the old days, professionals sat at their desks and clients came to them. They charged what they liked and clients paid. Professional services were a black art – clients didn't understand them and the professionals who provided them commanded great mystique. As a client you felt privileged if a professional person deigned to act for you.

No longer. Professionals have lost their mystique. Clients are demanding. They want to know what they are getting for their money. They are courted by other professionals offering more for less. Competition is on the increase (although it's still not, in most professions, as competitive as they think it is, and the degree of competition can only increase). Clients shop around and move around a lot more. So professionals need to be good at BD (also know as marketing).

You need to do the work well – that is what your professional training and qualifications will equip you to do. You need to be commercially aware when advising clients, so that you really understand what it is they are trying to achieve and where your advice fits in their bigger picture. And you need to be good at BD to gain more work from existing clients and to win new ones.

How do you do this?

NETWORKING

It's easier than you think. Just use all of the skills I've encouraged you to deploy so far when talking to clients generally: asking, listening, probing, building a relationship, managing expectations, building up a bank of goodwill and trust. You see, although PSFs these days talk about client relationship management (CRM), client service, branding and market positioning and although they have large BD and marketing departments, it is still down to the individual – you – to develop his or her practice and client following.

There are marketing or business development activities that over time you will be encouraged to do, such as speaking at conferences, writing articles and organising client seminars (see some tips in Chapter 8). These all help to raise your firm's – and your – profile, but they rarely of themselves lead to more work. Work comes from making contacts; in short, from networking.

Networking is a fancy term for getting out into the market and building a set of business relationships. Many professionals hate doing this. They think it's about selling, about trying to be friendly with people you don't know in order to get business from them. None of us likes doing this because it is insincere. However, effective networking is not like this. It begins as an attitude of mind.

ATTITUDE OF MIND

What professionals find over time is that their best clients, the ones they serve over a long period, keep coming back to them because the client and professional have points in common. At base it is because the client likes the professional. 'Like' is a feeble word that encompasses 'faith, trust and confidence', the qualities that David Maister sees as being at the heart of the successful professional/client relationship. It also embraces friendship – having things in common, possibly a shared outlook.

As I've mentioned elsewhere your best clients will be those with whom you feel you have something in common. Some will become actual friends. Professionals devote the bulk of their waking hours to work, so work is going to provide the most natural source of social contact. Those who keep clients and fellow professionals at arm's length are missing out on one of the greatest rewards that professional life provides: working with like-minded people.

Multipliers

The term 'multiplier' covers referrers of work who may not become clients themselves but who can endorse you and tell prospective clients how good you are. In other words, other professionals.

Some of the best new business comes from clients (1) having heard of you and (2) getting an endorsement from another professional in a different field. So cultivate those other professionals. They'll be doing the same to you (which is another reason for using networking occasions to meet as many people as possible – everyone's doing it).

And if you remember me saying this before, you're right (in Chapter 6) – an example of limited repetition.

HELPING OTHERS

Now, if you view networking, first, as a way of extending your circle of possible friends and, only second, as a possible source of future work, then you are developing the right mental approach. The professionals who are best at this do it as a way of helping others. For example, they give up evenings to have beers with people to discuss their careers and personal concerns. They do it not to get work, although that is often the indirect result – and I say indirect because you never really know where work comes from. Usually it's a combination of someone knowing you and a fellow professional recommending your firm. So it follows that the more people you know – the wider your network – the more work will result one way or another.

My point is this. You can make work pleasure and vice versa by having the right attitude to networking. You cultivate like-minded people because you want to, not because you feel you have to in the name of business. Having this sort of outgoing attitude, this generosity of spirit, will in any case make you a more interesting person – the sort of professional that clients are more likely to relate to. So get out there and get networking. Not because it's good for business, but because it's good for you and for the people you meet.

NOT ABOUT SELLING

The most important point to realise is that BD or marketing is not 'selling'. Selling implies trying to get someone to buy something he or should doesn't need or want. Marketing is about trying to understand someone's needs and demonstrating that you can meet them. In fact, a simple definition of marketing or business development was coined some years ago by Neil A Morgan. He said it was 'meeting clients' needs profitably' (see box below). I like this simple definition enormously. I don't think it's restricted to business development or marketing (which I see as more or less the same thing). I see it as defining the role of the professional generally: meeting clients' needs profitably.

STAYING IN TOUCH BETWEEN PROJECTS

I've already said a lot about client relationships. One thing I haven't said is that professionals are very poor at staying in touch with clients between projects. Again, they think it is insincere and smacks of selling. But imagine if your doctor or dentist rang you every so often and asked how you were; or if your garage rang every so often asking how the car was running. You'd be pleased they were showing an interest, *even if you knew they were doing it for business reasons.* As you know (because I've said it earlier) I believe the best clients become friends over time – not necessarily friends like your school friends or the neighbours, but friends nonetheless; people you like and like talking to; and they feel the same way about you. So it becomes natural to call them up from time to time to see how things are. They are part of your network

---

Marketing = meeting clients' needs profitably

Neil A Morgan's definition of marketing is: meeting clients' needs profitably.

The focus is on **clients' needs**, so you have to work out what these are – by using the asking and listening skills I've told you about.

It's about showing that you can **meet** those needs and actually do so. I like the word 'meeting' – it implies face-to-face contact. And that's what business is still about: personal contact. That's what makes it interesting – it's about people and meeting people. You demonstrate that you can meet the client's needs by talking about previous, similar projects you and the firm have worked on – your track record.

And you need to do it **profitably** – hence all the stuff in the last chapter about scoping, pricing and billing. It's no good doing work for clients unless you can make money doing so: unless a PSF can do it profitably it will go out of business and won't be around tomorrow to do the same again.

and some of the best new clients you get will come from **existing business contacts moving to new organisations**. They will bring their new employer to you.

An easy way of staying in touch between jobs is to look out for comments in the press about a client or the industry it is in, and calling the client up when you do. It shows them that (1) you are thinking of them and (2) are sufficiently interested in their business and industry to look out for these things. You'd be amazed how pleased they are.

All the research and literature will tell you that the **best source of new work and new business is existing clients**. They act as your ambassador, telling everyone how great you are. When individuals change jobs to a new organisation they bring their new employer to you. So a good question to ask a client in the post-completion review is '**What's next?** Where is the business going? What other work is there coming along?' Tell the client **how much you enjoyed working for them**. It all helps to encourage them to think that you will go that extra mile for them.

NEW CLIENTS

Yet – and it's only human nature – getting new clients is still regarded in all PSFs as sexy. If you can say that you have won a new client, you are a hero back at the ranch. Even though all the studies show that winning new clients is expensive: it takes a lot of time to win new clients (and time in a PSF is money).

It is true that PSFs do need to attract new clients for the reasons given in the previous chapter: as a PSF moves up the food chain it wants to attract bigger and better clients offering more complex, profitable work and paying bigger fees. And it needs to get rid of the tail of smaller, less profitable clients. Besides, clients are disappearing all the time – they get taken over or go bust or change the nature of their business; or a new management regime takes over that prefers to use other advisers. And clients for their part are shopping around more. So there's always a need to attract new clients, but PSFs tend to put an undue focus on it. Winning new business is often called 'pitching' because a prospective client will ask a number of competitors to pitch – i.e. each to put a proposal together with the prospective client choosing the one it likes best.

In an ideal world, you are so close to your clients that you never have to pitch – either for the client or for his or her work.

But let's assume that the firm is asked to pitch. Here's how it works. What follows is a simple methodology which is effective if properly followed. It's not the only one but what follows represents a good start.

CRM

Client relationship management is a systematic way for a PSF to manage relationships with its core clients.

In the past, when firms had only a few dozen partners and didn't have extensive international networks, the relationship between the PSF and a big client could be conducted through one or two partners in the firm. Now PSFs can have hundreds and even thousands of partners (PwC has over 7,500), many different areas of practice, and offices all over the world – and their clients are equally large and complex – so a more organised approach is necessary. It coincides with greater emphasis by PSFs on that small number of core clients who produce the largest proportion of a PSF's income (the 80/20 principle – 80% of your income from 20% of your clients which you remember is known as the Pareto Principle). Some investment banks for example focus on a maximum of 2,000 clients while other big PSFs struggle to service 20 times that number.

CRM makes use of databases to track and share information about the most important people at a client's organisation, who in the firm knows them, the degree and nature of activity between the PSF and the client, and the details and outcomes of marketing initiatives by the PSF towards the client. Professionals in the PSF will meet regularly to share information about the client and devise and pursue business development strategies. The aim throughout is to widen and deepen relations with the client, to make the relationship stronger and more 'institutionalised' with the aim of getting better, more profitable work from a wide selection of people at the client's organisation, feeding a wider number of practice areas in the PSF.

Getting involved in these CRM activities is a good way for you to develop your own BD skills. It also impresses your supervisor.

The typical scenario is that a company invites the firm to submit a proposal setting out how the firm would do a given piece of work and at what price. The invitation/process is called a **pitch** or **tender** or **beauty parade**.

PITCH PROCESS

The usual way in which it works is that:

- A prospective client organisation (let's call it X) draws up a **long list** of possible firms that could do the work
- It sends each one an ITT (**invitation to tender**) or RFP (**request for particulars**), inviting each firm to explain how it would do the work, who would be on the team, how much the work would cost and examples of previous experience
- Each bidder sends in a formal **tender** containing this information
- X then uses these submissions to narrow the long list down to a **short list** of candidates, then asks each shortlisted firm to attend an interview or meeting
- X uses the **interview** to find out more information and ask questions
- Then it decides which is **the winning firm** and awards that firm the work
- There may be post-tender negotiations, for instance on price, before the winner is announced

Variations:

- Some are **paper bids** where X decides which firm to use on the basis of the written proposals alone, without interviewing the firms
- Sometimes X may narrow the list down to two, then give each the same small job as a pilot or trial and the one who performs better gets the mandate
- X may use this process to set up a **panel** consisting of a small number of firms. Then when it has a job it asks each panel member to quote a price and the cheapest wins. Unless a firm is on the panel, it can't bid; but, even once it is on the panel, unless it provides competitive quotes it won't get any work. Every so often X will review the panel and eject any firm that is failing to win work, to make room for new additions

TIPS AND TECHNIQUES

1. Decide whether to pitch or not Sounds obvious, but many PSFs are so flattered to be invited to tender that they do so without thinking through some key questions:

- Should we win this?
- Should we, at the very least, be shortlisted?
- Do we have the relevant expertise and track record?
- Are we prepared to invest the time to win?
- Who are our competitors likely to be?
- What are our USPs?

To pitch successfully – and there is little point in doing so unless you are going to win – requires an enormous amount of time, especially in researching X's hot buttons (see below). So unless a firm is prepared to invest this time (which in a big pitch can run to hundreds of man-hours) don't bother. A firm needs to be convinced that it should win before deciding to tender. If it is in any doubt – usually because it lacks expertise, track record or resource – it should decline. Instead, it should write to X, telling X which types of work and projects the firm does want to be considered for in the future. I have done this and it works, because it shows X that the firm knows where its strengths lie.

There are exceptional circumstances, for instance where the firm is building a new area of expertise and deliberately low-balls (undercuts the competition in price) to win the work in order to develop its expertise on the job. But a firm needs to be prepared to invest in such speculative pitches with little chance of immediate success, and to do so over a period: in other words, the firm needs to take the strategic decision to do so, using profits generated in other areas of the business to support this effort. Once the firm has decided to tender, respond to X as quickly as possible confirming that the firm will take part: X will be judging the firm from the moment the ITT leaves X's building.

2. Talk to X Do not tender unless X is prepared to have a pre-pitch dialogue. This is because the firm needs to understand exactly what X's drivers are, and these are unlikely to emerge from the ITT documentation itself. If X isn't prepared to talk (even to have a conversation over the phone), don't pitch. The firm is making a hefty investment in making the pitch, so a few minutes of X's time is the least X can spare. If X isn't prepared to reciprocate, don't proceed.

Such a pre-pitch interview will help you work out what X's real concerns are. It can also help you to move the goal posts – often X does not actually know what it wants until someone comes along and helps it to define its needs; the firm which does that has an edge over the rest. Sometimes X will refuse for legal reasons (e.g. public procurement regulations which affect public-sector bodies and privatised entities and require them to give the same information to all potential suppliers). But there are ways round that: for instance, if the gist of the conversation is published to the other tenderers, most legal requirements are satisfied.

Do not embark on this discussion with X lightly. You need to have done your research and found out as much about X as possible from sources ranging from X's own website and financial statements to informal sources in and outside your firm – people who know people at X. You need to use the discussion with X to test your assumptions about its hot buttons.

3. Identify X's hot buttons These are the critical drivers (and there are usually no more than five or six) behind X's decision to go out to tender. These usually have little to do with the firm's expertise and everything to do with X's own situation, its own anxieties and concerns. Professionals, in pitches, major on their own expertise and track record. But clients tend to take that as read. If you aren't up to the job it is unlikely that you would have been on the long list. What X wants is a professional who understands what is keeping X's people awake at night and addresses those issues. Simple to say but, in practice, very difficult to do; it requires a lot of information (research) about X as well as deep analysis and imagination.

For example, X may be asking a law firm to tender for its legal work. But its hot buttons may be:

- The business is becoming increasingly international
- X is subject to increased regulation
- X is worried that it may prove attractive to a competitor
- Its own legal department is small and under-resourced
- It has a new CEO who used a different law firm at his old company

The law firm can respond by addressing these as follows:

- The law firm is itself international and has offices or strong contacts with local law firms in each of X's markets
- The law firm has relevant regulatory expertise and advises other companies in similar sectors
- There are legal defences that can be put in place to protect against takeover
- The firm is used to working alongside in-house legal departments and can provide complementary resources and skills where either are lacking internally
- The law firm has just been joined by a lateral partner (a partner moving between two firms at the same level of seniority) from the firm the CEO used previously – this new partner will help with relationship management between the firm and X

The same technique applies to all PSFs in all pitches.

4. Design the interview first The hot buttons provide the structure for the interview and the tender document. But work out what you are going to say in the interview before drafting the tender. Assume that, whatever time you will be allowed for the interview, a third is used for the firm to present and two-thirds for Q&A. This a good rule of thumb. This will give you between 10 minutes and half-an-hour depending on the total time allotted to each firm, which may range from 30 minutes to 90 (if you don't know, ask when talking to X).

An interview or meeting is a notoriously inefficient medium for transferring information from one person to another. At best, you will be able to get five major points across. These should address X's real concerns (the hot buttons). A simple template for such an interview is this: tell X what the five points are; get each member of the team to lead on one or more of them; open the discussion up for questions from X (the Q&A bit); recap the five points and, by then, you will have exhausted the time you have been allotted. Make this structure the basis of your written tender: the structure of the presentation will be dictated by the hot buttons. Those four to six points are the ones to major on: identifying what they are; and how the firm can meet them.

You may be thinking that this is presumptuous, that the firm doesn't know if it will be shortlisted and asked to attend an interview. If so, don't proceed (see point 1 above). At least this way you know what you will say at the interview before you have sent off the tender. Too often, firms put in a tender, learn (to their delight) that they are shortlisted and then (horror) start having to plan the presentation. The result is that the tender does not support the presentation and the presentation is itself ill-planned.

5. Then draft the tender Work backwards from the interview to draft the tender so that the tender document supports and follows the structure of the presentation in the interview. This is because:

- The tender process is a poor way of communicating information – you need to make a number of simple points several times to be sure they have been received by X.
- People from X attending the interview may not have read the tender. Strange but true! Don't assume the people you meet will have read your document through properly, or even at all.
- Some Xs lay down the format of the tender document, so that all firms are required to follow exactly the same structure, to make comparisons between them easier. Even if you have to do this, subvert the process by setting out the hot buttons in a short covering letter; or attach the information X has requested as appendices to the five points.

Once you've drafted the tender, read through it. Do sentences and paragraphs start with 'we' all the time? If so, recast them to put the emphasis on 'you' (i.e. X).

6. So what/which means that Anything you say in the tender must pass two tests. The first is the 'so what?' test. 'We have the latest technology.' So what? To answer that, you have to explain why the latest technology should mean anything to X, given X's set of circumstances. The second test (which helps answer the first) is 'which means that...' So: 'We have the latest technology, which means that we will be able to set up an extranet so that we can communicate efficiently with you.' This turns a feature of the firm (technology) into a benefit for X (efficient communication). Hey presto.

7. Analyse the competition/move the goalposts Professionals are poor at this. Work out who the competitors are (try asking X; at worst X will say no; often X will tell you who else is tendering). Then work out what they will claim as their USPs. Then make sure that in your tender you demonstrate that your USP is what matters.

For example, let's say that you are an engineer and X is responsible for the construction of a toll road in a less-developed country called Ruritania. Your firm has plenty of expertise in toll roads but has never done a project in Ruritania. Your competitor has experience of projects in Ruritania but is weak on toll roads. Your pitch – from tender to interview – must be designed to stress that what matters is knowledge of toll roads, not the particular country where the road is being built: that local conditions are secondary to toll-road know-how.

You need to do this to outflank your competitor, because you can predict exactly what it will be majoring on (the importance of having previous knowledge of Ruritania). Doing this will move the goalposts in X's mind: what will matter is knowledge of toll roads not previous experience of Ruritania.

8. Rehearse the interview/meeting In particular:

- The firm must take along **the team who will do the work and one of the firm's leaders** – clients like to see the people they will be working with; and they like to feel flattered that they are important. X will always say that it wants to see the team who will do the work – but don't make the mistake of thinking that X doesn't want to be flattered too.
- Make sure **everyone has something to say** – even the most

junior team member (who may be you).

- **Rehearse the FAQs** – the firm needs to put a lot of thought into the questions X's representatives are likely to ask, and how to answer them, especially on price (see below).

- Don't script the presentation – instead, try to **turn the interview into the first meeting after the firm has been appointed**. In other words, turn it into a discussion with the client, especially in the Q&A bit. This has three benefits: it shows them how you interact with each other (how the team will work together); it encourages your team to relax; and it makes X's people think at the end that they have already effectively appointed you.

- Assuming, however, that each team member has something to say in the presentation, make sure you **don't all thank each other** – so as Robin stops and Tom takes over, Tom mustn't say 'thank you' to Robin – it sounds false.

- Do thank X's representatives for seeing you and use that to enable one of you to **chair the interview**: 'Thank you very much for agreeing to see us. We will talk for 15 minutes and then allow you to ask questions, but please ask questions as we go along if you like.' This way you can stage-manage the presentation and, crucially, go over any question X's people have asked which your team hasn't dealt with. 'I think we're reaching the end of our allotted time, but just to emphasise what Bill said: we would only charge you if the sale goes through.' This gives your team two bites at the cherry. Keeping control in this way enables you to recap.

- **End by repeating the hot buttons**: 'So, to reiterate, the five key reasons for appointing us are:...'

- **Price** Be upfront about discussing price and say you are happy to discuss it further after this stage. Offer options (at the dialogue stage you should ask X what it wants in terms of price; ask if it has a budget).

- **Don't take business cards** Otherwise you find out in the taxi to X that everyone has a slightly different one. Instead, take a photo-card, a sheet with everyone's photo on it (and, underneath, name, position and team role) in the order in which you intend to sit round the table. Leave plenty of space under the photos and captions for notes – X's interviewers will write notes underneath and you will stick more firmly in their minds.

- **Find out in advance** You need to know the size of room, seating space around the table, type of presentation required, how many from X will be there and their functions – make sure the presentation addresses a concern of each function represented.

- **Do not use audiovisual aids if possible** They get in the way and can go wrong. They don't allow eye-contact and encourage professionals to 'lecture'. If necessary take along hard-copies of PowerPoint slides (enough for X's people and your team) and talk to those. This allows you to go back and forth at will and encourages more of a discussion. However, do be visual – diagrams are better than words.

- **Do not look out of the window** When one of your team is speaking, look at him or her and nod in support (don't all do it otherwise you look like donkeys) or look at the X people to detect any resistance to what is being said (rather than looking down). Smile rather than looking glum or bored. Move your chair back from the table so your team forms a slight semi-circle around the team member speaking, allowing everyone to see him/her.

9. Afterwards, call X Ask whether there is anything else the interviewers need to know: if you are not the last to be seen, it's possible that a competitor presenting after you has raised an issue in their minds that they haven't considered before so you need the chance to be able to cover it. Also, be prepared to have a further discussion about fees: the firm may be asked for its 'best and final' price.

10. Ask for feedback If the firm loses, ask X for a meeting to discuss why. This helps to maintain an ongoing relationship. But don't use this meeting to try to reopen the bid. X won't like that. Use this meeting to show you do listen and want to improve. By the way, for the same reason, ask for feedback even if you win.

11. Do stay in touch If you lose, don't back away in embarrassment. After all, the firm made it to the short list so X must like you. Besides, given that the whole pitching process is such an inefficient way of selecting firms, often X may end up making the wrong choice anyway and a year down the road will want to talk to you again. You have invested hugely in making the pitch and X will understand that. X owes you, at the very least to be prepared to maintain a dialogue. It's in X's interest to do so.

Final point. If your relationship building is good, you shouldn't have to pitch at all, or at the very least you should have an inside track. Equally, don't assume that a selection process isn't going on just because there isn't an ITT and formal tendering process. X may just pick up the phone and want to chat through a possible project. Treat that innocent-sounding call like an ITT and respond using some of what you have learnt above.

Which leads us to the penultimate chapter: selling yourself.

PART 3: Understanding You

Chapter 11

YOUR FUTURE – THE ROAD AHEAD

SPEED-READ SUMMARY

- Decide how far you want to get in your profession

- Become a 'reflective professional' – able to improve incrementally and learn from what you have done before

- Demand opportunities to develop your skills

- Keep a diary to check your progress

- Make a note of your goals and then assess whether you are achieving them

- Don't get depressed by the short-comings of the organisation you're in – the better its market reputation the more shambolic in practice it often is

You need to do three things:

- Decide whether being a professional is for you and, if it is, how far you want to progress
- Work out what you need to do to get there (or anywhere else your future takes you) and then do it
- Think 'client' all the time – and by client I mean your internal clients (colleagues, supervisor, bosses) as well as your external clients and contacts that you build up over time

In short you need to work out what others want from you and what you want in the long run.

Two things may help you. The first is the concept of the 'reflective professional' based on Kolb's learning cycle.

REFLECTIVE PROFESSIONAL

Kolb's learning cycle consists of (1) doing, (2) reviewing, (3) learning from the review and then (4) applying what has been learnt in order to (re)do, and so on round the circle again. This, says Kolb and others, is the way we learn: by doing something, learning from it, and modifying what we do when we repeat it.

The reflective nature of this process is helped by asking questions. After the 'doing' stage, ask **'what?'** questions such as 'what happened?', 'what did I or others do or not do?' and 'what are the key aspects of this situation or experience?'. Then in order to learn, ask **'so what'** questions such as 'so what were the effects of what I did/did not do?' and then move on to applying what has been learnt by posing **'now what'** questions, such as 'now what are the implications of what has or has not happened?', 'now what do I need to change?', 'now what will happen if I do nothing?' and 'now what am I going to do differently?' and so on.

My own version of the learning cycle or circle starts with the word 'Do' at the top, then moves clockwise to 'Review' (at 3 o'clock) then 'Conclude' (at 6 o'clock) and then 'Ensue' (at 9 o'clock). It sort of rhymes, which helps to fix it in the grey matter.

The point is to be conscious of what you are doing, how well you are doing it and where you could improve (hence the desire for feedback, proper appraisals and post-completion reviews). This is the true nature of learning-by-doing or **experiential learning** as it is called.

The reason for giving you all the advice in this book is so you can try it out, practise and find what works for you. Learning by, from and through experience requires reflection. This requires a critical look at the what and why of practice. But professionals are by nature doers, so you must learn to reflect.

The old adage has it that learning is a change in ability, while insanity is the repetition of the same actions in the expectation of achieving a different result. In reflecting on what you have done you are not looking for radical change – just incremental improvement (every day, in every way...), the sort of performance improvements that Formula One racing teams seek to give them that extra edge.

One way of doing this is by keeping a diary of how you are doing professionally. Reflect on the work you have done and whether you could improve and, if so, where and how. Write these thoughts down, either in hard copy on the back of an envelope which you can then file using a simple treasury tag in a folder; or electronically on a laptop or PDA. Every few months pull out your accumulated thoughts and reflections. It helps you consider your own development and where you need to focus.

Another way is suggested by Peter Drucker. He says that you should, when making a decision, record where you expect it to have led you in 12 months' time. Then, 12 months later, compare where you are with where you expected to be. Drucker took this idea from a medieval monk. Plus ça change...

FROM PUSH-TRAINING TO PULL-LEARNING-AND-DEVELOPMENT

The second idea is to demand the sort of development opportunities you want to enhance your skills and expertise. The relationship between employer and employee has changed. In the old days, jobs were more or less for life and in return the employer 'owned' you and at the end they gave you a pension for good service. Now, however, no employer can offer a job for life and most people wouldn't want it (remember the 'psychological contract' in Chapter 5?).

Even in PSFs, some people are turning their back on partnership for work/life balance reasons. Employees for their part feel less loyalty to the organisation. Each job is, in a sense, a staging post to the next. What matters is how marketable a job makes you. This means you can be demanding of your employer: you want opportunities to increase your skills and make yourself marketable. My advice is: demand them.

Employers used to offer 'push' training – employees got it whether or not they wanted it. Now employers offer 'pull' learning and development – lifelong learning which it is up to the employee to seek out.

So start now. Do some of the personality-type tests that are available – such as Myers Briggs (what's Myers Briggs, I hear you ask. Go and look it up – you're responsible now for your own lifelong learning).

Work out who you are and what you want. Then go for it. You owe it to yourself and no one else is responsible.

The Theory of Shambolic Organisations

Everybody wants to think they are working in the best firm for them. Too often we can get depressed by poor organisation, lack of communication and poor management. But don't get too depressed.

In my experience the more successful an organisation appears to be on the outside, the more shambolic it appears when you're on the inside – which can sound quite depressing but is meant to be encouraging. Part of your job is to make your firm as effective as possible.

CHAPTER 12

WHAT ELSE TO READ, WHERE ELSE TO LOOK

This book may have turned you on or off. If off, then all I suggest you do is scan the pages of:

- *The Economist* – the weekly magazine (it calls itself a newspaper) devoted to current affairs. It has two sections towards the back on business and finance that are a wonderfully quick way of staying abreast of what's happening. There are regular in-bound supplements on industries, trends and technological change that are must-reads.
- *Harvard Business Review* – this, like *The Economist*, is read by senior people in business. It's more academic and contains articles based on research into perennial subjects like strategy, leadership, management and so on.
- *Financial Times* or *Wall Street Journal* – I take newspapers in fits and starts. Sometimes I read the FT every day for a few weeks then get bored and stop. Then a few weeks later I take it up again. I suggest you scan it. Your firm probably has an information service that circulates press cuttings about clients. Make sure you are on that.
- *Wikipedia* (the free online web-based encyclopedia) is a valuable first port-of-call. It's not always right (nor is this book) but it's close enough: a rough idea is better than no idea – it's better to be roughly right than precisely wrong.

But if reading this book has given you a taste for this stuff, there is plenty more out there. Thousands of business titles are published every year and most are riding a fad. Here are some that have stood the test of time.

BUSINESS

The Witch Doctors (Mandarin) by John Micklethwait and Adrian Wooldridge is subtitled *What the management gurus are saying, why it matters and how to make sense of it* and is a terrific guide to the world of management, strategy and management consulting as befits two writers from *The Economist*.

Understanding Organisations (Penguin) by Charles Handy is less dry than it sounds and has practical models on how people in business interact with each other.

I'm particularly keen on *The Richer Way* by Julian Richer (EMAP Business Communications). Richer is a hippy at heart but that hasn't stopped him building the highly successful chain of hi-fi retailers that bears his name (Richer Sounds). In this book he sets out his philosophy of customer service and people management. It also contains a wonderful account of how he built his business and the mistakes he made on the way. Read chapter 9 of his book if you are still unsure about cashflow and profit and can't quite grasp why small, fast-growing businesses are peculiarly susceptible to lack of cash.

I also like *Maverick* by Ricardo Semler (Penguin) which is his account of how he turned round his father's Brazilian steel company.

Anything by Peter Drucker is worth reading.

BEING A SUCCESSFUL PROFESSIONAL

Why Lawyers Should Eat Bananas by Simon Tupman applies equally to all professions. It contains 101 ideas designed to enhance your various marketing and management skills and to make the job of being a professional more enjoyable and satisfying.

Books by David Maister are always worth reading. Two I particularly recommend are: *Managing The Professional Service Firm* (Free Press) and *True Professionalism* (Free Press). The first is a collection of articles about management and marketing for professionals and should be mandatory reading for every professional. The second builds on the first. If you only read one of the books listed here, make sure it's *Managing The Professional Service Firm*. It's a classic and is more about managing yourself and your client relationships than anything else. Don't worry about when these books were published. They are timeless.

PSF MANAGEMENT THEORY

Another book that's been out for a while is *Making Sense of Law Firms* (Blackstone Press) by Stephen Mayson. Being a former lawyer turned management consultant, he wrote it about law firms but it applies equally to all PSFs. In it Mayson synthesises much mainstream management literature and applies it to PSFs. Many of the management models in this book are drawn from it. Mayson has also devised a number of his own management models (RULES, the levers of profitability, is one of his) which are in the book. They and it are timeless.

FINANCIAL MARKETS

There's a companion volume to this called *All You Need To Know About The City* that expands upon the first few chapters of this book. I recommend the books on the *City, Wall Street And Financial Markets* published by Profile under the Economist imprint. You could also try *The Financial Times Guide To Using The Financial Pages* (FT Pitman Publishing/Pearson) by Romesh Vaitlingam.

ECONOMICS

I'm not sure businessmen of the red-blooded variety give much of a fig about economics, but undoubtedly it helps to know about it. Take a look at *Free Lunch: Easily Digestible Economics* (Profile) by David Smith, the economics editor of the *Sunday Times*. If you want a basic reader, have a look at those available on Amazon (search against 'Economics'). You might also try the books *Everlasting Lightbulbs* and *The Truth About Markets* by John Kay, the FT columnist.

GO WEST...

Finally *The Soul Of A New Machine* by Tracy Kidder, available in the Modern Library series published by Random House, reads like a novel but is a true story about the building of a computer: how an engineer called Tom West inspired a group of college graduates to turn out a leading-edge machine. It's a book about professionals driven by passion, belief and single-minded determination.

David Maister (above) refers to it when giving examples of the effective management of professionals. If you become fascinated by Tom West (as I did) you can follow his subsequent career by searching the web.

I hope that in your working life you do chance upon one or more Tom Wests and perhaps even work for one. Like the best clients, they may not be the easiest of people but they make life worthwhile and interesting. And that's what it's all about. Safe journey.

JARGON BUSTER

Abort fee	Where the professional adviser charges less than a full fee because the client's transaction (on which the professional is advising) fails to complete
Accounts payable	Amounts due to suppliers That part of a company's finance department that deals with payments to suppliers
Accounts receivable	Amounts due from customers or clients That part of a company's finance department that chases payments due from customers
Acquisition finance	Debt funding for a takeover by one company of another
Active listening	Skills (Engage, Ask, Reaffirm, Silence) which help professionals focus on client needs
Active management	A style of portfolio management where the fund manager actively looks for investment opportunities (as opposed to passive management)
Actuary	A professional who advises pension funds by using statistics to forecast the incidence of death amongst a pool of pensioners in order to determine the level of investment required to pay their pensions
Agent	Legally-speaking, someone who acts on behalf of someone else (the principal) with the latter's full authority and is able to bind the principal in any contracts the agent enters with third parties. More generally, anyone who acts as an intermediary (e.g. estate agent)
Amortisation	Banking term meaning the reduction in debt principal by

	paying it off in instalments; accounting term meaning the amount deducted each year from the book value of an asset
Annuity	An annual amount paid out to a pensioner (usually paid in monthly instalments) until death
Appraisal	Periodic assessment of an employee's career progress
Arbitrage	Exploiting the difference in price between two goods or services of identical value which can be bought in one market and sold for more in another – the act of arbitrage brings the two markets into equilibrium
Asset finance	Tax-favoured way of funding an asset where a bank (lessor) buys the asset and leases it to the borrower (lessee) for the asset's useful economic life in return for regular payments (rental) paid by the lessee over the life of the lease to reimburse the lessor for the capital cost of the asset plus interest – same as *finance lease*
Asset management	Fund management
Asset sale	The sale of assets employed in a business (as opposed to selling off an entire subsidiary)
Associate	A nebulous term (like 'agent') with various meanings, such as a mid-ranking professional or a business partner or crony
B2B	Business-to-business (aka 'wholesale')
B2C	Business-to-consumer (aka 'retail')
Back office	Those administrative operations of a company which do not add to its *USP* or market differentiation
Balance of payments	How much a country owes or is owed by other countries, depending on whether it imports more than it exports by way of international trade
Balanced scorecard	A method devised by Kaplan and Norton of monitoring those factors which have an impact on a business's successful development
Balance sheet	A periodic snapshot of the capital (equity and debt) employed

	in a business and the assets which that capital is funding
Baltic Exchange	London's shipping market in which ship capacity (charters) is traded
Bancassurance	The provision of banking and insurance by a single financial institution
Bank	An institution that is licensed to conduct banking business – see *Commercial bank* and *Investment bank*
Bankrupt	An individual who is unable to meet his liabilities (a company is said to be 'insolvent' not bankrupt)
Base rate	The rate of interest set by a central authority such as a central bank
Basis point	Financial term meaning one hundredth of a per cent
BCG	Boston Consulting Group, a management consultancy
Bearer instrument	A share or bond that is not registered so the holder is treated as the owner
Beauty parade	Colloquial term for an ITT (invitation to tender) where a company asks a number of competing suppliers to submit a tender and appoints one or more of them
Belbin	A method devised by R M Belbin of assessing the roles critical to the effective functioning of a team
Below investment grade	A share or bond that pension funds are not allowed to hold (aka 'junk' or 'high-yield')
Benchmark	Used as a verb ('to benchmark') and a noun meaning to compare against like – for example, companies benchmark their performance against that of rivals
Best-in-class	A term applied by consultants to assess systems against their peers (others include 'best-of-breed')
Beta	A measure of how closely a particular share moves up and down with the market

Bidder	A company bidding to take over another
Bill	A money market (i.e. short-term) financial instrument – contrast with a bond which is longer term (duration of more than a year)
Bi-lateral	Between two parties
Billings	A professional service firm's turnover – i.e. how much it has invoiced clients; also applies to an individual professional ('billing targets'). Although professionals talk about 'billing a client' the bill itself is always called an 'invoice'
Blended rate	A pricing structure used by professionals where the client is billed the same average hourly rate for all professionals on a project, regardless of their seniority or expertise
Bond	An IOU issued by a corporate or bank (the terms 'bond' and 'note' are virtually interchangeable)
BOOST	A model for providing feedback (Balanced, Objective, Observed, Specific, Timely)
Boutique	Usually refers to a small, specialist financial company – a bank, broker, fund manager or venture capital provider (sometimes referred to as a 'house')
BPO	Business Process Outsourcing – a form of BPR but specifically through outsourcing and/or offshoring
BPR	Business Process Re-engineering – the fundamental reorganisation of a company's operations to reduce costs and increase efficiency
Brainstorm	Colloquial term to mean 'discuss'. Actually a structured way of developing solutions to a specific issue
Brand	A company's image or identifiable product – often more valuable than the fixed assets reflected in its balance sheet; part of its IPR and its USP; often seen as a business's soul
Brand management	The custodianship, protection and development of a company's brand – can be of totemic importance to a business (e.g. Coke)

Bricks 'n' clicks	Used to describe businesses that use the internet (click) as well as more traditional routes to market such as retail outlets (brick)
Broker	Intermediary In the financial markets, a member of a stock exchange who trades securities with and on behalf of clients
Budget	A plan setting out how much can be spent in a business over a set period
Bundled bank	A bank that combines both commercial and investment banking operations
Business angels	Wealthy individuals (usually successful entrepreneurs) who fund start-ups
Business continuity	A back-up plan that takes effect if a business is hit by events outside its normal activities – e.g. terrorist action, power cut, extreme weather
Business development	The marketing function and activities used to attract customers – often distinguished from 'sales' (getting a customer to buy a product or service). Business development focuses on segmenting the market, targeting the relevant segments and using different media to reach them – often hinges on strategies, plans to implement those strategies and budgets to support them
Business plan	A plan that sets out expected future income and expenditure (staff costs, premises, etc)
Business process outsourcing	See *BPO*
Business process re-engineering	See *BPR*
Buyer	An institution that buys securities. Also means the function in a company responsible for the purchase of raw materials and stock
Cap	Colloquial term used by fund managers when describing a particular company or investment – 'big cap stock' is usually a

	top 100 company by market capitalisation; 'small cap' is a venture capital investment or small public company; mid-cap is a medium-sized public company
Capital	Money invested in a business – it can be equity (shares) and/or debt (loans and/or bonds) but is generally used to mean equity
Capital call	When a company seeks further funds from shareholders; also when a professional service firm requires partners (i.e. those who own it) to pay in money or leave undrawn profits in the business to fund working capital or a particular investment
Captain of industry	The chairman, managing director or chief executive of a major business who has a particularly high profile
Cartels	Companies in the same sector that coordinate their activities often through a central organisation
Cash cow	Mature product or service that provides steady income which can be used to subsidise new product development
Cashflow	The strength of revenue or income flowing through a business; a business can be very profitable (i.e. make a large margin between its sales and its costs of production) but still go bust because its income lags its cost of sales; equally a business can have strong cashflow but only marginal profitability and still go on year after year
Ceiling	A maximum; a point above which something will not go – e.g. a ceiling on a company's opportunities; a ceiling on a professional's fee quote
Central bank	A country's lender of last resort which regulates banks and controls the money supply, usually meaning it plays an integral role in implementing government economic policy
CEO	Chief Executive Officer – the person in charge
Chairman	Often non-executive – doesn't have day-to-day control of the business but oversees the CEO and board on behalf of investors; usually plays a more strategic role; will remove the CEO on behalf of investors if the business does badly; the practice of combining the role of CEO and chairman is now frowned on

Channel to market	A way for a company to reach its customers – the internet is said to have provided an additional channel to market
Charge	The security that a bank takes over a borrower's assets which the bank can sell to recover any money due under the loan
Charter	A contract to use a ship to carry cargo
Cherry picking	Selecting the best assets of a company rather than buying it whole
Chinese wall	The invisible barrier between two functions in the same business to ensure that, for regulatory reasons, sensitive information isn't shared
CIO/CKO	Chief Information Officer/Chief Knowledge Officer – responsible for an organisation's know-how
Circular	A notification sent by a public company to its shareholders
Clicks 'n' mortar	The same as *Bricks 'n' clicks*
Client	The posh term used by professionals to refer to a customer
Collective investment scheme	A pool or fund in which each investor holds a unit or share entitling it to a corresponding share in the pool's investment gains/losses – a way of diversifying risk by investing in a fund that itself invests in a wide variety of securities
Comfort letter	An assurance that usually falls short of being a full guarantee from a parent company that it will stand behind its subsidiary
Commercial bank	A bank that takes in deposits and borrows in the wholesale market in order to make loans. The difference between the interest it receives and the interest it pays is the bank's margin. High street clearing banks are commercial banks
Commercial conflicts	Where a professional could, legally, act for two entities but is prevented by one from doing so because of its fear that commercially-sensitive information may be leaked to the other
Commercialisation	The exposure of a state-owned activity to private-sector ways of doing business

Commercial paper	A type of bond with a very short maturity – usually three months (called '90-day paper')
Commoditisation of services	Management theory coined by David Maister and others which holds that the value of specialist expertise reduces as it becomes standardised over time
Company secretary	That part of a company that deals with the regulatory aspects of being incorporated, such as the filing of corporate information at Companies House (in the UK), the calling of shareholders' meetings and the execution of company documents
Compliance	The function in a business which ensures it stays within regulatory constraints – applies to regulated businesses such as financial services
Compliance officer	Responsible for the *compliance* function in a business (especially banks)
Conditional fee	Pricing structure offered by a professional service firm to a client where a fee is charged only if there is a successful outcome. The amount of the fee includes a percentage mark-up to reflect the outcome. Like a *contingency fee* but where the scope for uplift is much smaller
Conditional sale	A sale with payment in instalments where title to the asset passes to the buyer only once all of the instalments have been paid
Conflict	Inability of a professional to act for two clients because they are on opposite sides in a transaction or dispute
Consolidation	Where businesses in the same sector merge; also means cutting costs, often following a merger
Content	The subject-matter of an initiative as opposed to the way in which it is agreed or implemented (process)
Contested bid	A bid from one company (bidder) for another (target) that the target has rejected; or where there is more than one bidder for the same target
Contingency	Allowance for the risk that something might happen – e.g. contingency planning (scenario or 'what if' planning) and

	contingencies (unexpected events) in project management
Contingency fee	Pricing structure offered by a professional service firm to a client where a fee is charged only if there is a successful outcome. The amount of the fee is a percentage of the amount the client gains from the project
Continuous improvement	A management technique that focuses on generating incremental and ongoing improvements to all of a business's processes
Convergence	The term used to describe the coming together of two or more industries or technologies
Convertible	A bond that gives the holder the right to switch it into equity (shares)
COO	Chief Operating Officer
Core assets	Those businesses or fixed assets in a business which are regarded as central to a company's strategy
Corporate finance	Advising a company on (1) raising finance and/or (2) an M&A transaction
Corporate governance	Regulations and principles that govern how a company is run by its directors for the benefit of its shareholders
Corporate social responsibility	A movement that requires companies to do more than make profit, but to have regard to their stakeholders (employees, customers, suppliers, local citizens) and their wider position in society as a whole
Cost of capital	Economist's term to assess whether the returns in a business are greater than the costs of doing business and, in particular, the income forgone on the capital invested in the business
Counterparty	The other side to a deal or transaction
Coupon	The rate of interest paid by a bond – traditionally bonds (other than debentures) were bearer so the issuer would pay interest only to the person bearing the coupon that came attached to the bond
Covenant	Legal term for a promise in a loan agreement

Credit control	That part of a company that chases customers (debtors) for unpaid bills; the act of controlling the level of debtors
Credit rating	The rating an issue of securities (usually bonds) is given by a credit rating agency (with triple-A being the best) to indicate the likelihood of default
Credit risk	The risk that a borrower may fail to repay the amount borrowed or interest due on it
Critical dependencies	A project management term that describes the relationship between those key parts of a project that are dependent on each other
CRM	Client Relationship Management
CSFs	Critical Success Factors – the key things a business needs to do well in order to succeed
Culture	The ethos/values of a business – what a company feels like to work in – common attitudes and behaviours – 'the way we do things around here' (McKinsey)
Customer value management	The business development technique of focusing on understanding the customer and his or her lifelong value to the business
Data mining	The use of algorithms to detect patterns of buying behaviour amongst a mass of customer data
Data warehousing	The storing and cleaning of data used in *data mining*
Debenture	A corporate bond listed on the London Stock Exchange, often secured on the issuer's assets
Debt	Any form of finance where the borrower agrees to repay the principal amount of the debt and in the meantime to pay interest on it (also known as 'servicing' the debt) which is tax-deductible; the only other form of finance is equity
Debtor days	The average number of days it takes a business to get paid from the date of the bill to the date of payment – the higher the average, the greater the working capital requirement

Debtors	Customers that owe a business money
Default	Failure to repay a loan or part of a loan on time – usually because the borrower is bust
Deferred earnings	Financial returns that are postponed – often used when acquiring a company or in an MBO where part of the price or return is dependent on future profit
Defined benefits	A pension scheme that specifies what an employee will get when he or she retires (usually expressed as a proportion of final salary) – these schemes are in decline because they are too expensive to fund
Defined contributions	A pension scheme that specifies what an employee must pay into the scheme with no guarantee of what he or she will receive by way of pension when they retire – also called a money purchase scheme because the resulting 'pot' is used to buy an annuity from (usually) a different pension provider such as an insurance company
Demographics	Statistics about the condition of communities; currently the most significant is the ageing of the population through people living longer and having fewer children
Demurrage	Shipping term for the penalty that a charterer pays for failing to load or unload a cargo on time
Depreciation	Reduction in the value attributed to an asset used in a business to reflect the wear and tear of usage and allow for its eventual replacement
Derivatives	Financial instruments, such as futures and options, that are derived from other financial instruments
Development bank	A supranational bank (i.e. not tied to any country) that funds infrastructural development in less-developed economies on advantageous terms; usually part of the World Bank
Dilution	The reduction in the proportion of a company's share capital held by a shareholder, usually caused by an issue of fresh shares none of which is allocated to that shareholder
Direct	The establishment of an operation or subsidiary in another

investment	country
Director	The person with legal responsibility for running a company
Disaster recovery	Plans/steps a business has to take to recover from a severe setback outside its normal course of trading such as a terrorist strike, power disruption or severe weather
Discount	The amount by which securities trade below their issue price
Discounted cashflow	Used to assess the present value of future projects by discounting future cashflows back to their present value by using an implicit rate of interest reflecting the value of money over that time if invested elsewhere
Discounted fee	A fee arrangement where the bill is reduced (discounted) usually because of the volume of work the client is providing (volume discount)
Discount to net asset value	Used in connection with investment trusts where the share price does not reflect the true value of the underlying investments (asset value) having stripped out the investment trust's borrowings (net)
Disintermediation	Where the usual intermediaries in a market are circumvented – e.g. corporate issuers going straight to bond investors and disintermediating banks; bloggers on the web disintermediating publishers
Distributed	Software applications that are stored on servers and downloaded for the duration of use only – used to describe anything that is made available over the internet rather than, say, on CD or DVD
Distribution	Financial term used to describe the way in which an investment bank places securities with institutional investors
Dividend cover	The ratio of profits to dividends – i.e. how many times a company's dividends are covered by the profits out of which they are being paid – the higher, the safer
Downstream private equity	The activity of spending money raised from institutional investors through private equity funds – the money usually being spent on taking public companies private

Due diligence	A detailed review of a borrower's financial position, made by a bank or lead manager in a bond or share issue, to satisfy lenders or investors of the borrower's credit standing
3 Es	Expertise, Experience, Efficiency – model developed by David Maister to describe the evolution of professional services
Earn out	Where the price paid for a company depends in part on future profits
Economic rent	Economist's term for a return that is greater than the cost of capital which generates it
Emergent strategy	A strategy that emerges from an organisation's interaction with its external environment, usually at grass-roots level through the staff who deal with clients (Mintzberg)
Entrant	A business that comes into the sector or market as a further competitor (Porter)
Entrepreneur	A person who starts one or more businesses, pursuing his/her own idea or someone else's
EPS	Earnings per share
Equilibrium point	Economics term for when the level of supply and demand balances and the market 'clears'
Equity	The form of finance where shareholders put up risk capital in return for the prospect of dividend payments and capital growth on their shares; dividends are paid out of the company's taxed income
Equity partner	The principal in a firm – equity partners in a partnership are the equivalent of shareholders in companies: they own it
ERP	Enterprise Resource Planning – systems and software that automate a company's back office
Estates management	That part of a company that manages its real estate and premises
Estimate	A fee quote that is not binding on the service provider

Eurobond	The traditional name for an international bond – i.e. issued by a corporate outside its domestic jurisdiction in a currency other than its domestic currency (note: here, 'euro' has nothing do with the euro currency)
EVA	Economic value added – a measure invented by Stern Stewart to assess a business's worth by subtracting from the value it creates the cost of that activity and the opportunity cost
Event of default	One of the events entitling a lender to terminate a loan agreement and ask for the borrowing to be repaid immediately
Executive	That part of a company that runs the business and takes decisions; the act of taking decisions; also (oddly) the title for mid-ranking employees
Exit route	The way in which an investment is realised – e.g. in venture capital
Face value	The nominal or par value printed on the face of a bond or note – may not be its actual (market) value
Facilities management	That part of a company that provides the administrative infrastructure
Factoring	A way of getting paid early by selling your receivables (what you are owed by customers) to a bank
Faith, trust and confidence	Phrase coined by David Maister to capture the relationship which clients have with the best professionals – a goal for us all to aspire to
Feedback	Immediate critique offered by a supervisor to a junior to help him/her improve
Finance director	The director who looks after a company's finances
Finance lease	A way of funding equipment used in a business other than by way of a loan – the bank buys the equipment and leases it to the business for its exclusive use in return for rental which amortises the cost of the equipment plus an implicit interest rate – same as *Asset finance*
Financial covenants	Promises made by a borrower in a loan or credit agreement about the continued state of its business that, if broken, allow

	the lender to accelerate the loan
Financial year	A company's 12-month accounting period (may or may not coincide with the calendar year)
Firm	Legally speaking, a partnership – but often used as shorthand for a company
Fixed assets	The assets permanently employed in a business without which it cannot function (such as premises, equipment)
Fixed fee	Pricing structure where the client will be charged a pre-agreed amount no matter how long (or short) the project is
Fixed income/ interest	Another name for a bond (mainly because the bulk of bonds pay a fixed rate of interest over their life) as opposed to an FRN – a Floating Rate Note
Floating, flotation	When a private company is listed on the London Stock Exchange and its shares are sold to the public; also known as 'listing' or 'going public' or an 'initial public offering' (IPO)
Floating rate note	FRN – a bond whose rate of interest 'floats' – i.e. is geared to a benchmark rate which itself fluctuates
Forecast	A prediction of future sales/turnover
Forex	Foreign exchange – overseas currencies
Forward	A contract made today at an agreed price for delivery (of the goods or service on one side and payment on the other) at a date in the future – usually three months away
Franchising	Allowing someone else to use a business idea, format and brand in return for a payment (usually a royalty)
Free cashflow	The cash generated by a business after deducting expenses, interest on loans and tax
Front-of-house	Those parts of a business responsible for direct contact with clients (e.g. reception, hospitality)
FTSE 100 FTSE 250	FTSE is the Financial Times Stock Exchange set of leading market indicators – FTSE 100 is the index of the top 100 UK

	listed companies by market capitalisation and the FTSE 250 the next 250
Function	Job, role, position in a company, a part of a company
Fund	A pool of money contributed by investors in expectation of a return (income and/or increase in value) in the future (see *Collective investment scheme*)
Fund manager	A person or business that manages by investing money belonging to others – also known as asset, money, portfolio, wealth manager
Fungible	Two or more securities that in terms of issuer, interest rate, par value and maturity are interchangeable
Future	A derivative that allows the holder to command a market position without actually holding the underlying security, by putting up a margin (a small percentage of the total exposure) and which is settled on expiry by payment or receipt of the difference between the future price and the underlying. Unlike an option which gives the holder the right but not the obligation, a future imposes the obligation which – together with the ability to trade on margin – is what makes futures so dangerous to novices
Futurologist	A consultant who helps companies predict future changes in their markets
GDP	Gross domestic product – used to describe a country's annual output, as if it were a business
Gearing	The ratio of a company's equity capital (shareholders' money invested in the business) to its debt (liabilities). In a professional service firm, its ratio between equity partners and other fee-earners, also known as *leverage*
Globalisation	The economic trend that is turning the world into a single market for similar products and services served by *multinationals* active worldwide
Going public	Same as *Floating*
Golden hello	A signing on fee paid to a senior executive

Golden parachute	A payment made to a senior executive if his/her company is taken over and he/she is sacked
Goodwill	The entry on the right hand of a *balance sheet* which represents the financial difference between a company's assets and its liabilities – i.e. the reason/reputation why customers come to it
Grey market	An international market in goods or services which are priced differently in different countries so encouraging them to be moved without the manufacturer or provider knowing from a cheap market to a more expensive market to gain the difference in price – this is a form of *arbitrage*
Guarantee	A legally binding commitment to step in and make good a shortfall in funds
H&S	Health & Safety – a set of regulations that govern everything from how you should sit at your desk to criminal liability imposed on companies for the negligent death of employees
Hedge fund	A collective investment scheme that takes high-risk positions in derivatives and currencies and uses short positions to generate high returns; the manager is usually on a performance-related fee
Hedging	The use of derivatives to protect an investment or market position against market fluctuations
High-net-worth	Rich person
High-yield bond	A bond that pays a high rate of interest in relation to its cost
Hire purchase	A form of conditional sale where the purchase price is paid by instalments
Hive down	To inject assets into a new subsidiary prior to selling it off
Hostile bid/takeover	An unwelcome bid rejected by the target
Hot buttons	The key factors driving a *pitch*
Hourly rate	The traditional way in which professional service firms charge for their work – usually an internal measure of cost-of-production

HR	Human Resources – that part of a company that looks after employee issues, from pay and holidays to disciplinary issues and dismissal
HRD	Human Resources Development – the discipline (and function) of increasing employee performance; also known as 'Training' and increasingly as 'Learning & Development'
ICT	Information, Communications and Technology – used to be 'IT' (computer hardware and software) then embraced the 'C' of telephones and the internet as these systems converged
Incentive billing	Fee structure that rewards the service provider by paying an increased fee for achieving pre-agreed outcomes
Incidence of mortality	A term that gets actuaries excited – a set of figures predicting when a proportion of a specified group of individuals is likely to die; important for calculating pension fund liabilities
Income	Revenue generated from sales
Income gearing	The ratio of interest payable on a company's debt to the profits out of which the interest is paid – the debt equivalent of *dividend cover*
Index tracking	See *Passive management*
Indirect investment	Gaining investment exposure to a market by buying shares in companies that do business there
Inflation	Increase in prices which reduces the real value of money – usually caused by an excess of demand over supply
Insider dealing/trading	Buying or selling securities on the basis of information not generally available to the public – usually a criminal offence
Insolvency	When a company is unable to meet its liabilities (viz. cannot pay interest on its debts) and has to cease. If the company continues it is said to be 'insolvent trading'. Usually it will be wound up but in certain circumstances may be allowed to restructure and continue (called 'Chapter 11' in the US after the relevant part of the insolvency code)

Institution	A substantial financial entity – usually an established bank or institutional investor
Institutional investors	The ultimate buyers of securities (equities and bonds) – insurance companies, pension funds and investment managers (who run unit trust and OEICs funds)
Insurance	Payment of a premium in return for the promise of the reinstatement of a loss should it occur over a 12-month period
Insurance company	A company providing *insurance* cover
Interest	Payments made on the loan principal
Interest rate	The amount (expressed as a percentage of the amount borrowed) due on a loan while it is outstanding
Interest rate risk	The risk that an interest rate will increase (if you are a borrower) or decrease (if you are an investor)
Interest rate swap	An agreement to exchange a floating rate liability for a fixed rate or vice versa – the two parties notionally swap an underlying principal amount then pay each other interest as if they had made the swap; in practice the amounts are netted so that only one payment passes from one to the other; the effect is to give each party a synthetic position as if it had borrowed at the swapped rate
Interim billing	Where the professional service firm bills the client in regular increments for the work as the project progresses – beneficial to the PSF's cashflow (working capital)
Inventory	Stock – either of components waiting to be part of the manufacturing process; or of finished products waiting to be sold. High inventory represents a lot of cash (working capital) invested in goods that are not being used, so is a cost to the business
Investment bank	Not really a bank at all but an institution that underwrites and distributes the issue of securities by companies, makes a market in those securities and trades them for its own account. Most are American

Investment grade	Securities above a certain credit rating which pension funds are permitted to buy
Investment management	Same as *Fund management*
Investment trust	A listed company that invests in the shares of other companies – a form of *collective investment scheme* which is said to be closed-ended since a specific number of shares are in issue at any one time
Investor relations	That part of a public company that deals with the shareholders, maintaining communication with them on a regular basis
Invoice discounting	A form of *Factoring*
IPO	Initial Public Offering – same as *Flotation*
IPR	Intellectual Property Rights – a business's know-how, image and brands, protected by law through copyright, trademarks and patents
Issuer	A company, bank or government that issues bonds or equities
ITT	Invitation to tender – part of a *pitch* process
Joint and several liability	The legal rule that says that each partner in a firm is liable for all of that firm's debts
Joint venture	A legal agreement between two businesses to pool resources to create a separate, third business which may be a separate company in its own right
Junk	Below-investment grade bonds which most pension funds are not permitted to buy
Just-in-time	Japanese management movement that ensures the components needed for a manufacturing process are provided 'just-in-time' as opposed to being stockpiled months in advance. Requires highly sophisticated *supply chain management* and has the benefit of reducing the *working capital requirement* by reducing the cash invested in *inventory*

Kaizen	Japanese management term that means *continuous improvement* – like many Japanese management techniques it is now part of standard business practice
Knockoff copy	A (often poor) copy of someone else's product – usually in breach of their *IPR*
Know-how	An individual's or organisation's knowledge
Knowledge economy	Term coined by Drucker suggesting that what we know is more valuable than what we make
Kolb	The person who invented the *learning cycle*
KPI	Key performance indicators – the principal financial measures which indicate whether a business is on target
LBO	Leveraged buy-out – like an *MBO* but where the ratio of debt funding to equity is high
Learning & Development	The current term for corporate training of employees to enhance their performance
Learning cycle	Also known as 'experiential learning' – how people learn from doing by acting on that experience to change what they do the next time
Legacy systems	Old computer systems which are superseded but are incompatible with the new system, and contain crucial data which must then be migrated to the new system. Sounds easy, but is often a nightmare. Most businesses have more than one incompatible computer system
Lender of last resort	The traditional role of a central bank, to stand behind the banks it supervises and step in to support any that go bust
Leverage	The ratio of equity partners to other fee-earners – a crucial component of the *levers of profitability*. Explains how big PSFs with large teams working on projects make money from doing so – provided the PSF has the right work and clients
Levers of profitability	Also known as RULES; devised by Stephen Mayson to demonstrate the limited number of factors that affect a professional service firm's profitability – Rates, Utilisation,

	Leverage, Expenses, Speed
LIBOR	London Inter-Bank Offered Rate – the rate of interest that creditworthy banks charge each other for inter-bank loans
Limited liability	The protection that shareholders and directors have from liability for a company's debts if it goes bust
Liquidity	A measure of the tradability of a company's shares – affected by the free-float of shares held by outside investors; the ease with which a security can be traded on the market
Listing	When a company goes public and its shares are listed on a stock exchange – also known as floating or doing an IPO
Listing requirements	The conditions laid down by a stock exchange which a company must satisfy in order to list and remain listed on that exchange
Lloyd's	The London insurance and reinsurance market
LLP	Limited liability partnership
Loan	A form of debt provided by a lender to a borrower
Lobbying	Canvassing politicians on behalf of business to ensure that legislation takes account of corporate interests
Logistics	See *Supply chain management*
Long bond	A bond of long duration – usually more than 10 years
Longtail effect	A term first coined by Chris Anderson in 2004 to mean niche markets that are profitable because of the internet
Low balling	Pricing a service at below-cost in order to undercut the competition and win market share
Lump of labour fallacy	Economics term meaning that the intuitively obvious answer isn't always correct; it comes from the idea that if people work shorter hours, this will provide work for the unemployed and so reduce unemployment – which isn't so
M&A	'Mergers and acquisitions' – i.e. the activity where companies take each other over

Macro-economic	Term used to describe 'big picture' economic factors
Management buy-out	The sale of a business to the people who run it (managers), who buy it (buy-out) usually with the help of venture capital
Managing agent	Person or firm running a Lloyd's insurance syndicate
Marcoms	Marketing communications – that part of business development that focuses on communications with the media (e.g. press releases) and through the media (advertising) as well as directly with clients (e.g. brochures)
Market capitalisation	How much a public company is worth (number of shares in issue x share price)
Market liberalisation	The opening up of a regulated market to competition
Market maker	A bank or broker that makes a market in a share – i.e. is always prepared to buy and sell at prices which it quotes continuously
Market risk	Exposure to moves in the market as a whole also known as *systemic risk* and the opposite of *specific risk*
Market value	The current price a bond or share commands in the market – what investors are prepared to pay for it
Marketing	See *Business development*
Mass customisation	An array of options that allow mass-produced goods to be tailored to a specific customer's specification
MBO	Management buy-out
Members' agents	Part of the Lloyd's insurance market that looks after the interests of investors (once called Names)
Mezzanine finance	Found in venture capital deals (e.g. MBOs and LBOs) where the capital is part-equity, part-debt, and ranks behind senior debt but ahead of junior debt and equity. Also used to describe debt that can flip into equity (e.g. convertible bond or loan)
Mid-market	Used to describe medium-sized public companies – e.g. 'mid-

	market brokers' don't act for the biggest companies
Mid-office	Part of a business that doesn't deal directly with clients but is critical to the business's well-being — in a bank includes compliance, legal and risk management
Migrate	To move computer data from legacy systems
Mission	The strategic roadmap to the organisation's vision
MNCs	Multinational companies that do business in several overseas markets and may be listed on more than one exchange
Money purchase	See *Defined contributions*
Monopoly	A market-dominant position that allows a company to inflate the price for its goods or services
MPC	The Bank of England's Monetary Policy Committee which sets interest rates
MTN	Medium term note — a bond of roughly 3–7 years' maturity
MTN programme	A pre-arranged package of different methods of financing open to a company, including issuing an *MTN*
Multilateral	A loan made by a *syndicate* of banks to a borrower; also, another name for a *supranational*
Multinational	See *MNC*
Multiplier	A professional who may refer new clients to you without becoming a client himself or herself
Name	An individual investor at Lloyd's — now in decline
Net present value	The discounted value of cashflows produced by an investment
Networked distribution	Originally, software applications sourced over a computer network rather than installed on individual servers; has come to mean 'download-on-demand' over the internet
Networking	Developing personal contacts for social and business purposes

NewCo	Favourite lawyers' term to mean a new company created as part of a project. Often given a code name which then sticks (e.g. when John Duffield left Jupiter to start New Star; and Railtrack in the UK privatisation of the rail network – how else do you explain the tautology of 'rail' and 'track'?)
NITA feedback	A simple model for offering feedback (Headline, Replay, Rationale, Prescription) devised by the US National Institute of Trial Advocacy
NLP	Neuro-Linguistic Programming – a method of increasing personal performance through, amongst other things, improved interpersonal communications
Nominal value	Same as *par value*
Non-core asset	A business or an asset employed in a business that is not central to a company's strategy
Non-executive	A senior role in a company that does not carry responsibility for day-to-day operations
Normative strategy	A company's purpose or sense of direction as informed and supported by its culture
NPD	New Product Development – part of R&D
OBS	Off-balance sheet – accounting term applicable to financial transactions (especially debt) which are not attributed to the company concerned; but has come to be pejorative following the collapse of Enron because of OBS transactions
OEIC	Open-ended investment company – like a unit trust but which is actually a company
Offshoring	Relocating back-office activities to another, lower-cost country
Operating lease	A lease for the short-term use of an asset (as opposed to a *finance lease*)
Operations	A company's activities
Opportunity cost	The return forgone by investing capital in a business rather than elsewhere (e.g. on deposit at a bank)

Option	A derivative that gives the holder the right to buy (call) or sell (put) an underlying security, but not the obligation. 'American' options are exercisable at any time up to expiry; 'European' options are exercisable only immediately prior to expiry
Organogram	Visual depiction of a business's structure including departments, functions and roles
Origination	The *primary market* investment banking activity of advising companies and governments on bond issues
OTC	Over The Counter – off-exchange financial instruments that are customised to a particular customer's needs
Outsourcing	The transfer of back-office activities to a third-party supplier
Overrun	Where a project has exceeded costs or deadline
Over-subscribed	Where demand for a bond or share is greater than the number on offer, so that applications have to be scaled back
P&I Clubs	Found in the shipping industry, mutual associations that provide insurance for members (shipowners)
P&L	Profit and loss account
Paper bid	A pitch, beauty parade or ITT where the prospective client makes its choice on the submissions of the tenderers, without actually meeting them
Paradigm shift	See *Secular trend*
Par value	The *nominal value* of a security – i.e. the value at which it will be redeemed which, if it is in hard-copy form, is printed on it – contrast with *market value*
Parallel imports	The movement of goods between markets to obtain a better price – see also *grey market* and *arbitrage*
Parent	A company which owns another (subsidiary)
Pareto Principle	Applies to widely different situations and is also known as the 80/20 rule: e.g. 80% of a business's income comes from 20% of its customer base. Essentially means that a

disproportionately large return comes from a disproportionately small part of one's effort – the trick is in identifying which makes the difference

Partner	Legally-speaking, a person or organisation that is in a partnership (also called a firm) and is liable for its debts; an equity partner is an owner of the business; a salaried partner is an employee and not really a true partner
Partnership	Legally-recognised entity that combines two or more people or institutions working to generate a common profit
Passive management	Also known as index-tracking, where a portfolio replicates a stock exchange index in order to follow the market average – can be computerised, making it cheaper than active management
Payment on account	Where a client is asked to make a payment in advance of the supplier doing any work
Pension fund	A pool of money used to finance the income paid to retired workers
Personality typing	The idea that people can be categorised into broad segments according to what they are like, their preferences, etc. There are many models that purport to do this
PEST	A business model that focuses on macro-economic factors: political, economic, social and technological
PFI/PPP	Private finance initiative/public-private partnership – both are methods of using private-sector funding to build public-sector projects
Pitch	A process in which a company or government asks competing providers to bid for new business (also known as an ITT or beauty parade)
Placing	Where shares or bonds are 'placed' with a small group of institutional investors so the issue is not public and less disclosure is required. Also known as a 'private placement'
Plain vanilla	A financing that is straightforward, e.g. a bond issue without any 'bells and whistles' (derivatives) attached

Plan	American term for pension fund
Plan sponsor	The company to which a particular pension fund is attached – i.e. for whose employees it provides pensions
Platform	Originally meant a computer system; now means any systematic business process
PLC	Public Limited Company
Plug-and-play	Software term meaning that an application can be used 'out of the box' without causing set-up or compatibility problems
Poison pill	A mechanism to prevent a company from being taken over – for instance it may involve the issue of shares with special rights to acquire shares in the bidder
Political risk	The risk of political impact – for instance through a change of party in government or through a policy of nationalisation
Porter's Five Forces	Strategy model devised by Porter which assesses competitive pressures to which a company is subject, from its industry competitors, buyers, suppliers, new entrants and substitutes
Portfolio management	The same as asset, fund, money and wealth management – investing other people's money and being paid for doing so
Portfolio worker	Term coined by Charles Handy meaning someone who is self-employed and does a variety of jobs (some more lucrative than others) usually for lifestyle reasons
PR	Public Relations or Press Relations
Premium	A surplus paid over and above the market price
Pre-pitch interview	Part of the process of responding to an ITT through which the tenderer obtains more information from the prospective client in order to increase its (the tenderer's) chances of success
Price-earnings ratio	The share price of a company divided by its earnings per share (*EPS*)
Price fixing	The anti-competitive practice of agreeing with apparent competitors the price at which a good or service will be

provided to the market

Price sensitive information	Information about a share that will affect its price in the market – usually any trades in a share based on such information is *insider dealing*
Primary markets	The investment banking activity of securities issue, distribution and underwriting
Principal	An amount borrowed; or a person or entity who is responsible for a business's liabilities
Private company	A company that isn't listed on an exchange and whose shares are therefore not publicly traded
Private equity	Using funds from institutional investors to buy public companies and take them private, usually with a view to breaking them up or on-selling them
Privatisation	The term covering the many ways in which public-sector activities are transferred to the private sector
Process	The way in which something is done, as opposed to what it actually comprises (content)
Procurement	That part of a company responsible for buying in goods and services; originally began in government (e.g. defence procurement) which is subject to public procurement rules ensuring equal treatment of competing suppliers
Product lifecycle	The theory that every product or service loses its attraction to customers over time as rival products and services with better features are introduced in competition to it
Profit	The surplus (if any) that remains when the costs of doing business are deducted from the revenues generated in that period
Project finance	Also known as 'limited recourse' or 'non-recourse' finance because the lenders have recourse only to the project itself; often used to finance third-world infrastructure projects where the state buys the output (e.g. hydro-electricity) which funds the lending, and the lenders have rights of 'step in' if the borrower (the project company) defaults

Project management	Techniques used to manage a project so that it is delivered on time and within budget
Prospectus	The brochure a company prepares prior to listing to encourage investors to buy its shares
PSBR	Public Sector Borrowing Requirement – what the government has to borrow to bridge any gap between tax receipts (income) and government expenditure (outgoings)
PSF	Professional service firm
Public affairs	Also known as *lobbying* – those agencies, and that part of a company, that seek to influence government over the content of future legislation
Public company	A company listed on a stock exchange
Public policy	Something done or not done supposedly in the interest of the general public
Public-to-private	A takeover of a public company whose shares are then delisted from a stock exchange
Quality systems	A management approach to manufacturing goods or providing services which reduces inconsistency to a small statistically insignificant level
Quarter	Three-month period – a company's financial year comprises four quarters
Quartile	25% of a pool or universe – used in fund management: upper quartile means being in the top 25%
Quota	An artificial limit imposed by the members of a *cartel* on how much each can produce or sell
Quote	A fee proposal which, if exceeded, may cause the customer to refuse to pay the excess – meant to be more binding on the supplier than an estimate
Rating	The rating conferred on a bond issue by a rating agency which indicates the likelihood that the issuer will repay it

Rating agency	Independent agencies (Standard & Poor's and Moody's are the best known) that assess an issuer's ability to service and repay a bond and provide a rating (triple A is the highest) to enable institutions and brokers to assess a bond's credit-worthiness quickly
R&D	Research and Development – that part of a company that develops new products and services
Realise an investment	To sell a security or property to extract any gain in value since it was acquired
Recommended offer/bid	A bid for a *target* that is recommended by the target's board to its shareholders
Regulatory risk	The risk that a business (1) contravenes the rules to which it is subject or (2) is investigated by government
Reinsurance company	A company to which an insurance company lays off some of the risk it has taken on from insureds
Remuneration package	The total of money, bonuses, share options and other benefits paid to a senior employee
Rental	Payment by the lessee to the lessor under a *finance* or *operating lease*
Representations and warranties	Contractual terms (promises) by one company to another, usually as part of a takeover
Rescheduling	Where lending banks agree to spread the repayment of a loan over a longer term to enable the borrower to repay it at all
Resource	Usually means people, time or money – i.e. what is required to get a task done
Restrictive practices	Anti-competitive ways of doing business
Retail	Where the customer is an individual
Retail banking	Banking services for consumers (i.e. individuals not businesses)
Retained profit	Profit that isn't paid out to shareholders but is kept in the business, to fund cashflow or investment projects

Reverse engineering	Taking someone else's product apart in order to find out how they made it, usually to create a *knockoff copy*
Reverse takeover	Where a small company takes over a larger one
Rights issue	A further issue of shares by a listed company – called a 'rights' issue because existing shareholders have a right to pre-emption in respect of the new shares in proportion to their existing holdings so that their stake in the company is not diluted
Risk	The exposure of a business to the chance of something (bad) happening – in itself not a bad thing: business is about taking risks but getting adequately rewarded for doing so
Risk management	The systems and procedures designed to identify, control and mitigate the risks to which a business is exposed
ROCE	Return On Capital Employed
Rocket science	Colloquial term to show that something is not complex, as in: 'This isn't rocket science'
ROI	Return On Investment
Roll over	To extend a debt by treating the expiry as the beginning of a further term of equal duration
Royalty	A regular income stream (which may vary in amount each time) generated by a business activity – e.g. song royalty
RULES	The levers of profitability, devised by Mayson: Rates, Utilisation, Leverage, Expenses and Speed
Salaried partner	Has the external status of being an equity partner (and the liability) but without the ownership stake in the partnership, so is effectively an employee
Sale-and-leaseback	A form of funding where a company sells an asset to a bank and then simultaneously leases it back in order to continue using it – often happens when a company owns the building it occupies and does a sale-and-leaseback to free up capital to use in the business

Sales force automation	Computerised system allowing the sales force of a business to gain real-time information on prices and inventory through continual updating of central data with the sales they are making
Scheme	Alternative name for *pension fund* or *plan*
Scoping	Assessing at the outset how big a project is, what *resource* will be required and what the cost to the client will be
Scenario planning	'What if' or contingency planning (part of strategy)
Seasoned equity offering	A fresh issue of shares by a company that is already listed – same as a secondary issue or rights issue
Secondary issue	See *seasoned equity offering*
Secondary markets	The markets for second-hand securities – shares and bonds that have already been issued and bought by an investor that is on-selling them – contrast with the *primary markets*
Sector	A market in which the same goods or services are made, provided or sold. Also used to indicate industrial development: primary (natural resource extraction), secondary (manufacturing) and tertiary (services)
Secular trend	Same as *paradigm shift, seismic shift and step change* – a cliché of management consultants, meaning a fundamental change in the world or the way we live or work
Securities	Shares or bonds
Security	An asset charged as security for a loan
Seismic shift	Same as *paradigm shift, secular trend* and *step change* – a cliché of management consultants, meaning a fundamental change in the world or the way we live or work
Servicing debt	Paying interest (and any fees) on a loan
Share	Evidence of equity ownership in a company
Share option	An option to buy a share – gives the option holder the right

	but not the obligation to buy the share
Ship finance	A form of *asset finance* used to fund ships and oil rigs
Shortlist	Part of an *ITT* or *pitch* process where the prospective customer draws up a short list of possible suppliers to interview, prior to making its choice
Short-listed	A supplier who makes it to the *short list*
SMEs	Small and medium-sized enterprises
Sole trader	A person in business on his or her own account
Specific risk	The risk specific to a particular company – the opposite of *market* or *systemic risk*
Spin-off	Demerger of one business from another
Spot market	The current market (for immediate delivery as opposed to the forward market)
Star	A product or service that is market-leading and generates top returns (BCG model)
Start-up	Young company
Step change	See *secular trend*
Stock	Same as a share – but originally meant a bond
Stock exchange	Regulated market on which company shares are listed
Strategy	A plan setting out a business goal and the path to achieving it
Subsidiary	A company that is wholly owned by another (parent)
Substitutes	Alternatives to buying a product or service (Porter)
Supplier	Commercial provider of goods or services (Porter)
Supply and demand	Economic term that covers buyers in a market (demand) and sellers (supply) to that market

Supply chain management	Also known as *logistics* – this is the unseen part of retail distribution which ensures the right quantities of the right goods are available in retail outlets at the right time; it's part of a function of optimising the mix of warehousing and transport; part of the science of predicting seasonal demand. Sounds boring but is fascinating. Ensures you can buy your favourite cereal from your local supermarket whenever you want
Supply-side economics	The use of incentives (e.g. lower tax) to increase the level of full employment
Supranational	A bank that is not tied to any particular country but has a supra (above) country role
Suspended	When a stock exchange halts trading in a share listed on it
Sustainable competitive advantage	The goal of all business – to achieve an advantage over competitors that cannot be easily replicated by them
Swap	A way of changing a floating-rate loan into a fixed-rate and vice versa; also a way of changing a loan into a different currency enabling each of the two counterparties to obtain a better rate or currency position than they would in their respective markets
SWOT	A basic strategy model – Strengths and Weaknesses (internal), Opportunities and Threats (external)
Syndicate	A group of banks; in the insurance market a vehicle backed by investors to underwrite risk
Syndicated loan	A loan to a single borrower made by a group of banks on the same terms – often used where the sum borrowed is more than a single bank would wish to lend
System	A computer network; or a process that provides a consistent output or result each time
Systemic risk	See *market risk*
Takeover	The acquisition of one company (target) by another (bidder) – also known as *M&A*

Takeover Code/Panel	The self-regulating body in the City of London that oversees *M&A* deals
Target	A company that is subject to a bid
Tasked-based billing	Fee structure that allows a project to be broken down into specific tasks and an agreed price to be put against each
Tender	A submission by a bidder or supplier in response to an ITT (invitation to tender) from a prospective customer
Time/cost/ quality	The three variable factors of project management
Time management	The tips and techniques deployed by a professional to make best use of his or her working day
Total shareholder return	Realised value of a share plus the dividend income less the purchase price
Trade association	A body that represents all the competitors in an industry – can give rise to the suspicion of a *cartel*
Trade finance	A method of ensuring that exporters get paid and buyers only pay when they have the goods, using letters of credit that are then discounted in the 'à forfait' market; in this sense a sophisticated form of factoring
Trade publication	A magazine or journal aimed at the participants in a particular trade – often subscription-only and not available in newsagents. One of the oldest is *The Grocer* for the food retail business
Tranche	A slice of a loan or bond – may apply to a particular part-repayment
Treasuries	US government bonds – the US government is the largest borrower in the world and is regarded as the safest (if it goes bust we might as well all pack up) so it commands the finest pricing of its bonds, which is the benchmark off which all international bond issues are priced
Treasury	That part of a (large) company that looks after money flows in and out and, in particular, executes foreign exchange trades,

	hedging operations and invests short-term surpluses in overnight money markets
Triple A	The top credit rating – a blue-chip borrower
Trophy client	A client which is a big name so looks good on a professional service firm's client list, even if it doesn't provide much work or much profitable work
Trust	Legal structure whereby an asset is held by trustees on behalf of a body of beneficiaries – especially useful where the beneficiaries may be changing all the time (e.g. pensioners in a pension fund; investors in a unit trust)
Trustees	The legal owners of an asset who may not have beneficial ownership of (actual entitlement to) that asset or its financial proceeds
Under-subscribed	Where the take-up of a share or bond issue is less than 100%
Underwriting	Taking on the risk that an issue of securities will not be sold in its entirety – a guarantee to the issuer that it will raise the money it expects
Unit trust	A collective investment scheme, described as open-ended
Universal bank	Same as a *bundled bank* – combines commercial and investment banking activities
Upstream private equity	Raising funds from institutional investors in order to finance public-to-private takeovers
Useful economic life	The life of an asset (such as a plane or ship) that is being leased before it needs to be replaced
USP	Unique selling proposition (marketing term) – what attracts a customer or client to buy from a particular business or professional service firm
US Treasuries	Bonds issued by the US government
Value-at-risk (VAR)	Computer-based risk analysis that enables a bank to gauge and manage its aggregate exposure to markets – done by

	devising models based on historic data of market movements, price volatility and correlations between markets
Value billing	Fee structure where the professional service firm lets the client decide after the project is done how much to pay for the services provided – requires great trust between the two
Venture capital	Equity finance provided by specialist 'venture capitalists' in return for a shareholding in the business (usually a relatively new and small one); they realise their investment when the company floats or is sold in a 'trade sale'; note that they also finance MBOs
VFM	Value for money
Vision	Part of a company's strategy – the picture of where it intends to end up – its goal
White elephant	A big project that is pointless and unwanted
Wholesale	Business-to-business – where the customer is a business or government
Wholesale banking	Lending to businesses
Wholesale money	Money managed on behalf of institutional investors
WIP	See *Work in progress*
Working capital	The money needed to bridge the gap between a business's outgoings and its income, without which it will go bust
Working capital requirement	The amount of *working capital* a business needs
Work in progress	Work that has been done for a client but hasn't yet been billed – the level of WIP has a major impact on a business's cashflow
Yield	The rate of interest a bond pays, expressed as a percentage in relation to its market value

Zero-coupon bond	Also known as deep discount bonds, where the interest element is wrapped up in the (higher) amount repaid on maturity

INDEX

3i	23	Architects	111-12
À Forfait Market	60	Articles	150
Accountants	XI, 109-10, 157	Asian Development Bank	57
Accounts	26, 32	Asset Finance	19, 58-60
Acquisition Finance	55, 58	Asset Sales	43
Active Listening	98	Assets	59
Actuaries	110-11	Assets, Non-Core	43
Advertising Agencies	112	Audiences	144
Advice	126-8, 136-7	Audiovisual Aids	191
		Auditors	109
African Development Bank	57	*Auto Trader*	22
Alliances	70	B2B (Business-to-Business)	41, 81
Amazon	72	B2C (Business-to-Consumer)	41, 81
Ambassadors	174, 182	Bad Debts	159
Amiables	100-2	Balance Sheet	25-6
Amortisation	25	Balanced Scorecard	14
Analyticals	100-2	Baltic Exchange	68
Annual Report	47	Bankers	112-13
Annuity	111	Bankruptcy	20
Anti-Trust Laws	40, 83	Banks	X, 23, 42, 56, 61, 158
Apologies	135-6		
Appraisals	128-9	Banks, Bundled	56
Arbitrage	67, 82		

Banks, Central — 57

Banks, Commercial — 56

Banks, Conglomorate — 56

Banks, Investment — 56

Banks, Merchant — 56

Banks, Retail — 56

Banks, Supranational — 57

Banks, Universal — 56

Banks, Wholesale — 56

Barriers to Entry — 6

Barristers — 116

Basis Points — 53

Bearer Instruments — 53

Beauty Parade — 184

Belbin — 130

Best Practice — 74

Best-In-Class — 74

Bid Timetable — 42

Bids, Hostile — 42

Bids, Recommended — 42

Big Picture, The — 18

Bills, Types Of — 163-5

Blogging — 73

Board of Directors — 104

Body Shop, The — 3

Bold — 147

Bond Yields — 65

Bonds — 52, 56

Bonds, High-Yield — 58

BOOST — 126

Boston Consulting Group Matrix — 13

Boutiques — 23

Boxes — 148

Brackets — 148

Brainstorm — 135

Brand Markets — 85

Brand Specialists — 113

Brands — 39

Branson, Richard — 102

Brick 'N' Click — 73

Briefing — 124

Brochures — 150

Brokers — 34, 69, 113

Budget — 25, 170

Builds — 144

Bullet Points — 144, 147

Burger King — 39

Burn-Out — 157

Business Angels — 23

Business Cards — 190

Business Development (BD) — 178-92

Business Formats — 21

Business Models – see Models

Business Plan — 25

Business Process Outsourcing — 74

Business Process Reengineering — 73-4

Business Structure — 103-9

Businessmen, Types of — 100-2

Buyers — 5

Candover	23
Capital Investment	20-1, 59
Capital Requirement	159
Captains of Industry	43
Cartels	40
Cash Cows	13-14
Cashflow	IX, 18-20, 34, 38, 158-9, 174
Cashflow Return On Investment (CFROI)	48
Certificates	57
Chairmen	104
Channels To Market	41
Charter Party	68
Charts	148
Cherry Picking	43
Chief Executive Officer (CEO)	2, 9, 43, 103-4, 187
Chief Information Officer (CIO)	85, 106
Chief Operating Officer (COO)	105
Churn	80
Circulars	35
City Code	42
Clarity	143
Client Base Segmentation	174
Client Expectations	133-4, 142
Client Relationships	168-9, 172
Client Relationship Management (CRM)	81, 178, 183
Client Satisfaction	134
Clients	X, 3-4, 14, 96
Clients, New	182-4
Closed Questions	98
Closed-Ended Trusts	36
Coca-Cola	41, 82
Comfort Letter	24
Commanders	100-2
Commas	148
Commercial Conflicts	103
Commercial Drivers	170
Commercial Paper	55
Commercialisation	86
Commoditisation	166
Company Structure	103-9
Competition	5, 40, 59-61, 189
Competition Authorities	38, 83
Competitive Environment	88
Complaints	134-6, 167-8
Completion	57
Conclusions	141-2
Conditional Sale	19
Conglomerates	38
Consumerism	80
Contacts	179
Content	8
Contingencies	172
Contingency Planning – see Scenario Planning	

Continuous Improvement
– see Kaizen

Convergence 72

Conversations 96-100

Convertability 58

Cooperative
Bank, The 3

Copywriters 112

Core Competencies 12

Corporate Finance 42, 56

Corporate
Governance 43, 84

Corporate Planning
Departments 10

Corporate Social
Responsibility 84

Corporatisation 88

Cost of Capital 48

Coupons 53, 65

Covenants 58

Covering Letters 188

Covey, Stephen 126

Creative Accounting 32

Creative Pricing 171

Credit Approval 57

Credit Cards 25, 80

Credit Control 159

Credit Rating Agency 54

Credit Risk 55

Creditors 27, 159

Critical
Dependencies 168

Critical Success
Factors 169, 172

Culture 3

Currency Brokers 61

Current Affairs 197

Current Assets 27

Customer Loyalty 80

Customer Value
Management IX, 75

Customers 38

Cute Clients 162

Dashes 148

Data Migration 77

Data Mining IX, 75-7, 80

Data Warehousing 76

Deadlines 125, 150, 172

Dealers 56

Debentures 53

Debt X, 19, 21, 24, 52, 158-9

Debt Refinancing 26

Debtor Days 158-9

Decisiveness 143

Deep Discount Bonds 57

Defaulting 24, 58

Defect 80

Defined Benefits 111

Defined Contributions 111

Deflation 63

Delegation 124

Dell 22, 76, 78

Deming, Edwards 79

Demurrage 68

Depreciation	25, 31	Editors	150
Derivatives	37, 67	Efficiency	48, 78-9
Diluted	37	Efficiency Work	167
Director of Administration	105	Electra	23
		Emails	142
Directors	21	Emergent Strategy	11-12
Discount	35	Engineers	113
Discounted Cashflow	49	Enterprise Resource Planning (ERP)	73-4
Discounting	19, 64	Entrants	5
Disintermediation	56, 73	Environment, The	84
Dividend Cover	26, 47	Equilibrium Point	91
Dividends	22, 31, 47	Equity	X, 21
Dogs	13	ERP	IX
Dot Com Boom	72	Estimates	161, 171
Dow Jones 30	45	Eurobond	54
Downrated	54	Eurodollar	54
Draw Down	57	European Investment Bank	57
Drucker, Peter	12, 84, 195, 198	European Union	83
Due Diligence	57	Event of Default	58
Dyson, James	22	Exchange Controls	61
Earn-Out	43	Executive, The	104
Earnings Per Share (EPS)	46	Exit Route	34
EARS	98	Expectations	133-4, 142
EBRD	57	Expenses	154, 157-8
Economic Rent	48	Expenses, Fixed	157
Economic Value Added (EVA)	49	Expenses, Variable	157
Economics	XI, 91	Experience	166
Economies of Scale	82	Experiential Learning	195
Economist, The	93, 146, 197-8	Expertise	174
		Experts	166

Exports	63, 91	Forward Contract	62, 68
Expressives	100-2	Forward Market	68
External Client		Franchises	39
Reporting	171	Franchising	22
External Environment	7, 12	Fraud	65, 69
Face Value	65	Free Cashflow	48
Facilitator	8	Free Trade	83
Factoring	19	Freeman, Christopher	90
Feedback	124-8, 191	FTSE 100	45-6
Fees, Types Of	163-5	Full Employment	91
Finance	105	Fund Management	35, 56
Finance Leasing	58-60	Fund Managers	114-15
Financial Pages	46	Futures Market	61-2, 68
Financial Times	197, 199	Gantt Charts	130
Financial Year	25	Gates, Bill	
Fines	40	*– see Microsoft*	
Fishbone Maps	135	GDP	91
Fitch	54	Gearing	47, 157
Fixed Assets	21, 27	General Electric (GE)	3, 45, 75
Fixed Charge	24	Gilts	53
Fixed Income		Globalisation	IX, 82-3
Instruments	53	Goals	132
Flipcharts	8, 132	Going Short	37
Floating Charge	24	Golden Hellos	43
Flotation	34	Golden Parachutes	43
Flow Diagrams	148	Golden Share	89
Food Chains	174	Goodwill	30
Ford	41, 82	Google	72
Forecasting	25	Government	89-91
Foreign Exchange	60	Grammar	148
Forex Markets	60, 63	Grant	7
Formula One	195	Graphic Designers	115

Graphs	148
Grey Markets	82
Gross Dividend Yield	46
Gross Revenue	18
Group Companies	41
Growth	47
Guarantor	24
Handy, Charles	2, 86, 198
Harvard Business Review, The	93, 197
Headings	147
Headline	141
Hedge Funds	37
Hedging	37, 66-8
Heinz	39
High-Value Goods	20
High-Yield Bond	54
Hire-Purchase	19, 60
Hive-Down	43
HM Revenue and Customs	18
Holding Company	41
House Prices	63
Hugely Geared	44
Human Resources	105
IBM	22, 73
Incidence of Mortality	110
Income	18, 20
Income Gearing	47
Incomplete Information	170
Index-Tracking	114
Individualistic School	90

Industry Conferences	109
Inflation	62, 91
Information and Communications Technology (ICT)	72
Initial Public Offering (IPO)	34
Innovation	14, 90-3, 166
Innovation Management	90
Insider Dealing	36
Insolvency	20
Institutional Investors	23, 35, 45, 56, 84
Insurance	67-8
Insurance Brokers	115
Insurance Companies	35
Intellectual Property Rights	85
Interest	19, 23-4, 158
Interest, Rate of	55, 62-5
Interim Billing	159-60, 171
Intermediaries	113
Internal Management	171-2
International Bond Market	52
International Trade	82
Interviews	184-92
Investment	23, 34, 91
Investment, Direct	61
Investment Funds	36

Investment, Indirect	61	Layouts	146-8
Investment Trusts	36	Learning Cycle	194-5
Investor Relations		Learning-By-Doing	195
Units	45	Leases	58
Investors	61	Lectures	191
Invitation to Tender	184	Legacy Systems	77
Invoice Discounting	19	Legal Opinions	57
IT Director	105	Legal Personality	23
ITC Consultants	115-16	Legal Requirements	186
Jargon	146	Leisure Activity	80
Joint and Several		Lender of Last Resort	57
Liability	21	Lenders	27
Joint Ventures	70	Letters	140
Junk Bond	54	Letters of Credit	56, 60
Just-In-Time		Leverage	154, 157,
Production	76		166-7
Kaizen	76	Leveraged Buy-Outs	
Kaplan & Norton	14	(LBOs)	44, 58
Kay, John	199	Liabilities	27
Key Performance		LIBOR	56
Indicators (KPI)	25	Lifelong Learning	86, 196
Kidder, Tracy	199	Lifetime Value	75, 173
Knowledge Economy	12, 84	Limited Liability	
Knowledge		Partnerships (LLPs)	21, 37
Management	IX, 85	Listing Requirements	34
Kohn, Alfie	85	Lloyd's of London	68-70
Kolb's Learning Cycle	194-5	Loan Acceleration	58
Labour	83	Loans	19, 24
Language	140-1	Lobbyist	116
Larson, Gary	10	Logistics	78
Lateral Thinking	11	London Stock	
Lawyers	116, 162,	Exchange	34, 45
	187	Long Bond	55

Longtail Effect	83	Market Researchers	117-18
Loss	29	Market Value	65
Loss Adjusters	115	Market Value Added	49
Low Balling	173	Marketing	92, 105, 181
Lump of Labour Fallacy	91	Marketplace	12
McDonald's	22, 39, 41, 82	Markets, Secondary	56
		Mass Customisation	78
Madejski, John – see Auto Trader	22	Mass Markets	82
Magazines	150, 197	Mature Products – see Cash Cows	
Maister, David	151, 166-7, 179, 198-200	Mayson, Stephen	154, 199
		McKinsey	3
Majority Control	42	Medium Term Notes	55
Management Buy-Out (MBO)	44, 58	Meetings	8, 132, 187
		Members' Agents	69
Management Consultancy	2, 117	Memos	140
Managers, Active	114	Mergers & Acquisitions (M&A)	38-40, 55-8
Managers, Passive	114	Merril, David	100
Managers, Types of	100-2	Mezzanine Finance	58
Managing Agents	69	Micklethwait, John	198
Managing Expectations	133-4	Microsoft	3, 22, 41
Mandate	184	Mind Maps	135
Manufacturing	85, 92	Minority Interests	42
Margins	56	Mintzberg, Henry	11-12
Market Capitalisation	46	Misfeasance	21
Market Clearing	91	Mission	3, 12
Market Liberalisation	87	Models	4-15
Market Presence (or penetration)	39	Monetary Policy Committee	62
Market Price	46	Monitoring	168-73
Market Pull Model	92	Monitoring Procedure	125

Monopoly 40
Monopoly, Horizontal 40
Monopoly, Vertical 40
Moody's 54
Moral Editing 155-6
Morale 157
Morgan, Neil 181
Mortgage 59
MTN Programme 55
Multinational
    Companies (MNCs) 41, 72, 82
Multipliers 180
Myers Briggs 196
Names 69-70
Narrative Lists 147
Negligence 154
Net Present Value 25, 49
Networked Distribution 72
Networking 178-83
Neuro Linguistic
    Programming (NLP) 99
New Product
    Development (NPD) 90
Newsletters 150
Newspapers 141-2,146,
    197
NHS 91
Nike 41, 74, 82
NITA 126-7
Nominal Value 65
Non-Executive Directors 84
Normative Strategy 3
Off Balance Sheet

(OBS) 86
Offer Document 42
Offshore BPO 75
Offshoring IX, 74
Oil 89-90
One-Off Benefit 160
Online Shopping 81
Open Questions 98
Open-Ended Trusts 36
Opportunity Cost 157
Options 68
Organograms 104
Origination 56
Orwell, George 146
OTC Market 67
Outgoings 18, 29
Output by Sector 91
Outsourcing IX, 74, 87
Over-promising 133
Over-subscribed 35
Over-utilisation 157
Overdraft 158
Overnight Money
Markets 62
Overtime 157
P&I Clubs 70
Panels 184
Paper Bids 184
Par Value 65
Paradigm Shifts 8, 72
Paragraphs 141, 147,
    188
Parallel Imports 82

Parent Company 41

Parent Company
   Guarantee 24

Pareto Principle 81, 183

Particulars 184

Partnerships 21

Patent Attorneys 118

Patience 151

Payment, On Account 160

Payment, Upfront 160

PCs 3

Pension Funds 35, 43

Pensions 25, 111,
196

People, Types of 100-2

Percentage Fees 169

Performance 195

Performance Fee 37

Personality Typing 100

PEST 8

Phone Conversations
   – see Telephone Calls

Photos 190

Pirsig, Robert 79

Pitch Process, The 182,
184-92

Pitching 121

Podcasting 73

Porter, Michael 5

Porter's Five Forces 5-7, 48

Portfolio Management 173

Portfolio of Patents 85

Portfolio Workers 86

Post 73

Post-Completion
   Reviewing 172

PowerPoint 144

PR Consultants 118

Pre-tax Profit 48

Premium 41, 69,
155, 162

Premium Trading 35

Presentations 121, 144

Price Change 46

Price Fixing 40

Price Movements 46

Price Sensitive
   Information 36

Price Volatility 46

Price/Earnings Ratio 46

Prices, Fixed 161

PricewaterhouseCoopers
   (PwC) 183

Pricing Structures 160-5

Primary Industries 84

Primary Market Activity 56

Principal 23

Private Companies 21, 38

Private Equity 44

Private Equity,
   Downstream 44

Private Equity,
   Upstream 44

Private Finance
   Initiative (PFI) 87

Privatisation 86-8

Process 8, 14

Product Lifecycle	13	Questions	98, 144, 188
Professional Relationships	X	Quotas	40
Professional Service Firms (PSFs)	6	Quotations	161
		Rates	154-7
Profit	14, 18-25, 28-31, 46, 157, 181	Rates, Headline	155
		Rates, Realised	155
Profit & Loss	25	Rates, Reduced	155
Profitability	63-4	Ratios	32
Profits	158	Receivables	19
Profits, Retained	159	Regulation	40
Project Management	129-31	Rental	59
Project Plan	168	Remuneration Package	43
Project Template	170	Reports, Financial	25
Prospectus	34	Reports, Presentation	140
Protectionism	61	Reputation	X
Psychological Contract	85, 196	Research & Development	14, 92, 106
Public Borrowing	87	Resourcing	168-73
Public Companies	21, 34, 38	Restrictive Practices	40
Public Relations (PR)	105, 150	Retail	41, 81
Public Sector Borrowing Requirement	91	Retail Investors	35
		Retail Markets	39
		Retail Price Index	91
Public-Private Partnerships (PPP)	87	Retained Earnings	31
Public-to-Private Deals	44	Return on Capital Employed (ROCE)	48
Pull-Learning-And-Development	195-6	Return on Investment (ROI)	23, 25
Punctuation	148	Revenue	18, 29
Push-Training	195-6	Revenue, Gross	18
Quality Systems	79-80	Revenue, Net	18
Quantity Surveyors	119	Reverse Engineering	76
Quarters	25		

Reverse Takeover	43	Service Economy	81, 85
Richer, Julian	198	Share Allocations	35
Right of Pre-Emption	37	Share Options	43
Rights Issues	37	Share Ownership	89
Risk	154, 171	Share Price	64
Risk Factors	169	Share-for-Share	
Risk Management	65-8, 106	Exchange	43
Risk, Types of	65-6	Shareholders	21, 23, 27, 31-2, 58, 88-9
Roll Over	55		
RULES	154, 199	Shares	56, 67
Sale-and-Leaseback	60	Ship Finance	68
Sales	18	Shopping	80
Sales Force		Short Lists	184
Automation	79	Shorting the Market	37
Scenario Planning	10-11	Six Sigma	79
Seasoned Equity		Skills	196
Offerings	37	Slides	144
Secondary Issues	37	Small and Medium	
Sector, Primary	41	Enterprises (SMEs)	23, 92-3
Sector, Quaternary	41	Smith, David	199
Sector, Secondary	41	Snakeskins	174
Sector, Tertiary	41	Social Deterministic	
Secular Trends	8, 72	School	92
Securities	52-3	Sole Trader	21
Security	24	Solicitors	116
Segment	6	Solutions	135
Seismic Shifts	72	Sony	10
Self-employed	21	Specialist Input	170
Selling	180-1	Speed	154, 158-60
Seminars	179		
Semler, Ricardo	198	Spot Market	61
Sentences	188	Stakeholders	84

Standard & Poor's	54		Tasks	124-6
Standby Guarantees	24		Tax-deductible	26
Statistics	91		Tax Avoidance	120
Step Changes	8		Tax Consultants	120
Strategy	X, 3-15		Tax Liability	120
Subsidiaries	61		Taxation	18, 58-9, 91
Substitutes	5			
Success Fee	162		Taxed Cover	26
Sunday Times	199		Taxed Profit	26
Supermarkets	80-1		Technology Push Model	90
Supervision	124-6		Technology, Role of	9, 197
Suppliers	5, 27, 38		Tectonic Shifts	72
Supply and Demand	91		Telecommunications	86
Supply Chain	IX, 78		Telephone Calls	137
Supply-Side Economics	91		Tendering	184-92
Surveyors	119		Text Boxes	148
Suspension	35		Theory of Shambolic Organisations	196
Sustainable Competitive Advantage (SCA)	14, 48		Theory of the Business	12
Sustainable Return	48		Time Charge	154
Swaps	67		Time Management	131-3
SWOT	6, 11		Time Recording	156
Syndicate	57		Time Sheets	156
Syndicated Loan Agreement	57		Time Zone	162
Syndicates	69		Timetables	172
Takeover Panel	42		Tobacco Companies	83
Takeovers, Hostile	42		Total Business Return	48
Takeovers, Recommended	42		Total Shareholder Return	49
Target	58		Toyota	82
Targets	38, 42		Track Record	161
			Trade Finance	56, 60

Trade Publications 109

Trade-Off Triangle 131

Trademarks 85

Training 174

Transaction Log 172

Treasury, The 61-2

Trophy Contract 173-4

Tupman, Simon 198

Turn 56

Turnover 18, 20

Twain, Mark 142

Under-delivering 133

Underwriters 69

Underwriting Arrangements 34

Unique Selling Proposition (USP) 2, 4

Unit Trusts 36

Upper Quartile 114

Utilisation 154, 156-7

Vaitlingam, Romesh 199

Value-For-Money (VFM) 168

Values 3

VAR (Value-at-Risk) 67

Venture Capitalists 23, 34, 44

Vision 3

Volvo 78

Wal-Mart 77-8

Wall Street Journal 197

Websites 104

Wholesale 41, 81

Wholesale Money 35

Wikipedia 73, 197

Wooldridge, Adrian 198

Words, Active 146

Words, Foreign 146

Words, Passive 146

Work-In-Progress (WIP) 158

Work/Life Balance 196

Working Capital Requirement 20-1, 158-9

Working Hours 156

Working Names 69

World Bank 57

Write Off 155

Writing 150

Yield 65

Zero Coupon Bonds 57